D0712913

Swedish Folk Music in the Twenty-First Century

Swedish Folk Music in the Twenty-First Century

On the Nature of Tradition in a Folkless Nation

David Kaminsky

WITHDRAWN
UTSA Libraries

LEXINGTON BOOKS
Lanham • Boulder • New York • Toronto • Plymouth, UK

Published by Lexington Books
A wholly owned subsidiary of The Rowman & Littlefield Publishing Group, Inc.
4501 Forbes Boulevard, Suite 200, Lanham, Maryland 20706
http://www.lexingtonbooks.com

Estover Road, Plymouth PL6 7PY, United Kingdom

Copyright © 2012 by Lexington Books

All rights reserved. No part of this book may be reproduced in any form or by any
electronic or mechanical means, including information storage and retrieval systems,
without written permission from the publisher, except by a reviewer who may quote
passages in a review.

British Library Cataloguing in Publication Information Available

Library of Congress Cataloging-in-Publication Data
Kaminsky, David, 1974-
 Swedish folk music in the twenty-first century : on the nature of tradition in a folkless
nation / David Kaminsky.
    p. cm.
 Includes bibliographical references and index.
 ISBN 978-0-7391-6722-9 (cloth : alk. paper) -- ISBN 978-0-7391-7291-9 (electronic)
 1. Folk music--Sweden--History and criticism. I. Title.
 ML3706.6.K36 2012
 781.62'397009051--dc23
                            2011042207

⊖™ The paper used in this publication meets the minimum requirements of American
National Standard for Information Sciences—Permanence of Paper for Printed Library
Materials, ANSI/NISO Z39.48-1992.

Printed in the United States of America

Library
University of Texas
at San Antonio

For my parents
Amy and Ken Kaminsky

my brother
Jonathan Kaminsky

and my grandmother
Florence Katz

Table of Contents

Preface and Acknowledgments   ix

Chapter 1: Toward an Insiders' Definition of Folk Music   1

Chapter 2: Reinventing Tradition   19

Chapter 3: Geographical Boundaries (and their Limits)   45

Chapter 4: Folk Music and the Public Eye   75

Chapter 5: A Natural Art   107

Chapter 6: Three Definitions of Folk Music   129

Chapter 7: Two Public Performances   143

Postscript: Return of the Nationalist Right   161

Appendix A: List of Interviews   165

Appendix B: Glossary of Terms   167

Bibliography   171

Discography and Videography   185

Index   187

About the Author   197

Preface and Acknowledgments

My conscious entry into the world of Swedish folk music was initiated, as things occasionally are, with the filling out of a form. I was a sophomore music major at Macalester college at the time, and while my coursework in the department dealt exclusively with Western art music traditions, as a musician I was already in the process of moving away from the classical music of my youth. I had quit the college orchestra at the end of my first year in order to concentrate more fully on playing with the African Music Ensemble, and to join Flying Fingers, the school's student-run Celtic and American folk music group. I have some recollection of sitting in a school computer lab, over whatever paperwork Macalester deemed necessary for me to fill out in application for permission to study in a country with which they had no established exchange program. Something at a loss for justifications, I composed some words regarding the opportunities I would have to learn about Swedish folk music. I do not recall the exact ratio of my desire to fill the page relative to the sincerity of the words with which I filled it. Neither do I have any clear recollection of whether or not I had any idea what Swedish folk music might be, though I had already spent several of my younger years in Sweden.

Some months later, on my way to or from one class or another at the Gothenburg School of Music, I passed a sign advertising for new members in Lekarlaget, the school's folk music ensemble.[1] Curiosity, combined (no doubt) with a dutiful sense of retroactive honesty regarding my study abroad application, prompted me to join the first rehearsal. I was one of a handful of musicians in attendance. We began by dragging benches to the middle of the mirrored dance space, where we sat in a square formation. Most if not all of the others played fiddle; I was the only flutist. Leadership for the month had been granted to Karin Eriksson, who taught dance tunes from the nearby province of Halland. The first we learned was Gösta Rackares polska, which Eriksson gave us initially as a series of short melodic fragments. As we started to assemble these into a melodic whole, the musicians began tapping their feet in a regular rhythm: one two (pause) one two (pause).

ix

Despite a rhythmic structure quite foreign to my early training as a classical flutist, I picked up the tune easily. For the last two years at Macalester I had been taking private bamboo flute lessons with Ghanaian master drummer and ethnomusicologist Sowah Mensah. His approach to teaching had favored an understanding of melodic lines as unfolding relative to a bell/clave timeline pattern, rather than regular pulses or beats. This, my primary previous exposure to aural musical learning, proved extremely helpful in allowing me to understand the uneven polska's melodic rhythm, which I also came to conceptualize as relative to the regular foot-tapping pattern that accompanied it.[2]

The language with which Swedish musicians tend to discuss the rhythm of polska music, however, is essentially notation-based, culled from that of the Western art music tradition. The foot-tapping occurs on beats one and three, while the timing of beat two may be variable according to regional style and dance variations. Most of these regional variations can be classified under one of three rubrics: Triplet polskor have a strong 9/8 feel. Sixteenth-note polskor, which generally betray the strongest kinship with Baroque-era art music traditions, are in 3/4, each beat receiving equal spacing. Eighth-note polskor, lastly, are sometimes described as rhythmically uneven, occupying a position between 3/4 and 9/8.[3] These are served least well by transcription, and sometimes involve a certain amount of rhythmic rubato against the stable foot-stomping metrical frame.[4]

My first scholarly interest in Swedish folk music involved questions regarding the uneven polskor. Inspired by my African bamboo flute lessons, I wondered at the rhythmic construction of these Swedish tunes, and whether or not the notation-based language with which my friends described them might be camouflaging its organic connection to the dance (which, with the music, literally revolves around that regular tap-tap-pause pulsation). My sub-Saharan Minnesota backdoor entry into polska awareness just might, I thought, have afforded me some felicitously unique insight into the question of rhythmic construction. I abandoned this line of reasoning fairly early on, however, and have only revived the question of the relationship between polska music and dance in my most recent research. My thoughts on the matter have shifted considerably in the intervening years, but that is a matter for a different piece of writing.

What I can say in retrospect is that the familiarity with which I experienced Gösta Rackares polska on that first day of rehearsal might be explained as a function not only of my Ghanaian bamboo flute lessons, but also of my past experiences living in Sweden. Between the ages of seven and nine, from 1982–1984, I had lived with my family in Umeå, a small northern city on the Baltic. My father had language tapes filled with musical interludes by Jan Johansson, Swedish folk tunes arranged for jazz piano and bass. Those same recordings, mostly from the album *Jazz på svenska*, were also frequently played in the dead air time between shows on the two Swedish television channels that were available in the early eighties.[5] When I returned to Sweden with my family in 1991, this time to Gothenburg, a fellow student in my high school music class did a presentation on *Jazz på svenska*. Reminded of its existence, I bought the CD reissue. The following year, back in the States, I transcribed many of the melodies so that I could play them on the flute. Yet returning to Gothenburg in 1995, those first days with Lekarlaget, I had not quite yet made the conscious connection between Jan Johansson and Gösta Rackare.

The resulting unfamiliar familiarity that marked my conscious introduction to Swedish folk music is actually a fairly common experience in folk music Sweden. Many who discover the music as adults speak of having had no idea of its existence before stumbling upon it, yet also report the experience as a sort of homecoming. Some explain this as an effect of a kind of cultural memory, though my reading is somewhat more banal. A number of my consultants have cited ubiquitous Swedish Christmas songs and midsummer children's song games as examples of popularly known polska melodies, unbeknownst to the populace at large. As I self-consciously listen for traces of folk music in Sweden's mass-media soundscape I hear it slipping through in other places as well. Spelman group music is piped into the background at the Liseberg amusement park in Gothenburg.[6] A synthesized folk melody makes itself heard in a TV ad for a trance CD.[7] Jan Johansson generates background melancholy in any number of contexts. In television advertising, snippets of folk music tend to recur in certain situations, fulfilling predictable functions. They might signify the pure and natural (cows in a field producing a popular butter spread), the anachronistic (the old man who refuses to get broadband), or the quaintly comical (the middle-aged cross-country runner making an enthusiastic but unambitious attempt at a comeback).[8] This public folk music is usually marked by some twentieth-century adaptation or fusion, and is often an unobtrusive background presence, foregrounded only on the rarest occasions. The bare-bones pre-industrial forms are far less apparent today, limited essentially to a subcultural niche. That smaller musical world of enthusiasts is generally concealed enough to be identified as something new to the Swede who stumbles into it, yet just hinted-at enough in the broader soundscape to be recognized as something familiar when that occurs.

I played with Lekarlaget for a year. In the summer of 1996 we performed at the Kaustinen folk music festival in northern Finland, and some weeks later a number of us attended the Korrö festival in the south of Sweden. When I returned home to the States I kept playing Swedish music, integrating tunes into my senior recital at Macalester, alongside the Ghanaian and Celtic. Sowah Mensah encouraged me to go into ethnomusicology, and the following year I applied to several programs with a mind to study Swedish folk music.

I do not recall exactly when I began to develop the idea of looking at the concept of folk music in Sweden. It may well have been, again, in the filling out of the appropriate forms, the grant applications that would return me to the field. I was inspired, in any case, by the ethnographic tradition of allowing the field to dictate the topic, championed by Nicole Beaudry among others.[9] I recalled clearly that the most common topic of conversation among the Swedish folk musicians I had known was the very question of the nature of folk music. My declared intention was to return to Gothenburg and rejoin Lekarlaget, and from there to insinuate myself into various other corners of the local folk music scene, from the practical to the academic. Finding the group defunct upon my arrival in 2001, I was nevertheless able to make use of the contacts I had established within it. I joined Karin Eriksson in the biweekly graduate musicology seminars at the University, and began playing with Bagaregården's spelman group, an ensemble led by two former Lekarlaget members, Martin Hillbratt and Dan Olsson. Joar Skorpen, one of Lekarlaget's co-founders, was to become a key consultant for the dissertation. I began volunteering weekly at the Folk Music Café, something of a local hub for folk music life, which I had also come to know through the group. Other contacts followed. In the spring I joined a polska dance group, Skjortor och Särkar, and began private lessons with folk flutist Jonas Simonson. During the summer I moved within the season's expanded sphere of local folk music life, traveling the national circuit of gatherings, summer camps, and festivals, capped by a return to Korrö in the end of July. I have returned to that circuit each summer since my initial fieldwork year. I also spent the 2006–2007 Academic year in Tobo, Sweden, studying folk dance pedagogy at the Eric Sahlström Institute.

In my interviews I did my best to get a representative sampling of Gothenburg-area musicians, dancers, academics, and event organizers. The professional and academic spheres were small enough that I was able to interview everyone. In seeking consultants within the broader amateur sphere I made every attempt to maintain a balance of both interest (dancing, playing, singing) and gender. All my consultants were Swedes, most middle-class, all white.[10]

I would like to thank my consultants: Håkan Bengtsson, Göran Berg, Anders Bergsten, Ulla Bergsten, Alf Bergstrand, Anders Dahlgren, Ida Heinö Djunovic, Olle Edström, Helena Ek, Magnus Ek, Karin Eriksson, Ulf Henningson, Martin Hillbratt, Johan Hogenäs, Lilian Håkansson, Gunnel Johansson, Pers Nils Johansson, Hans Kennemark, Ulf Kinding, Joanna Kober, Sten Källman, Kjell Leidhammar, Urban Lind, Jan Ling, Karl Malbert, Svante Mannervik, Lennart Mellgren, Göran Månsson, "Dans" Mats Nilsson, "Sax" Mats Nilsson, Vivi Nilsson, Rose-Marie Landén Nord, Annika Nordström, Ida Norrlöf, Gunilla Ohlsson, Dan Olsson, Kajsa Paulsson, Rolf Persson, Harald Pettersson, Göran Premberg, Emma Rydberg, Inger Rydberg, Per Sandberg, Greger Siljebo, Jonas Simonsson, Joar Skorpen, Åsa Grogarn Sol, Ingvar Strömblad, Sara Uneback, Anders Waernelius, Bernt Wennberg, Annelie Westerlund, Lotta Vesterlund, Margareta Lundquister Wignall, and Hanna Wiskari. Their interviews are the foundation upon which this book is built, and their generosity is what made it possible.

I have also had considerable help from "insider" readers, several of whom have earlier served as consultants. Thanks go to Per-Ulf Allmo, Alf Bergstrand, Jonas Ericson, Lars-Gunnar Franzén, Ulf Kinding, Jan Ling, Svante Mannervik,

Sheila Morris, "Dans" Mats Nilsson, Lars Olson, Dan Olsson, Göran Premberg, Tommy Sjöberg, Eva Thestrup, and Tony Wrethling for keeping me honest. In some cases I have made changes based upon their comments, in others not. For instance, my explicit classification of Polska Dancers as a category separate from spelman gathering and traditional folk dance group spheres came as a result of comments from Lars-Gunnar Franzén and Jonas Ericson, among others.[11]

This book would not have been possible without the aid of the granting organizations that funded its research and writing. Thanks go to the American Scandinavian Foundation Thord-Gray Memorial Fellowship fund and the Harvard Center for European Studies Krupp Fellowship, which funded a year of research between 2001 and 2002. Summer research funding was provided by the Harvard Music Department's Richard F. French Prize Fellowships, John Knowles Paine Travelling Fellowships, and the Harvard Graduate Student Council. Finally, thanks go to the Harvard Graduate Society Dissertation Fellowship fund and the John and Elizabeth Armstrong Graduate Dissertation Fellowship for supporting the writing of the dissertation that would later become this book.

Finally I would like to thank Richard Wolf and Kiri Miller, brilliant scholarly writers who provided useful comments on this work, and especially my graduate adviser, Kay Shelemay, whose tireless and timely readings of multiple drafts in the face of her own daunting schedule was a godsend.

Notes

1. The University of Gothenburg School of Music merged with schools of opera and theater to become the Academy of Music and Drama in 2005. In this work I use the older name consistently throughout, in order to avoid confusion.

2. Jan-Petter Blom and Tellef Kvifte have also noted that foot-tapping patterns in Norwegian music might have a timeline-like relationship to the melody, in "On the Problem of Inferential Ambivalence in Musical Meter," *Ethnomusicology* 30, no. 3 (1986): 511.

3. See, e.g., Jan Ling, Erik Kjellberg, and Owe Ronström. "Sweden," in *The Garland Encyclopedia of World Music*, Vol 8, *Europe*, ed. Timothy Rice, James Porter and Chris Goertzen (New York: Garland, 2000), 435.

4. Mats Johansson calls this phenomenon "rhythmic tolerance" in his "The Concept of Rhythmic Tolerance: Examining Flexible Grooves in Scandinavian Folk Fiddling," in *Musical Rhythm in the Age of Digital Reproduction*, ed. Anne Danielsen (Burlington: Ashgate, 2010), 69. Similarly, Cynthia Tse Kimberlin remarks on a "rubato effect" relative to covert timelines in Ethiopian music in her "Traditions and Transitions in Ethiopian Music: Event as a Catalyst for Change," *Intercultural Music* I (1995): 136–137. Ali Jihad Racy makes a comparable argument about rhythmic flexibility within a strict metrical frame in Arab music, in *Making Music in the Arab World: The Culture and Artistry of Tarab* (Cambridge: Cambridge University Press, 2003), 118–119.

5. Jan Johansson, *Jazz på svenska*, 1964, Megafon MFLP S4, 33rpm vinyl LP.

6. For definitions of "spelman" and "spelman group," see glossary, page 169.

7. The track in question is Galaxee's "The Crow Song," from the collection *Trance 2001, The 3rd Edition*, 2001, EMG Records Sweden AB 5002, 2 compact discs.

8. Advertisements for Bregott, Bredbandsbolaget, and McDonald's, respectively. For more on Swedish folk music in advertising see Märta Ramsten, "'Genuint svenskt' med folkmusikaliska förtecken," in *Folkmusik Och Etnicitet*, ed. Johanna Björkholm (Vasa: Finlands svenska folkmusikinstitut, 2005), 22–29.

9. See, e.g., Nicole Beaudry, "The Challenges of Human Relations in Ethnographic Enquiry," in *Shadows in the Field: New Perspectives for Fieldwork in Ethnomusicology*, ed. Timothy Cooley and Gregory Barz (New York: Oxford University Press, 1997), 68–70; and Kay Kaufman Shelemay, *Let Jasmine Rain Down: Song and Remembrance among Syrian Jews* (Chicago: University of Chicago Press, 1998).

10. The racial make-up of folk music Sweden is far whiter than that of the country as a whole. While there are a handful of people of color involved in the national scene, I knew none in Gothenburg during my initial fieldwork year. There may very well have been none in the city at the time.

11. In other cases I have not made changes for practical reasons. For instance, Jonas Ericson also commented that I underplay the significance of Skeppsholmsgården, Stockholm's main folk music club, by not mentioning it at all. I am certain he is correct in citing that institution as a powerful influence on the national folk music scene, but given its marginality to the experience of my Gothenburg consultants, I have not seen reason to mention it. The localized nature of my fieldwork, a practical necessity, is thus in this sense an unavoidable disadvantage. This is not to suggest, however, that any other single locality would have given a fuller picture. For instance, Ericson's Stockholm-centered perspective caused him to wonder why I would focus so much upon a small, local event like Korrö (actually southern Sweden's largest folk music festival). His perspective on the matter relates to the fact that the Stockholm folk music pathway does not always extend to Korrö, just as that of Gothenburg may not always extend to Skeppsholmsgården.

CHAPTER 1

—∿∿—

Toward an Insiders' Definition of Folk Music

A senior center by day, on Friday nights Allégården becomes the social nexus for much of Gothenburg's small folk music community. A handful of volunteer workers appear in the early evening in order to prepare for the venue's weekly transformation into the Folk Music Café. The work consists primarily of some minor food and coffee preparation, the setting up of chairs (if a concert is planned), and the strategic draping of cloths over the most egregious photographic evidence of the building's regular patrons.

On the second night of the fall 2001 season, I was granted an interview with Åsa Grogarn Sol, the volunteer president of the Café.[1] Just before the interview I wrote down my opening question in my notebook, careful to phrase the Swedish as precisely as possible: "My dissertation will be one of the first extended works on Swedish folk music written entirely in English, and will thus have the opportunity to be read by a broader audience. What should it say about Swedish folk music?" It was to be the first ethnographic interview of my Swedish fieldwork. What better beginning than to ask my first consultant what a dissertation about folk music should look like?

> *Kaminsky:* I thought that I could ask about this, this dissertation that I'm doing. That I'm writing. It will be one of the first—there isn't much written in English about Swedish folk music, right? And I thought I'd like to ask what people think that it's important to, what should be written, like, in a dissertation like this. It's a pretty general question, but it's, the idea is that it should be pretty open.
> *Sol:* Yeah, it's nice, I can talk about that for a long time.
> *Kaminsky:* Well, go ahead.

1

Sol: Well, I can do it if I concentrate. I guess the first thing I think English-speaking readers should know about Swedish folk music is what's particular to it. For example, the enormous treasure trove of melodies. I can't talk for very long about that, I mean there are so many great melodies. And the fact that almost all the music is modal is interesting. And then you should make it clear that Swedish folk music is a genre category. And you might possibly say that it's the music of rural peasant society. But then, I already feel like I want to take back everything I've just said, because what do we know, really? And then you get into all these emblematic things, like why do people wear folk costumes? And why don't we wear them here in the Folk Music Café? The folk costume is formalwear, so why do people wear it when they're going out to dance? Yeah, there's so much of this stuff that—I'm really happy that I'm not the one who has to write this dissertation. It seems really tough.[2]

Sol's tentative answer is indicative of the central problem that shapes this book. As I continued to conduct interviews I soon discovered that her difficulty grappling with the concept would not be the exception but the rule among my consultants. More often than not they found it impossible to come to some way to define or describe folk music that they themselves found entirely satisfactory, much less that came to a consensus with any others.

My goal in this work is to explicate the folk music concept as it is understood by members of a specific community who associate themselves in one way or another with something they would call folk music. One of my central tasks, then, must be to determine some way to describe a concept whose meaning is not agreed upon by the set of people who share it.

The Concept of "Folk Music"

The ethnographic approach to the study of folk music as a concept has a fairly limited tradition within ethnomusicology. While twentieth-century folk music scholars for years wrestled with the problem of defining folk music, they were predominantly concerned with its usage as a scholarly term.[3] In the present day, however, "folk music" as an etic category has largely fallen out of favor within mainstream ethnomusicology. Scholars have come to realize that "folk" may had been a dubious designation even in the eighteenth and nineteenth centuries, an idealized rural population in whose name the upper classes could justify political action, yet whose authenticity somehow withered the moment they developed their own political voice.[4] (Hence the "folkless nation" of my own title; the myopically innocent Swedish rural folk of the nineteenth-century urban imagination simply do not exist today, if they ever existed.) More than thirty years have now passed since the International Folk Music Council changed its name to the International Council for Traditional Music, a move that Philip Bohlman suggests signaled the general academic abandonment of the concept to all but the most conservative scholars.[5]

This has created a dilemma for me in my work. My ethnomusicological training distances me from the people I study, who, having based a music-cultural revival on the research of an earlier generation of scholars, have also maintained their now-outdated terminology. I have found myself so conditioned by my scholarly training to react against certain outmoded language that when people talk about "authenticity" or "the genuine" I experience an immediate reflex to bracket them as unsophisticated preservationists. I imagine that for some ethnographers even the use of the term "folk music" itself might provoke a similar response.[6] My impulse to separate myself in this way from my consultants has been powered, I think, by the sense of discomfort I have felt upon recognizing that my interest in "ethnic music" has been encouraged in part by the same sort of exoticism and sense of authenticity that likely motivated early comparative musicologists, folklorists, and anthropologists. In hermetically sealing off my consultants' position from my own I seek to protect myself against the manifested specters of my disciplinary past, proving to myself that I have matured beyond authenticity.

My coming to terms with that element of my relationship with the music I study has been aided by this realization: that similar romanticizing forces have for many of my consultants—especially those who discovered folk music late in life—guided much of their self-discovery of ethnic identity through music. Thus, while I have hardly embraced these forces as unproblematic, I fear them less having recognized that they may function in processes of selfing as well as Othering. This discovery of mutual experience with my consultants has done much to aid in my ability to empathize with them when their struggle with the folk music concept brings them to places my training dissuades me from treading.

I also find their struggle very recognizable, because just as I and those I study trace the same intellectual-historical roots, so do we share similar misgivings about them. My sense is that this commonality is informed strongly by an information feedback loop between scholars and practitioners of Swedish folk music. The two worlds became especially close during the early revival in the late 1960s, a time during which new practitioners relied heavily upon the scholarly world for material, given the extent to which traditional forms had fallen out of practice. By the peak of the revival in the late seventies, as scholars began seriously to question the paradigms of their predecessors, so still-connected practitioners must have felt the reverberations of these discussions. Conversely, the various creative musical developments of the revival were doubtless instrumental in pushing scholars in their reevaluation of traditional notions of what folk music could be. The connection between theoretical and practical worlds during the revival was reinforced, finally, by the increasing number of scholars who were also players, and the number of players who engaged in amateur scholarship and collection work.[7]

The most influential academic in terms of having a direct effect on the Swedish revival was probably sociomusicologist Jan Ling. His 1964 *Svensk folkmusik* became something of a bible for revivalists. His 1967 dissertation *Nyckelharpan* was an equally holy text to new players and builders of the keyed fiddle, Sweden's unofficial national instrument. *Svensk folkmusik* was based on a lecture series given by Ling in the late fifties in Uppsala. It provided an overview of various elements of nineteenth-century Swedish peasant music culture, with chapters on organology, yearly festivals, social dancing, and so forth. Little attention was paid to the twentieth century, and even those few pages framed recent developments in terms of their relationship and fidelity to the music of pre-industrial peasant culture.[8] As a central text of the revival, *Svensk folkmusik* thus helped establish folk music among revivalists as a historical genre based in the musical practices of nineteenth-century rural society.

Ling was probably also responsible to a certain degree for initiating the more analytically critical discussion of the folk music concept as the Swedish revival reached its peak.[9] In his landmark essay "Folkmusik—En brygd," he wrote:

> As I understand it the word "folk music" itself is an ideological concept: it is coined by representatives of the eighteenth and nineteenth century bourgeois class as a label for music of "the Others," the folk, which they observe, study, and try to incorporate into their culture, or reintroduce back to the folk in order to counteract the homogenizing influence of mass culture.[10]

The publication of this essay in 1979 marked a defining moment in the literature on Swedish folk music, much of which after this point would take Ling's lead and engage with the concept in a more critical way.[11]

Ethnomusicologist Owe Ronström, for instance, has examined the shifting political uses to which the term "folk" has been put, and the cumulative effects of those shifts in meaning on the folk music concept.[12] He points to the confusion generated by a folk music that belonged first to an entire nation's populace and later to a specific rural peasant class.[13] Dan Lundberg and Gunnar Ternhag, meanwhile, have focused on the difficulty of a folk music concept that "has moved from a social categorization to a question of style. If the pioneers of collection only searched for folk music among the lower strata of society, almost without regard to how it sounded, today we seek folk music with the help of our ears in all social strata."[14] Together, these scholars have traced a series of shifts in meaning: Swedish folk music was first the representative music of a nation, then that of a more narrowly defined peasant society, and finally a musical genre with roots in that now-vanished rural culture. These conceptual shifts have been powerful generators of ambiguity, however, in that they can never entirely erase previously held definitions. The presentist approach of defining folk music as a genre category may be accurate in some sense, yet is not particularly useful for practitioners (or scholars) who are invested in amassing cultural capital to the concept. For this reason it cannot entirely replace those definitions which, by emphasizing function or social context, suggest closer connections to older traditions. These older definitions, in turn, are less adequate in describing modern Swedish folk music in all its iterations, from the conservatory to the concert stage and recording studio. As such, the various and contradictory ways of meaning "folk music" all remain useful in one context or another, and so they must be resigned to their coexistence, vying to make logical sense out of their constant juxtaposition. Hence Lundberg and Ternhag's observation that most surveys on Swedish folk music (including their own) do not use the term in a consistent way. Most modern scholars make explicit cases for not defining the term at all.[15]

The common scholarly solution has been simply to allow folk music to mean whatever its users mean it to mean.[16] Owe Ronström writes:

> The question of what folk music "really is," or what is "typical Gotlandic folk music," is impossible to answer. But it is clear that the concept carries a cultural charge that has encouraged many to make the attempt regardless. Ultimately, folk music is nothing other than *what we call folk music*. It is often those people who use the word who determine what it should mean. Musicians, researchers, politicians, audience, all are involved in a never-ending tug-of-war to determine in which direction and to what length its contents can be stretched.[17]

Swedish scholars have generally not continued their analyses of the concept past this point. But what Ronström frames as a conclusion I read as a call to ethnography. I accept and proceed from the notion that the term "folk music" is defined by its use.

Toward an Analytical Framework

The central purpose of this ethnography is the detailed analysis of what Swedish folk music scholar Karin Eriksson, citing Lydia Goehr and W.B. Gallie, has referred to as "an open and essentially contested concept."[18] To this end I have assembled a patchwork of theoretical approaches to conceptualization, culled from the fields of anthropology, philosophy, education, and literary criticism, beginning with those same philosophers cited by Eriksson in her discussion of the folk music concept.

Despite their apparent eclecticism, the constituent patches of my theoretical apparatus all seem to find their common threading in the work of Ludwig Wittgenstein.[19] The central strand that fundamentally underpins not only these theories, but also many of the above-cited Swedish writings on the concept of folk music, is Wittgenstein's notion that "the meaning of a word is its use in language."[20] A secondary and related thread is his suggestion that a concept may be described in terms of its "family resemblances," markers of identification which when assembled to a critical mass exemplify it, yet none of which are fundamental to it.[21] This second thread is contingent upon the first; markers of identification are accumulated to a term by its continuous use in language. Lydia

Goehr's description of "open" concepts outlines how this process works over time: A concept may change and be adapted to new phenomena by its users, yet at the same time remains constrained by the parameters of its established usage. As time passes, new definitions of the term may be added, but their effect is cumulative, in that earlier ones can never actually be replaced.[22]

One side effect of such a process is the forced coexistence of simultaneous conflicting definitions, born of the needs of different users separated by time, space, and/or purpose. Thus is produced what W.B. Gallie calls an "essentially contested concept," one whose internal contradictions are perpetual and ir-resolvable.[23] Gallie lists a set of characteristics according to which a concept might be identified as essentially contested:

> (I) it must be *appraisive* in the sense that it signifies or accredits some kind of valued achievement. (II) This achievement must be of an internally complex character, for all that its worth is attributed to it as a whole. (III) Any explanation of its worth must therefore include reference to the respective contributions of its various parts or features; yet prior to experimentation there is nothing absurd or contradictory in any one of a number of possible rival descriptions of its total worth, one such description setting its component parts or features in one order of importance, a second setting them in a second order, and so on. In fine, the accredited achievement is *initially* variously describable. (IV) The accredited achievement must be of a kind that admits of considerable modification in the light of changing circumstances; and such modification cannot be prescribed or predicted in advance. For convenience I shall call the concept of any such achievement "open" in character.[24]

These criteria should already seem familiar. Point (I) relates to the cultural currency that makes the concept worth contesting. Points (II) and (III) effectively describe Wittgenstein's set of family resemblances, and suggest that the contestedness of a concept involves a conflict not over the makeup of that set, but rather as to its internal hierarchy. Point (IV) is essentially an alternate phrasing of Goehr's later definition of open concepts.[25]

Gallie immediately goes on, however, to add a fifth criterion:

> These seem to me to be the four most important necessary conditions to which any essentially contested concept must comply. But they do not define what it is to be a concept of this kind. For this purpose we should have to say not only that different persons or parties adhere to different views of the correct use of some concept but (V) that each party recognizes the fact that its own use of it is contested by those of other parties, and that each party must have at least some appreciation of the different criteria in the light of which the other parties claim to be applying the concept in question. More simply, to use an essentially contested concept means to use it against other uses and to recognize that one's own use of it has to be maintained against these other uses.[26]

This defining feature of essentially contested concepts introduces a new set of issues. Gallie argues that all parties must recognize their mutual participation in the contestation of a single concept in order for that concept to be considered a unitary entity.[27] He does not, however, elaborate on why all parties must be familiar with the specific viewpoints of their conceptual opponents. My extension of his argument would be that the fragmentation of a contested concept is such that familiarity with only a single viewpoint upon it would not allow its user to summon the requisite "parts or features" (Wittgenstein's "family resemblances") for the concept to be considered in play. Put another way, the territory of the concept is so internally divided among the different parties that no single fenced-off area would be sufficient to identify the broader landscape on its own.

A key rhetorical technique for traversing the entire territory of a concept regardless of its internal divisions and contradictions is the exploitation of a feature of language Mikhael Bakhtin has termed "heteroglossia." Bakhtin's description of heteroglossia, a certain multi-voiced character to prose and everyday language, may be read as an analysis of the dialectical force behind the creation of open and contested concepts:

> Instead of the virginal fullness and inexhaustibility of the object itself, the prose writer confronts a multitude of routes, roads and paths that have been laid down in the object by social consciousness. Along with the internal contradictions inside the object itself, the prose writer witnesses as well the unfolding of social heteroglossia *surrounding* the object, the Tower-of-Babel mixing of languages that goes on around any object; the dialectics of the object are interwoven with the social dialogue surrounding it. For the prose writer, the object is a focal point for heteroglot voices among which his own voice must also sound; these voices create the background necessary for his own voice; outside of which his artistic prose nuances cannot be perceived; and without which they "do not sound."[28]

If we read Bakhtin's "prose writer" instead as "any speaker," the first half of this citation may be read as a description of the general linguistic mechanics of concept formation, and the second of the principles guiding concept usage.[29] The background voices Bakhtin describes form something like a sonic image of the general terrain of a concept, in the absence of which the speaker could not claim a position. The speaker's voice is like a "you are here" sticker whose meaning is entirely contingent upon its placement on that sonic map.

Heteroglossia as Bakhtin describes it is common to all everyday language.[30] The specific aspect of heteroglossia most useful in the description of essentially contested concepts, however, is the explicit or implicit appeal to alternate points of view, what a linguistic anthropologist might call "reported speech."[31] The major advantage of being able to cite multiple opposing viewpoints in describing a concept is that the segregation of signifying markers thus summoned permits their logical inconsistency. Put in more concrete terms, when an interview subject asked to define concept X says "some would define it Y, but I say Z," she effectively manages to invoke both Y and Z, circumnavigating any logical incompatibility that might otherwise deny their coexistence in X. This type of heteroglossic rhetorical technique supercedes logical/territorial constraints, and thus becomes a key tool for mapping the contested terrain of open concepts. Such tools are necessary because the standard technique for describing concepts, definition, requires that they be circumscribable; whereas the defining feature of open concepts is their lack definable external boundaries. Thus any satisfactory description of an open concept must rely not upon definition, but the extended traversal of its inner terrain, travel requiring rhetorical techniques that allow the speaker to cross its internal borders freely.

The exploitation of heteroglossia is not the only rhetorical method that allows this sort of border crossing, however. Another is the tentative and experimental personal exploration of the conceptual terrain exemplified in the Åsa Grogarn Sol quotation at the beginning of this chapter. This technique involves exploratory attempts at finding gates between fenced-off areas, and failing that, simple fence-jumping (i.e., logical leaps). The difficulty of the terrain combined with the maintenance of a unitary subjectivity can make this process frustrating for the speaker: "And then you should make it clear that Swedish folk music is a genre category. And you might possibly say that it's the music of rural peasant society. But then, I already feel like I want to take back everything I've just said, because what do we know, really?"[32] Yet an extended discussion of a contested concept using this technique allows as much or more of the terrain to be covered as does that of heteroglossic refraction.[33]

This exploratory way of discussing concepts has been examined in depth by education theorists Ference Marton and Wing-yan Pong. In their analyses of interview transcripts, Marton and Pong point to what they call "intra-contextual conceptual shifts," moments when a subject leaps from one way of understanding a concept to another.[34] They proceed from a view of conceptualization based in phenomenography, a branch of education theory that sees the understanding of any phenomenon as the total command of a finite number of "ways of comprehending" it.[35] I find this final phenomenographic ways-of-understanding model a useful tool for following the tectonic shifts that have formed the contested terrain of the modern Swedish folk music concept.

Ways of Understanding "Folk Music"

Most of the elements that make up the Swedish concept of folk music can already be discerned in two formative pieces of writing from the beginning of the nineteenth century. The journal *Iduna* was the mouthpiece of the Gothic Society, the first organization to engage in the systematic collection of Swedish peasant music. The opening statement of the premier issue in 1811 included this creed:

Every generation reproduces itself not merely physically but also morally in another: it leaves on to it its customs, its concepts. It is this continuous tradition, which in different times nevertheless always unifies the Folk, it constitutes its uninterrupted consciousness of itself as a Nation; it constitutes, so to speak, its personality.[36]

Tradition, the Folk, and the Nation are all seamlessly interwoven according to the European bourgeois national-romantic logic of the time. All three remain essential ways of understanding folk music to this day. When in this work I follow the example of the above *Iduna* citation in capitalizing these key concepts, I mean it as shorthand to signal their being in play as "ways of comprehending" folk music in the phenomenographic sense.

The other key piece of writing was Carl Envallson's definition of "National Music" in his 1802 *Svenskt musikaliskt lexikon*, a full twenty-one years before the term "folk music" would see print in Sweden.[37] Envallson defined the term as "[s]uch a music or song, that is most generally used by a certain Nation, and belongs to its character and temperament."[38] As the text continues, Tradition and the Folk also come into play, if not quite as explicitly:

One should thus distinguish between Provincial tones and National music. The Dal-kars' Song is also such a one, and like that of several Provinces in Minor; but it becomes in any case difficult to deny, that the genuine Swedish National music has been in Major. For if one in some way wishes to acknowledge the area around Sigtuna and Upsala, where the Upsviars' rightful home has been, one finds them still today to have most of their melodies and dances with their central tone in Major. . . . It is true, that many tones also exist in minor; but cannot the reason for this be in the composer's temperament, his taste and other circumstances, while we know that these minor tones are not so ancient, but for the most part composed by King Erik XIV in his days of melancholy. The reason for the minor tone of many may also be found in the district's location and the pasture's isolation.[39]

Where the *Iduna* statement simply distills and blends Tradition, the Nation, and the Folk, Envallson goes further by portending their volatility. The timelessness of Tradition is challenged by the history of composition, the stability of the National by regional variability, and the coherence of the Folk by individual and provincial idiosyncrasies.

The contradictions inherent to these three elements would soon also be exasperated by conflicts between them. For Envallson, National music was legitimated as a function of its being older and more of-the-folk than those provincial tones subject to the vagaries of individuality and isolation. The collection work of the Gothic Society, to begin about a decade later, would prove him quite wrong with regard to his suppositions about a unifying nationally characteristic Major mode.[40] Thus do Tradition and the Folk come into conflict with Nation, undermining the musical evidence supporting an ancient and unified National Folk Tradition.

A fourth element, too, would arise over the early half of the nineteenth century, further complicating the picture. Nature plays a minor role in Envallson's definition of National Music, the "pasture's isolation" that undermines National unity. Over the course of the nineteenth century in Sweden, however, the Natural would become an increasingly familiar trope within the folk-culture master narrative, alongside and intermingling with those exemplified in the above citations.[41] Its entry during this period into the Swedish folk music concept could only have been facilitated by its early presence in that of other nations, where "folk music" was born as a logical opposite of art music; an expression of nature as opposed to artifice.[42]

Each of these four elements of folk music—Tradition, Nation, Folk, Nature—have over time faced internal challenges, forcing constant tectonic shifts that have undermined the general integrity of the conceptual terrain. I have labeled the lines along which these internal shifts occur, calling them axes of time, place, commonality, and quality, respectively.[43] Along the time axis lies the perpetual conflict between cultural preservationism, which insists on the heritage of an unchanging past, and innovationism, which privileges musical growth and creativity. Along the place axis lies the tension between the sense of national identity bound up with the construction of a "Swedish" folk music, and the musically and politically motivated pull away from the national to both regional and international group identifications. Along the commonality axis lies the contradiction of a folk music generally unknown to the Swedish populace at large, and the concomitant question of whether or not the current obscurity of a music affects its right to be labeled "folk." Along the quality axis lies the issue of an increasing professionalization and formalization of a musical genre originally posited to exist in opposition to high art music.[44]

The true complexity of the concept has to do with the ways in which the axes intersect, overlap, and come into conflict with one another. In the early days of working out how to describe the phenomenon, I was determined literally to sketch out an actual map, showing exactly where these points of conflict and intersection were. In retrospect, I was fooled by my own use of metaphors like "conceptual terrain" into imagining that such a map might be feasible. One reader's frustrated response that my supposed axes seemed to be intersecting "like a plate of spaghetti" suggests that I might be misleading others into hoping for this sort of clarity as well. To be explicit, then: Any act of debating or defining Swedish folk music generally involves at least some amount of creative and strategic axial repositioning. By virtue of its essential contestedness, there can be no static and definitive map of the concept.

Instead, arguments about the nature of folk music may best be understood as a kind of language game. The point of this game is, generally, to maintain as much of the concept's cultural currency as possible. This currency consists of the four elements I have mentioned: Tradition, Nation, Folk, and Nature. Each element manifests in one end of a binarism. The challenge of the game comes with piecing the binarisms together so that they make logical sense, while simultaneously bringing as many of the four elements together. No ultimate winner can be declared, because all four elements can never coexist logically.

Occasionally in this game, the logical consistency of the greater part of the conceptual terrain is reinforced by the abandonment of a lesser part; or one element is challenged on the basis of its incompatibility with the other three. In some cases, for instance, individuals in interviews and in conversation will question the notion of a Nationally bounded Swedish folk music as a late, top-down, artificial construction, thus reinforcing its position as a Traditional, Folk, Natural phenomenon. Considering the new possibilities of international communications facilitated by globalization and mass media, modern world music might seem the most logical phenomenon upon which to base such an argument. Instead, however, this challenge to the significance of national boundaries draws without exception upon the border's pre-twentieth-century irrelevance to traditions of cultural exchange. To challenge national boundaries with an argument based on modern world music would mean a simultaneous abandonment of both Nation and Tradition as ways of understanding folk music, and thus the surrender of too much conceptual terrain at once. Similarly, when people make the argument that modern popular music is the true Swedish folk music, the musics they refer to are almost without exception genres made by and for Swedes like dance band or schlager, rather than the international pop music that actually tops the Swedish charts. As they challenge Tradition in favor of the Folk, they must maintain the National boundary or once again risk the abandonment of too much of that original terrain. Even today, the initial four elements of folk music claim their monopoly upon all of the cultural currency associated with the concept. What this also suggests is that the modern folk music concept in its unuttered state retains its affinity with all four original ways of understanding it. In many cases, the challenges people make to these elements must be the simple result of verbalization's demand for logical and ideological consistency.

The game is also complicated by the fact that its players can have situational motives, based in differing backgrounds and perspectives. They may be trying to legitimize or delegitimize a particular tune, genre, instrument, player, or ensemble. They may be attempting to align themselves with or distance themselves from a particular political ideology. They may simply be taking a given position for the sake of arguing. Each new round of the game thus has the potential to bring a fresh take on the concept. The map is constantly being redrawn. The ethnographic study of the concept then, what I put forth in this book, must simply be an overview of how the game has been played.

The next four chapters in this book address each of the axes of time, place, commonality, and quality, in turn. In chapter 2 I begin with a discussion of how the relationship between worlds of scholarship and practice have affected the discourse on "traditional" music. I then compare the discursive strategies of musicians who situate themselves upon various points along the axis of time, as they balance conflicting impulses for tradition and innovation. I conclude with a discussion of how that discourse of tradition vs. innovation has manifested in debates over the revival-era integration of non-traditional and historically reconstructed instruments to the world of Swedish folk music.

In chapter 3 I address the axis of place, examining the tensions at play between identities national, provincial, and international. I begin with a discussion of polska, a Swedish music and dance form with multiple regional variations. I argue that the central position of the polska as a marker for Swedish folk music is a function not only of its perceived age, but also its capacity to allow for the mutual coexistence of provincial and national identities. I then chronicle how Swedish anti-nationalist skepticism has over time redirected to the province much of the cultural currency historically granted to the nation as a whole. I discuss how folk musicians from the marginalized coastal province of Bohuslän have used their historical international connections with the British Isles in order to advance their standing and counteract the perceived hegemony of Dalarna, the province generally most associated with Swedish folk music and culture. I then compare that historical internationalism with a newer world-music-oriented project of international diplomacy and intercommunication associated with Dalarna's Ethno folk music camp and now-defunct Falun Folk Festival. Finally, I direct my attention to the tension between the rural and the urban in the imagination of Swedish folk music. This tension, while it plays out spatially, actually reflects shifts in the remaining three axes, whereby the historical processes of industrialization and urbanization placed the Natural and Traditional in opposition to a populace (Folk) increasingly engaged in modern city life.

Chapter 4 continues the preceding discussion with an analysis of the dual conception of the "common" (*folklig*) generated as a result of these shifts. One version retains its connection to rural heritage, whereas the other becomes associated with a modern life generally imagined as cultureless and soulless.[45] The frequent discussions among Swedish folk music insiders lamenting the current obscurity of folk music within Sweden often reveal an implicit desire to cure the ills of the newer forms of *folklig* culture with the medicine of forgotten rural traditions. A significant obstacle here, however, is the parallel between that impulse today and a similar one connected to Swedish cultural preservationism of the early twentieth century, whose historical association with German nationalism for many remains an issue of some discomfort. I examine a number of other obstacles that have inhibited the popularization of folk music as well. These include its reliance on a cultural context no recording or concert performance can convey, a secret-club mentality among insiders, and the obscuring effect of its more visible sister genres: accordion music, folkloric dance music, and Swedish world music fusion. Leading into the next chapter is a discussion of one final obstacle, an inaccessibility brought about by the unpolished rawness of the music itself.

Chapter 5 engages the central musical signifier of folk music, a raw, "natural" quality that finds its opposite in the polished artifice of art music. I discuss how a popular and scholarly view of folk music as musical antithesis to art music inspired revivalist constructions of a fiddle style that hypercorrected for traditional elements like glissando, vibrato, and second-fiddle harmonization, and instead exaggerated droning, foot-stomping, and "dirty" sound. I argue that this aesthetic was especially prevalent in the urban-centered folk music fusion scene, a bulwark against the classical to compensate for the loss of other musical boundaries of nation and genre. A related issue, also addressed in this chapter, is the tendency within the Swedish folk music subculture to privilege amateur over professional involvement.

The following two chapters engage specific case studies, in order to examine more closely how individuals negotiate the interactions between axes of time, place, commonality, and quality. In chapter 6 I undertake in-depth analyses of three interviews in which I have asked my consultants for definitions of folk music. I discuss their use of rhetorical strategies like heteroglossic refraction and discursive wandering, as described in this introduction.

In chapter 7 I examine two stagings of folk music events in Gothenburg, both of which in one way or another reflected attempts to reconcile some of the axial conflicts discussed in earlier chapters. The first was an exhibition by a local folk dance youth group, who addressed the concept of "folk dance" in a performance narrating the history of the creation of the stage form itself. The second was a concert by the folk music group Raun, whose theatrical approach to live shows involved the comical juxtaposition of various obviously conflicting elements of the folk music concept.

I close the book by introducing a dilemma, namely that the four-element folk music concept may be structurally xenophobic. Folk plus Tradition plus Nation defines a group of people whose ancestors lived in Sweden, and Nature constructs that complex as its own biotope, against which too much foreign influence becomes threatening. This problem has been brought into focus by the recent election of an anti-immigrant political party to Swedish parliament, with a campaign to divert funding from multicultural programs to the preservation of Swedish folk music and culture. This campaign has been met with open protest by the mostly left-leaning Swedish folk music community, yet for me it forces introspection regarding the ideological implications of my own love of the genre.

Notes

1. The Folk Music Café has a fall and a spring season, and is closed for Christmas and summer.

2. Åsa Grogarn Sol, interview by author, September 28, 2001. All translations of interview and field recording quotes are my own. Translations of written sources are mine as well, unless otherwise noted in the bibliography. For purposes of conserving space, I have not included the original Swedish quotations. Most of these can be found in the footnotes to my dissertation, "Hidden Traditions: Conceptualizing Swedish Folk Music in the Twenty-First Century," (Ph.D. diss., Harvard, 2005).

14   CHAPTER 1

3. See, e.g., Cecil J. Sharp, *English Folk-Song: Some Conclusions*, 2nd ed. (London: Novello & Co., Ltd., 1936 [1907]); Walter Wiora, "Concerning the Conception of Authentic Folk Music," *Journal of the International Folk Music Council* 1 (1949), 14–19; Maud Karpeles, "Some Reflections on Authenticity in Folk Music," *Journal of the International Folk Music Council* 3 (1951): 11–14; "Definition of Folk Music," *Journal of the International Folk Music Council* 7 (1955): 6; "The Distinction between Folk Music and Popular Music," *Journal of the International Folk Music Council* 20 (1968): 9–10; Bruno Nettl, *Folk Music in the United States: An Introduction*, 3rd ed. (Detroit: Wayne State University Press, 1976 [1960]), 20–27; Roger Elbourne, "The Question of Definition," *Yearbook of the International Folk Music Council* 7 (1976): 9–29; and Richard Middleton, "Editor's Introduction to Volume 1," *Popular Music* 1 (1981): 3–7.

4. See, e.g., David Whisnant, *All That Is Native and Fine: The Politics of Culture in an American Region* (Chapel Hill: University of North Carolina Press, 2009 [1983]), 6–16; William Roy, *Reds, Whites, and Blues: Social Movements, Folk Music, and Race in the United States* (Princeton, Princeton University Press, 2010), 49–78; Owe Ronström, "Making Use of History: Revival of the Bagpipe in Sweden in the 1980s," *Yearbook for Traditional Music* 21 (1989): 100-101.

5. Philip Bohlman, *The Study of Folk Music in the Modern World* (Bloomington: Indiana University Press, 1998), xiii–xiv.

6. I am reminded, for instance, of my first meeting of the Society for Ethnomusicology, where an attendee chided me when I told him I was studying Swedish folk music. It was 1998, and "folk music" was no longer a valid category.

7. The close connections between worlds of scholarship and practice are not unique to Swedish folk music, of course. They are probably common to any movement that seeks to reconstruct the musical life of a distant past. Kay Shelemay has noted similar phenomena in the early music movement, for instance, in her "Toward an Ethnomusicology of the Early Music Movement: Thoughts on Bridging Disciplines and Musical Worlds," *Ethnomusicology* 45, no. 1 (2001): 7–8. Neil Rosenberg has observed also that "[m]any of today's professional scholars in folklore, ethnomusicology, and related fields first became interested in these subjects not at school but through informal involvement with musics variously called 'folk' or 'traditional'" ("Introduction," in *Transforming Tradition: Folk Music Revivals Examined* (Urbana: University of Illinois Press, 1993): 2). See also Jeff Todd Titon, "Knowing Fieldwork," in *Shadows in the Field: New Perspectives for Fieldwork in Ethnomusicology*, ed. Gregory F. Barz and Timothy J. Cooley (New York: Oxford University Press, 1997): 87–88.

8. Jan Ling, *Svensk folkmusik* (Stockholm: Prisma, 1964), 131–134. This was the first general text on Swedish folk music since Tobias Norlind's *Svensk folkmusik och folkdans* (Stockholm: Natur och Kultur, 1930), which also focused heavily on the nineteenth century.

9. Previous to 1979 the question of a "folk music concept" had been discussed in a number of different contexts in Sweden; see, e.g., Ling's own *Svensk folkmusik*, 9; Katarina Nilsson and Elisabet Classon, "Folkmusiken och dess utövare!," *Hembygden* 51, no. 4 (1972): 12; and Rune Holmberg, "Vad menas med begreppet folkmusik?," *Hembygden* 51, no. 5 (1972): 13. Märta Ramsten references summer seminars at which the concept was discussed in 1976 and 1977 in her "Med rötter i medeltiden—Mönster och ideal hos 1960- och 1970–talets balladsångare," in *Återklang: Svensk folkmusik i förändring 1950–1980* (Stockholm: Svenskt Visarkiv, 1992), 7. The earliest Swedish writer that I have found to philosophize about the meaning of the term was Karl Sporr in "Om vår folkmusik och arbetet för dess bevarande," *Nordisk Folkdans* Julnummer (1921): 20. To

the best of my knowledge, however, Ling was the first, in 1979, to frame the concept explicitly as an ideological construct.

10. Jan Ling, "Folkmusik—En brygd," *Fataburen* (1979): 10.

11. The next general text on Swedish folk music was *Folkmusikboken*, edited by Jan Ling, Gunnar Ternhag, and Märta Ramsten (Stockholm: Prisma, 1980). This was a collaborative work based loosely upon the chapter outline of *Svensk folkmusik*, with the addition of some entirely new chapters dedicated to twentieth-century developments and critical scholarship issues. The new introduction was written by Jan Ling, and dealt, again, with the ideological underpinnings of folk music. The next general survey after *Folkmusikboken* also begins with a discussion about the folk music concept and its ideological implications, Dan Lundberg and Gunnar Ternhag's *Folkmusik i Sverige* (Smedjebacken: Gidlunds, 1996), 12–13. Similarly, Swedish scholars who have written monographs on folk music-related subjects in recent decades have generally dedicated some space to a critical examination of the folk music concept, e.g. Märta Ramsten, *Återklang: Svensk folkmusik i förändring 1950–1980* (Stockholm: Svenskt Visarkiv, 1992), 7–8; Gunnar Ternhag, *Hjort Anders Olsson: Spelman, artist* (Hedemora: Gidlunds, 1992), 14–18; Karin Eriksson, *Bland polskor, gånglåtar och valser: Hallands spelmansförbund och den halländska folkmusiken* (Gothenburg: Gothenburg University Press, 2004), 45–49; Niklas Nyqvist, *Från bondson till folkmusikikon: Otto Andersson och formandet av 'finlandssvensk folkmusik'* (Åbo: Åbo Akademis förlag, 2007), 16–17; and Ingrid Åkesson, *Med rösten som instrument: Perspektiv på nutida svensk vokal folkmusik* (Stockholm: Svenskt visarkiv, 2007), 18–23.

12. Owe Ronström, "Nationell musik? Bondemusik? Om folkmusik begreppet," in *Gimaint u bänskt*, ed. Bengt Arwidsson (Visby: Länsmuséet Gotlands Fornsal, 1989).

13. The dual meaning of the word "folk" as both an entire nation's populace and a particular substratum of that populace has been traced at least as far back as the late eighteenth century in Sweden by ethnologist Mats Rehnberg in his *Folk: Kaleidoskopiska anteckningar kring ett ord, dess innebörd och användning under skilda tider* (Stockholm: Akademilitteratur, 1976), 24.

14. Lundberg and Ternhag, *Folkmusik i Sverige*, 14.

15. Ronström, "Nationell Musik?," 17–18; "Inledning," in *Texter om svensk folkmusik—Från Haeffner till Ling*, ed. Owe Ronström and Gunnar Ternhag (Stockholm: Kungliga Musikaliska Akademien, 1994), 9; Lundberg and Ternhag, *Folkmusik i Sverige*, 14; Eriksson, *Bland polskor*, 44–45; Åkesson, *Med rösten som instrument*, 18; cf. Bohlman, *Study of Folk Music*, xviii.

16. Märta Ramsten has written that, for her, "the term folk music here stands for what it conceptually and analytically means in whatever context it is used" (*Återklang*, 7–8). Dance ethnologist Mats Nilsson has given me a similar definition, though he credits it to Jan Ling (interview by author, December 7, 2001).

17. Ronström, "Nationell musik?," 18, italics in original.

18. Eriksson, *Bland polskor*, 46; cf. *Lydia Goehr, The Imaginary Museum of Musical Works: An Essay in the Philosophy of Music* (Oxford: Clarendon Press, 1992), 90–94; and W.B. Gallie, "Essentially Contested Concepts," *Meeting of the Aristotelian Society* 56 (1956): 171–172.

19. I will not be the first ethnographer to cite a Wittgensteinian influence, of course. For instance, ethnomusicologist Jocelyne Guilbault has described the musical genre zouk as identifiable by its "family resemblances" after Wittgenstein in her *Zouk: World Music in the West Indies* (Chicago: University of Chicago Press, 1993), 48–49. Rodney Needham has famously cited Wittgenstein's family resemblances to argue for a reinven-

tion of anthropological classification systems in his "Polythetic Classification: Convergence and Consequences," *Man* 10, no. 3 (1975). Ernest Gellner went so far as to credit Wittgenstein with laying the groundwork for anthropology's massive disciplinary shift toward postmodernism, relativism, and reflexivity (which is to say, everything Gellner found deplorable in modern anthropology) in his *Language and Solitude: Wittgenstein, Malinowski, and the Habsburg Dilemma* (Cambridge: Cambridge UP, 1998).

20. Ludwig Wittgenstein, *Philosophical Investigations*, 3rd ed. (Malen: Blackwell, 2001 [1953]), §43.

21. Wittgenstein, *Philosophical Investigations*, §66–67.

22. Goehr, *Imaginary Museum*, 93–94.

23. Gallie, "Essentially Contested Concepts," 169.

24. Gallie, "Essentially Contested Concepts," 171–172, italics in original.

25. Goehr also notes that open concepts have sometimes been called "essentially contestable," though she does not cite Gallie specifically (*Imaginary Museum*, 91).

26. Gallie, "Essentially Contested Concepts," 172.

27. Gallie, "Essentially Contested Concepts," 175–180.

28. Mikhail Mikhailovich Bakhtin, "Discourse in the Novel," in *The Dialogic Imagination*, (Austin: University of Texas Press, 1981 [1934–1935]), italics in original. The essential contestedness of open concepts may further be read as the result of a feature of the "internal dialogism of authentic prose discourse" that cannot allow it to be "brought to an authentic end," since "it is not ultimately divisible into verbal exchanges possessing precisely marked boundaries" (326).

29. Bakhtin's line of reasoning does support such a reading in that he argues heteroglossia to be fundamental to "actual language" ("Discourse in the Novel," 327); his essay just happens to be focused upon the stylistic usage of this aspect of language by the novelist. For a broader anthropological discussion of heteroglossia and its relation to language and culture, see Dennis Tedlock and Bruce Mannheim, eds., *The Dialogic Emergence of Culture* (Urbana: University of Illinois Press, 1995).

30. Bakhtin, "Discourse in the Novel," 272, 327.

31. John A. Lucy, "General Introduction," in *Reflexive Language: Reported Speech and Metapragmatics*, ed. John A. Lucy (Cambridge: Cambridge University Press, 1993), 2.

32. Åsa Grogan Sol, interview by author, September 28, 2001.

33. Bakhtin describes "refraction" in the following way: "The prose writer as a novelist does not strip away the intentions of others from the heteroglot language of his works, he does not violate those socio-ideological cultural horizons (big and little worlds) that open up behind heteroglot languages—rather, he welcomes them into his work. The prose writer makes use of words that are already populated with the social intentions of others and compels them to serve his own new intentions, to serve a second master. Therefore the intentions of the prose writer are refracted, and refracted *at different angles*, depending on the degree to which the refracted, heteroglot languages he deals with are socio-ideologically alien, already embodied and already objectivized" ("Discourse in the Novel," 299–300, italics in original).

34. Ference Marton and Wing-yan Pong, "Conceptions as Ways of Being Aware of Something—Accounting for Inter- and Intra-Contextual Shifts in the Meaning of Two Economic Phenomena" (paper read at the symposium: New Challenges to Research and Learning, Helsinki, March 22, 2001), 14–18.

35. Ference Marton and Shirley Booth, *Learning and Awareness* (Mahwah: Erlbaum, 1997), 112; Marton and Pong, "Conceptions," 3–5. "In our presentation, and in

other phenomenographic studies, terms such as 'conceptions,' 'ways of understanding,' 'ways of comprehending,' and 'conceptualizations' have been used as synonyms for 'ways of experiencing'" (Marton and Booth, *Learning and Awareness*, 114).

36. Erik Gustaf Geijer, "Anmälan," *Iduna* 1 (1811): 5, capitalizations in original.

37. See, e.g., Rehnberg, *Folk*, 42; Ramsten, *Återklang*, 7. Musicologist Matthew Gelbart has noted a similar order of terminological evolution from "national" to "folk" some decades earlier in Scotland in his *The Invention of "Folk Music" and "Art Music": Emerging Categories from Ossian to Wagner* (New York: Cambridge UP, 2007), 98–102. He argues that qualities associated with folk vs. art musics there by the turn of the nineteenth century had been inherited from their late-eighteenth-century mapping onto nationally bounded musical identities: the Scottish/British vs. Italian/foreign.

38. Quoted in Jan Ling, "'Upp, bröder, kring bildningens fana': Om folkmusikens historia och ideologi," in *Folkmusikboken*, ed. Jan Ling, Gunnar Ternhag and Märta Ramsten (Stockholm: Prisma, 1980), 18.

39. Quoted in Ling, "Upp, bröder," 18; and Carl-Allan Moberg, "Tonalitetsproblem i svensk folkmusik," in *Texter om svensk folkmusik—Från Haeffner till Ling*, ed. Owe Ronström and Gunnar Ternhag (Stockholm: Kungliga Musikaliska Akademien, 1994 [1949]), 173.

40. Moberg, "Tonalitetsproblem," 173–174.

41. Orvar Löfgren, "The Nature Lovers," in *Culture Builders: A Historical Anthropology of Middle-Class Life*, ed. Jonas Frykman and Orvar Löfgren (New Brunswick: Rutgers University Press, 1987), 50–63.

42. Bohlman, *Study of Folk Music*, xix; Lundberg and Ternhag, *Folkmusik i Sverige*, 12; Gelbart, *Invention*, 40–79.

43. I have earlier labeled these axes "time, space, sight, and sound." The earlier terminology was more elegant and easier to remember, but not quite as descriptively accurate.

44. The conflicts that inhabit and confuse the Swedish folk music concept number greater than four. Yet the axes I posit, grounded as they are in the four essential ways of understanding the concept, form a solid foundation for classifying all relevant dichotomies. Most of these binarisms coincide with or fall under one of the main axes, while a few (e.g., urban/rural) may be found under several.

45. In English-speaking contexts this might be referenced as a folk/popular division (see, for example, Karpeles, "Distinction"; Peter Narváez and Martin Laba, eds., *Media Sense: The Folklore-Popular Cultural Continuum* (Bowling Green: Bowling Green State University Press, 1987). In Swedish, however, the single term *folklig* signifies both sides of the split.

CHAPTER 2

—*m*—

Reinventing Tradition

When members of the Gothic Society first took an interest in collecting peasant music in the early nineteenth century, they, like their international counterparts, were primarily interested in saving a tradition that had existed for ages and was about to go lost. In so doing, they were laying the epistemological foundations of a "Swedish folk music" on fundamental cultural products for which change could only mean decay. Especially given the ascendancy of the "work" concept at the time, it makes sense that the rescue operation should focus on melodies that could be preserved and disseminated through transcription, rather than on the ephemeral details of style and function.[1]

The rescuers of folk music created a genre that already at its inception was quite distinct from its peasant roots. Their focus on preservation meant that the repertoire was cherry-picked according to its perceived age, so that any "modern" trends were weeded out. The focus on dissemination meant that the music was arranged for piano with simple harmony accompaniments for the salon environment.[2] Songs were bowlderized and moved up to soprano range according to the stylistic standards of bourgeois music-making circles.[3]

The industrialization, emigration, modernization, and urbanization that took place over the nineteenth century did much to make the functions and music of Swedish peasant life obsolete. The champions of folk music were especially troubled by the rise of the diatonic accordion toward the end of the nineteenth century. Its scalar limitations and chordal underpinnings suited it better to newer pan-European styles than older Swedish ones. The instrument helped cement the popularity of new major-mode schottisches, mazurkas, polkas, waltzes, and the like, and homogenized the older polska dances into a more standardized form called hambo. Collectively this new accordion-associated repertoire would later come to be known as *gammeldans*, or old-time dance, when it in turn was over-shadowed by the modern dances of the early twentieth century.[4]

Meanwhile, until the last decade of the nineteenth century, the performance of "folk music" as a named genre was the exclusive domain of amateur and professional art musicians. It was really only in the first years of the twentieth century that the rescuers of this vanishing repertoire, in seeking potential bearers, turned to peasant folk musicians or *"spelmän"* (sing. *"spelman")*.[5] The first Swedish folk music contest was arranged by the painter Anders Zorn in 1906, for players of the cow horn and fiddle. Accordionists and brass instruments were explicitly barred from participation. Similar local events were held around the country in the years that followed.[6] In 1910 Zorn and a few other champions of folk music organized a national spelmans' gathering at Skansen, Stockholm's outdoor museum of Swedish folklife. This event was not a contest, but simply an opportunity for the invited spelmän to present themselves. All sixty-five musicians who answered the call were presented with a silver badge designed by Anders Zorn himself. Over the following years, smaller local "gatherings" would soon overshadow and eventually replace the contest format altogether.

The National spelmans' gathering was revived as an annual event in 1933, each year to be held in a different location in Sweden. Anders Zorn's silver badge would now be reserved for those participants who attained the highest distinction in a closed solo performance before a panel of expert adjudicators. Lesser awards would also be granted at these week-long "Zorn trials," at the ranks of certificate, bronze badge, and post-bronze certificate. In addition, one gold badge (or more rarely, two) would be presented to an individual of special distinction, pre-selected months in advance by the adjudicators.[7] Those who attained the silver or gold badge would be known as "riksspelmän" (national spelmän), an honor that even today carries significant weight both within the folk music community and in Swedish society at large.[8]

Over the first half of the twentieth century, public performances by folk musicians were dominated by virtuosic solo fiddlers from the province of Hälsingland, representatives of an innovative, crowd-pleasing style. In the 1940s, however, a new style of group fiddling was established by spelmän from the neighboring province of Dalarna. These newly founded spelman groups (*spelmanslag*) were both social clubs and performing ensembles. Their music combined the recent Dala development of second-fiddle harmonization with large-group unison fiddling, a phenomenon associated with contests and gatherings.[9] The Dala spelman group phenomenon was also foundational for the creation of a new National Organization of Swedish Spelmän in 1947, *Sveriges Spelmäns Riksförbund* (SSR). By the 1950s new spelman groups were popping up throughout throughout Sweden, and had surpassed the Hälsinge fiddlers as bearers of the iconic Swedish fiddle sound.

The Reinvention of Tradition

In the preface to his landmark 1964 survey *Svensk folkmusik*, Jan Ling opens by stating as his purpose "to present different types of music and instruments in the old Swedish peasant society as well as to clarify what seems to belong to the environment and what can be designated as outside stylistic influences."[10] Ling's concern with isolating outside influences from music that "belonged," expressed here in the mid-sixties, did not last long into his scholarship, however. On the contrary, much of the work he published from the late seventies to early nineties carried the explicit or implicit argument that outside influence, perhaps more than any other element, itself belonged as an essential feature of Swedish folk music.[11]

This change in Ling's approach was doubtless catalyzed by his growing concern with the ideological baggage tied to the folk music concept, and what he perceived to be problematic conceptual links between its reactionary past and supposedly progressive present.[12] Ling's marriage of tradition and adaptability was part of an attempt at severing folk music from its historical connections to a paranoid xenophobia that had sought since the early nineteenth century to preserve native cultural traditions against the threat of foreign contamination.[13] A critical aspect of Ling's solution, however, was that it did not force the abandonment of the native traditions that still today lay claim to the cultural capital associated with the folk music concept. In making outside influence an essential ingredient of traditional folk music, Ling gracefully negotiated a tension between the tradition that granted folk music its currency, and the innovation that could free it from the suffocating effects of history.

Ling's efforts at redefining what tradition could mean were also part of a broader trend, in Sweden and elsewhere, toward a general reconceptualization of the term.[14] In 1960, Albert Lord endeavored to reclaim for oral traditions some of the currency of creativity and authorship he considered to be unfairly monopolized by written culture. To this purpose he redefined tradition "not as the inert acceptance of a fossilized corpus of themes and conventions, but as an organic habit of re-creating what has been received and is handed on."[15] While scholars to this day may persist in using the term in the sense of unchanging cultural product, those who engage with it critically for the purpose of definition have generally followed Lord's example, seeing continuity and change as coexisting elements within it.[16]

Such definitions are more prescriptive than descriptive, however. They chart the course for a desired paradigm shift, for ethnographers especially, away from those of our scholarly predecessors who sought the civilized world's living pre-history among isolated tribes, groups whose value was thereby made contingent on their uncontaminated and unchanging customs.[17] Proactive redefinitions of "tradition" have thus saved the term from the fate of its less fortunate cousin, "authenticity," which having benefited from no such reconceptualization, was long ago banished to less enlightened halls.[18] Yet analysis of how the term "tradition" is actually used will reveal that its reinvented meaning is by no means ubiquitous.[19] Many continue to use it in reference to cultural product.[20] Further, the fact that "tradition" now has multiple possible meanings actually makes ethnographically-based critical analysis of relevant utterances more difficult. A person may use the term in that older sense of ancient custom, and when asked about it, define it using its reinvented meaning. In this way the specter of authenticity will always haunt, constantly threatening to take possession of tradition, only to flee when the light of interrogation is turned directly upon it. This ambiguity may have a beneficial aspect as well: The opposing internal meanings of the term may serve to remind us of the conflicted relationship we maintain with the ghosts of our own scholarly traditions.

Part of the impulse among scholars to protect the currency associated with their subject of study may relate to their own professional self-interests. The fact that the vast majority of Swedish scholars of folk music are practitioners as well can only add incentive. Those scholars who have flirted with denying legitimacy to the concept are, in fact, the same few who are not themselves players of the music.[21] Even these scholars must feel a closeness to the broader folk music community, however, given that much of their colleague and student base is made up of practitioners.

The connections between scholarly and academic realms have both influenced the development of the tradition concept among academics and allowed it to be echoed back to—and further developed by—the Swedish folk music community at large. Jan Ling has been both influenced and influential in this respect. His ideas about innovation as an aspect of tradition were inspired largely by the close watch he kept on the Swedish folk music revival, which was at its peak when he first began publishing on the subject. He reacted strongly against what he saw as reactionary romantic tendencies among many revivalists, and embraced the innovative musical practices of the likes of Groupa and jazz pianist Jan Johansson, whose staying power he attributed to a lack of fixation on any ideology of romanticism or authenticity.[22]

As I have argued in the previous chapter, these writings later influenced a new generation of practitioner-academics who would then echo them out to the broader Swedish folk music community. Fiddler/scholar Dan Olsson has communicated to me in interviews and other conversations that he owes a great deal to Ling in this respect, on more than one occasion referring me to Ling's articles and citing his definitions of the term. I have witnessed this influence borne out in Olsson's work as a teacher at the Gothenburg School of Music, as a musician talking casually with other musicians, and as president of the Swedish Folk Music and Dance Association.[23] It was in this last capacity that Olsson was honored with the inaugural speech at the 2004 Falun Folk Festival, where his theme was innovation as an essential aspect of tradition. I did not hear this speech myself (though Olsson has since supplied me with a copy). Rather, I saw it cited later that night before a packed community center hall by Sten Sandahl, producer of folk and world music for Concerts Sweden in his introduction to the Festival's opening concert.[24] Sandahl then went on to frame the series of concert acts (Klacklek, Väsen, and Frifot) as representatives of various and equally valuable points along the spectrum of innovation and tradition.

I cannot prove conclusively that this sort of echo effect is entirely responsible for the reconceptualization of tradition in the broader folk music community. I do know, however, from my field experience, that the reinvented tradition concept is very much at play in that wider arena. The word "authentic" came up very rarely in my interviews. Over the course of my first fieldwork year, in over sixty hours and 540,000 words it surfaced six times. Five times were in a discussion with ethnomusicologist and riksspelman Karin Eriksson, who positioned herself critically against it after I brought it up. Only once was it used uncritically, by fiddler Ulf Kinding.[25] The word "genuine" was slightly more common, with thirty-five occurrences, sometimes sincere, sometimes with critical distance, and sometimes in less relevant contexts.[26] Another Swedish synonym, "äkta," was used seventeen times.[27] "Tradition," on the other hand, was mentioned 653 times, and consistently betrayed tensions along lines similar to those discussed above.[28]

What follows is a discussion of some of the ways in which different musicians have positioned themselves and their music in relation to the tradition concept. Where folk music scholars tend primarily to be concerned with defining their terms and limiting their field of study, folk musicians must deal with the practical concern of how to create a personal relationship to the music. Very broadly, I have discerned four different approaches among practitioners. I have labeled them preservationism, neomedievalism, neotraditionalism, and innovationism.[29]

The preservationist sees tradition as both static and of great intrinsic value. Musicians who take this view are typically fiddlers for whom the rescue and maintenance of cultural heritage take precedence over specifically musical qualities of the material. Some of the older Gothenburg spelman groups maintain an explicit ideology of preservation, and learn hundreds if not thousands of tunes primarily to that end. When they gather to play, these groups spend little if any time focusing on music as a means of expression, or addressing issues of musicality, but rather tend to shuffle quickly through their extensive repertoire. This approach to tradition sets fairly strict limitations on personal creativity, and cannot be said to be ubiquitous even in these specific contexts. Because of the conservatism of this position, and because it does not allow for much in the way of musical development, those who hold it tend to be taken less seriously by others, serving as straw men for the more irreverent musicians, and kept at an ideological distance by those who hold a more moderately conservative position.

The neomedievalist is a musician who imagines and reinvents a lost, ancient music culture, from a time before credible source materials. Here, innovation generates tradition. The repertoire is generally a combination of new compositions and the most ancient-sounding traditional tunes. Instrumentation may vary greatly, but often includes reconstructed historical instruments such as bagpipes, hurdy-gurdies, and early nyckelharpor.[30] This approach is probably the least common of the four, and the most peripheral to the subculture.

Perhaps most common is the neotraditionalist, who views tradition as a frame within which a limited range of motion is allowed. This strategy seems most prevalent among those fiddlers whose primary interest is in the music, rather than the heritage. Where preservationism corresponds to the older sense of static tradition or authenticity, neotraditionalism is related to the reinvented tradition concept, with all its inner conflicts. The following statement by fiddler Greger Siljebo illustrates some of the tensions that define the neotraditionalist philosophy:

> On the question of styles and traditions and everything, it's hard to talk about right and wrong, because there are so many different variants, and it's difficult to isolate an original source. As a result you have certain freedoms to operate within that framework. . . . On the other hand, I don't think you should take any liberties you want; I mean we owe the music to try to ground ourselves in it in some way.[31]

Musicians who take the fourth, innovationist approach see tradition as either static or slow-changing, and conceptualize it in opposition to the modern and mutable. They situate themselves somewhere in between, where they must negotiate the two. Often these musicians are not fiddlers, but play instruments that were brought into the world of Swedish folk music during the folk music revival and after: saxophone, guitar, percussion, and the like. This positioning may create a kind of constant back and forth between tradition and innovation. Percussionist Anders Waernelius describes his relationship to tradition in his music-making: "I think it's kind of cyclical. You begin from tradition, and then you break free, and you come around to something modern or electronic, then you go back to tradition again, and it just goes around and around."[32]

These last two approaches have much in common, in that they both allow for limited movement within some kind of frame. Both permit the musicians to negotiate a personal creative space while retaining some connection to the tradition concept. These two approaches may also overlap and intersect in various ways. In order to better illustrate some of the similarities and differences between these latter two positions, I compare the utterances of two musicians who I feel represent their respective perspectives: fiddler Joar Skorpen and saxophonist Mats Nilsson. Both are professional players for whom the province of Bohuslän is an area of musical specialization and interest that complements a much broader repertoire.

The Neotraditionalist Approach

Though born and raised in Sweden, Joar Skorpen has family roots in Norway, and espouses a dual Swedish/Norwegian musical identity. Like many fiddlers of his post-revival generation, Skorpen has a strong background in art music as well as folk music traditions. He started classical violin at age nine, and as of the time of his interview split his time playing in Norway's Kristiansund Opera and studying twentieth-century music at the Gothenburg School of Music. Skorpen began playing *hardingfela* at around age sixteen, and has since frequently engaged himself in Norwegian spelman competitions, called *kappleikar*.[33] He made his first forays into Swedish folk music at the Gothenburg School of Music with his friend and fellow fiddler Henrik Silverhjelm, with whom he founded the ensemble Lekarlaget in 1994. When I interviewed him in November of 2001, Skorpen had within the past two years become very interested in the music of Bohuslän, the province of his birth. That summer he had gained the title of riksspelman for the playing of fiddle tunes from southern Bohuslän, an area of Sweden that has traditionally received little attention from either scholars or players.

According to Skorpen, lines drawn between Norwegian and Swedish traditions are not as clear as those that can be found between "weak" tradition areas, like southern Bohuslän, and "strong" areas like Dalarna in Sweden and Telemark in Norway. For Skorpen, the folk musician's loyalty to the tradition is far more critical in weak tradition areas. His or her impact on the future of the local tradition will be greater in such places, where cultural heritage has not been maintained continuously.

Nevertheless, Skorpen does speak of situations in which he as a musician and scholar has had the opportunity to express personal creativity in terms of his relationship to the folk music of southern Bohuslän. Firstly, he sees as the folk musician's goal in a weak tradition area not to slavishly reproduce a previous style, but rather to reconstruct the tradition as if it had been continuous and strong all along:

> The point isn't to get it to sound exactly like it sounded before. It's to get it to sound as if there had been an unbroken major tradition, as if there had been a bunch of spelmän all along the way. Which isn't the case in southern Bohuslän. ... You can hear the difference clearly in those areas where there is an unbroken tradition, because in those places there's a big difference if you just go back fifty years, between how they played then and how they play now. Playing styles and ideals have changed a lot. So for me there's no point in playing like they did in 1920. But on the other hand it's important to find, it gets very abstract, but to find whatever is essential. And I have this perspective very much from Sigmund Eikås, who taught me *hardingfela*.[34]

Again, this approach is related to the reinvented tradition concept, which posits change as a defining characteristic of tradition.

The approach also allows for a certain amount of personal creativity in its focus on musical reconstruction. The research process that Skorpen describes further justifies this limited freedom. He tries to crack the southern Bohuslän "code" by listening to old field recordings and analyzing old transcriptions, and bouncing theories off of fellow players and scholars. Eventually, informed by these processes, Skorpen creates his personal Bohuslän style:

> I'm interested in going as far as I can find sources. And when I get to the point where I can't find any more sources, that's when I try to find a reasonable solution for myself. I'll happily talk to other people about it too, and see if they also think that "yeah, that sounds probable, that's the way it might have been."[35]

According to Skorpen, the ability to crack a local "code" is the key to being able to play the music of any tradition, weak or strong. Skorpen compares the relative merits of different methods for internalizing regional codes in a way consistent with the reinvented tradition paradigm, placing focus on process rather than product. His ideal method is to learn directly from other players. Only after doing this will he have confidence in his interpretations of recordings and transcriptions. Thus, the ease with which he can learn regional codes is directly related to the strength of the local tradition. Where many fiddlers are available to play with, codes may be learned more quickly and with greater authority.

The cracking of a code for a given region entails awareness of which musical elements are central and which can be dispensed with or varied. Only after Skorpen has achieved this awareness does he have the ability to express himself creatively within that tradition without fear of breaking its bounds. In places where the tradition is strong, he can experiment with the boundaries with greater confidence, because he can be more secure in his knowledge, and because he knows he will have less of an impact on the future of the tradition.

Thus, where weak tradition areas grant Skorpen opportunities for creative expression by forcing him to postulate missing pieces of the puzzle and to project what would have been, the strong areas grant him creative license due to their greater authority and resilience. Skorpen describes how the competitive Norwegian *kappleik* system, precisely because it represents such a strong force for tradition, allows him to test the limits of what tradition permits in his own compositions:

> [H]ere in Sweden I meet a lot of skepticism against Norwegian *kappleikar* . . . that it's an artificial system, and that there aren't any variables in it. I actually think that's completely wrong, because I've discovered that there's actually a lot of room for variation. It's just that you have to follow the rules of the game. But if you find an opening there, you can get incredibly far away. I've done that sometimes, just for fun, at smaller *kappleikar*. I've tested the boundaries every now and again to see what they'll accept, and it turns out you can do a lot.

Kaminsky: But is it that you still keep that, what you were talking about before, this central importing thing, whatever it is?
Skorpen: Yes, exactly. I can give you an example of something I did once. I'm almost embarrassed, but then, it was good to try it. It wasn't really about what you could do, but rather to test if I had found that core. For example, you can play a tune that's commonly used in tradition, but if you play it with completely alien bowing, or with unintelligible rhythm, you get reamed, even though it's very conventional. But what I wanted to do—I had been doing my military service. Our first month we were at Evjemoen, in southern Norway. Near Setesdal. So –
Kaminsky: You did your military service in Norway?
Skorpen: Yeah, I'm a Norwegian citizen. So we had a big band in the music platoon there, and they wanted *hardingfela* during one of their numbers. It was "Final Countdown," and they were going to do a break in the middle, and I was going to come in and play *hardingfela*. So I took the theme from "Final Countdown" and I made a tune out of it. I tried to make it like a Setesdal *gangar* with these typical double foot stomps. And the theme was pretty submerged, so if you didn't know about it you wouldn't have heard it. And to complete the package I named it *Täljaren*, because their tunes have names like that: *Klunkaren* and *Tjuvaren*. I had never even intended to play it, but then I thought, I have to try this at a *kappleik*. So I was at a little *kappleik*, where I had been a lot and knew the people a little. And I didn't say what it was, I just said it was *Täljaren*, a tune from Evjen, in Setesdal. And because of the respect that I have for the judges, I thought that if they accept it, well, it doesn't matter who wrote it, I mean then the style is right. So I wasn't out to provoke or test the *kappleik*, it was really the tune I wanted to test. And it worked, because I placed just about where I usually do.[36]

Skorpen has tested multiple original tunes in this way. His habit of bouncing new ideas off the *kappleik*'s traditionalist wall is just one manifestation of how he plays tradition and innovation against one another.

Another relates directly to his dual identity as a simultaneously Swedish and Norwegian fiddler. Skorpen draws a picture of stark contrasts between his two motherlands and their folk music spheres. The Norwegian system, centered around the *kappleik*, has a density of tradition, a seriousness of endeavor, and strict categories for defining and ranking folk music.[37] The Swedish folk music system is more haphazard, loosely revolving around gatherings and festivals. This subculture is less in the public eye than in Norway, relying upon an inclusive definition of itself that welcomes various kinds of fusion and refuses to draw strict boundaries of any kind. As someone who travels in both worlds, Skorpen observes that his perspective changes based on his location:

I'm always in the opposition in some strange way. And I guess that's what's fun about having a foot in each camp, in Sweden and Norway. When I'm in Sweden it's just like I sound right now, I sound very categorical and very "this is the way it should be," all about preserving the tradition. When I go to Norway I'm just the opposite, because there there's enough of it from before, so some kind of counterbalance is needed.[38]

Skorpen's statement here about needing to act as a counterbalance is critical. It reveals that he is doing more than simply occupying a neutral position somewhere between an overly conservative Norway and a loose-with-the-rules Sweden. He positions himself on different points of the spectrum with self-aware intentionality, shifting his weight to balance out the imbalances he sees in each country's attitude toward folk music. In Sweden he argues as a Norwegian, and in Norway as a Swede. The boundary between the countries cannot be occupied ideologically any more than it can be occupied geographically, and thus no possibility exists of a coherent argument that might proceeded from any kind of center or neutral zone. There is no center, and the act of balancing for Skorpen is an interminable one.[39]

The Innovationist Approach

Saxophonist and recorder player Mats Nilsson expresses a somewhat different relationship to tradition than does Skorpen, though they do share the same dilemma of how to balance tradition and innovation. Nilsson has a broad repertoire of Swedish folk music he has learned from other musicians and recordings, grounded primarily in the west coast tunes taught to him by accordionist and band mate Per Sandberg. He had his first major exposure to Swedish folk music in 1989, when he took his family to the Falun Folk Festival on a tip from a friend. He describes the experience as illuminating:

> I went to Falun with my family, and I was completely taken; I really got into it. And what I really got into was how different the music-making was, compared to rock music. I usually put it this way: When you have a rock band, you have drums and bass, guitar and vocals. You can really take away the vocals, and you can take away the guitar too, but you still get a sense of energy from the drums and the bass. But you can't take away drums and bass. Because then you don't have much power left. What became clear to me that week in Falun was that the energy in folk music was in a completely different place. The energy was in the melody playing—in the tune itself, and the way it was played.[40]

Upon their return home, Nilsson and his family became regulars at the Gothenburg Folk Music Café. Nilsson and Sandberg started playing together as a duo in 1990 under the name RÅ-mantik (RAW-mance). In 1993 they added percussionist Anders Waernelius and today RÅmantik—they have since dropped the dash—is still active as a trio, with a repertoire that centers around, but does not limit itself to, Swedish folk music.[41]

As with Skorpen, Nilsson's view of tradition changes based on his perspective, though for Nilsson the relevant split lies not along the Swedish/Norwegian border, but between Sweden's folk music subculture on the one hand and general society on the other. When discussing Swedish society at large, tradition is to Nilsson something intrinsically valuable, under threat from the apathetic stance that most Swedes hold toward their cultural heritage. When he discusses issues specific to the small world of Swedish folk music, however, Nilsson places value on innovative performance, and tradition becomes either something conservative from which he distances himself, or a rich source of materials to mine. These apparently conflicting perspectives may also be tied to two separate concerns of the professional folk musician: as an artist Nilsson reacts against the conservatism of the folk music movement, while as a gigging musician he reacts against a mainstream that seems indifferent to his music.

In that smaller folk music sphere, the main element that distances Nilsson from tradition is an interest in musical practices he identifies as non-existent within traditional Swedish folk music. The musical arrangements of RÅmantik reflect this approach to the music:

> Swedish folk music has a little problem, because traditionally a whole acousti-
> cal space is missing from it. And that's the lower frequencies, the lower regis-
> ter. Traditionally there's no bass; there's no percussion either, really. And I
> really like it when you use that space, especially when you use it in a personal
> way. . . . I think Per is a very good example there. Because he has a way of
> playing bass lines on his accordion that nobody else has. I think he's found a
> completely personal way to be down there in that register, that actually doesn't
> exist. It just doesn't exist. Traditionally that register doesn't exist.[42]

This sort of observation is common among innovationists. Every percussionist, guitarist, and accordionist I have interviewed speaks of the challenge of having to develop a personal musical style in relationship to the Swedish fiddle tradition. The difficulty of adding new elements to a tradition that has previously developed in such a way as to not leave space for them forces a practice of constant innovation. Thus, for Nilsson, mixed-instrument groups become the living element within Swedish folk music:

> I'm thinking now of modern ensemble playing in Swedish folk music, which I
> think is a little genre of its own that's very unique, and very interesting, and
> pretty new. That's the one that's alive, you could say. In traditional fiddle play-
> ing—one fiddle, two fiddles, many fiddles—what happens there is you can
> have more or less talented fiddlers, and they can play the music more or less
> well, in a way that's more or less interesting. But that form is pretty fixed.
> Where folk music lives is in some kind of ensemble playing.[43]

Even within that smaller subcultural folk music sphere, however, Nilsson considers the tradition of critical import from an aesthetic point of view. He likens the folk musician's knowledge of the various kinds of ornamentation used in different areas of Sweden to the chef's knowledge of spices from different areas of the world. But Nilsson's interest is more in the spice than in the region, and in this sense his perspective on tradition remains one of a self-identified outsider.

This perspective changes when he begins to talk about the general Swedish populace and their obliviousness to folk music:

> Many people are familiar with a little gammeldans music around Christmas. And there are old tunes there too, to be sure—"Hej Tomtegubbar" and polskor and so on, of course there are. But this whole sphere that we're involved in, going around to polska clubs and playing a living traditional music, it's completely unknown among most people. They don't know it exists.[44]

When the context becomes Swedish society at large, the differences between "traditional" fiddle and "living" ensemble music lose much of their significance. The polska club environment Nilsson describes includes all branches of folk music, old and new. His use of the construction "living traditional music" collapses these various musical forms together as a single conceptual entity, unified in the giant mass-cultural blind spot they together occupy.

When looking at Swedish folk music from this broader perspective as a marginalized tradition among other dominant traditions (Nilsson uses phrases like "the Western tradition," "the gammeldans tradition," and "traditional pop"), the critical distinguishing musical factor becomes mode, rather than instrumentation and arrangement:

> Western music has developed a harmonic system that doesn't exist in Swedish folk music, in fiddle spelman music. . . . 98 percent of the music we hear in the world today is written based on those rules. And many people call [accordionist] Calle Jularbo Swedish folk music also, which of course it is, even if I'm interested in the one that's older. But this harmonic music has a huge impact in Sweden at the end of the nineteenth century, when the accordion comes. You know about this stuff, right? And you can also hear it in the tunes that come with that music. They're completely harmonically constructed. . . . The set of rules for making melodies in the Swedish fiddle spelman tradition is entirely different. We call it "modal," we have names for it, but that's the difference I mean.[45]

Here the older fiddle tradition and the newer ensemble folk music are unified in their common stock of modal tunes, and placed in opposition to an otherwise nearly ubiquitous harmonically-based music. The harmonic underpinnings of Swedish accordion music represent a significant logical obstacle here, as Nilsson must acknowledge its inclusion under the folk music banner, even as he posits modality as a core characteristic of Swedish folk music.[46]

Skorpen and Nilsson have very different approaches, but what they do share in common is this dual positioning along the time axis that shifts according to context, from Norway to Sweden in Skorpen's case, and subculture to mass culture for Nilsson. In a sense, Nilsson's approach can also be said to contain Skorpen's. When Nilsson broadens his scope to discuss folk music within the context of Swedish society at large, he places himself within the tradition and thus occupies something of a neotraditionalist stance.

The Neomedievalist Approach

The neomedievalist approach is also very much informed by the simultaneous drive for tradition and innovation. It rests on the basic principle that projecting your musical roots back to a time when authoritative sources are few has the dual effect of granting the currency of a romantic past while freeing you from the responsibility of loyalty to a continuous tradition. Percussionist Magnus Ek expresses this point of view in a critique of the old field recordings that have been so important to the reconstruction of Swedish folk music:

> I've made my attempts to listen to old music. But I realize I might not be the most sympathetic candidate—I think you can find gold here, even though I poke fun at it, I do think you can. It depends on who you are. And maybe you're the only one who can see the gold. But I mean, sometimes you can't even tell what they're playing. And then I can also get a little tired of it: "What the hell is this? He can't even play!" And "So what, let me get my inspiration from somewhere else; I only have the patience to dig so deep." Tradition is important from a certain standpoint; it is important to feel a connection back in time. But I feel it farther back. I mean, personally I feel that contact from what I imagine is somewhere around the eleventh century. And at that point there isn't anyone who knows how it sounded anyway. So then you have free reign; you can do what you like.[47]

Märta Ramsten has noted that the Swedish folk music revival was marked by the rise of a new, self-consciously archaic style, characterized by "sonorous play on multiple strings with drone and almost exaggerated rhythmic marking by way of stomping."[48] According to Ramsten, this style "spread during the seventies at spelman gatherings, classes, and through gramophone releases and can without a doubt be said to be one of the most audible and tangible manifestations of the folk music vogue among fiddlers."[49]

In order to analyze this new style and its ideological underpinnings, Ramsten examined contemporaneous folk music albums and their sleeve jackets. She demonstrates that in the liner notes specifically

> we can read a reaction against high culture's presentational music and dance, cultivated in concert situations, in folk dance associations, and in older folk music organizations. Function and community are keywords. The dance should be a natural element within everyday culture. One does not look to the contemporary music of youth culture, but back in history where one finds the music and dance that grows out of community in work and play in the old village society—a lifestyle to identify with.[50]

In distancing themselves from the high-culture trappings of the previous generation's folk music institutions, the revivalist rebels positioned themselves closer to the Natural and the Folk. And ingeniously, by appealing to an even earlier generation's village life, they constructed themselves as more Traditional than their more recent cultural predecessors.

A related trend of the late 1970s and early 1980s, which Ramsten has also noted, was an increased interest in reviving early Swedish instruments like the bow harp, hurdy-gurdy, bagpipe, and various early nyckelharpor.[51] This movement achieved its greatest visibility with Hedningarna, a folk rock group formed as a trio in 1987 by multi-instrumentalists Anders Norudde (nee Stake), Björn Tollin, and Hållbus Totte Mattsson. The group grew in membership and remained active until around 2003.[52] Throughout the nineties they were one of a very few Scandinavian folk groups with relatively broad name recognition among the wider Swedish populace. Their musical approach, though it varied from album to album, usually relied on some kind of fusion of the oldest and the newest musics; hypnotic small-range modal melodies that, even when original, recall a deep and mystical past, over dance grooves that sometimes suggest the techno club.[53] The liner notes to their second album, written by journalist Lars Nylin, are a perfect expression of the neomedievalist sentiment:

> It's easy to make this into a kind of hypothetical soundtrack to the Swedish middle ages. The problem is that such fantasy images are *too* easy, almost sloppy. The truth is clear: This is no aged music. The real question is whether any music made in Sweden today is more border- and timeless? Despite that the point of departure is the ur-Swedish northern lands' folk music, the end result is fascinatingly impossible to classify and place geographically. Or to date.[54]

This statement again reveals something of the efficacy of the neomedievalist approach: The band can appropriate the currency of an ancient Swedish music without operating in the shadow of the tradition of any particular time or place. On the other hand, this does not preclude the group from being loyal to specific traditions. Rather, it allows complete freedom in choosing which traditions to honor and how far to follow them.

The Politics of Instrumentation

Nineteenth-century collectors privileged music from three different contexts, each with its own repertoire, instrumentation, and gender associations. Fiddles, clarinets, and nyckelharpor were primarily male, associated with public music for dancing, celebrations, holidays, and life cycle events. Here polska was the dance form *par excellence*, while marches and walking tunes were staples of the celebratory genres. Of the forest instruments, animal horns went with the female herding tradition, while simple instruments of bark and wood were male-gendered, like the knives that whittled them.[55] Here the women's herding calls and horn tunes were of primary interest.[56] Finally, collectors went to women primarily for the mostly-domestic singing tradition: ballads, lullabies, hymns, and song games.[57]

These standard traditional forms as defined by nineteenth-century collectors have not seen significant challenge since that time.[58] They still make up the core folk music repertoire. In the dance realm, the polskor have come to be supplemented to a certain extent by gammeldans elements, especially schottisches and waltzes. But other than this minor addition, little change has occurred with respect to the basic forms. Most musical innovations engendered by the revival can be linked directly to new instrumentation and orchestration.

Musicians who entered the revival in its early days did so with relatively few experienced folk musicians to emulate. This paucity of tradition bearers no doubt contributed to the easy purchase found in the revival world by proto-neomedievalists, who enjoyed the advantage of having no need for them. It also meant that, in the absence of elders, much of the revival's leadership would have to come from musical traditions outside of Swedish folk music. As players of rock, jazz, pop, Western classical, and various international traditions came to fill out these roles, they brought not only their musical sensibilities, but in many cases also their instruments with them. Fiddles and clarinets thus came to be joined not only by the neomedievalists' bagpipes and hurdy-gurdies, but also by (the short list:) electric guitars and basses, drum kits, saxophones, trumpets, flutes, violas, cellos, acoustic guitars, recorders, bouzoukis, mandolas, didgeridoos, and a panoply of percussion instruments from around the world.

I have found from my interviews that players of such instruments today have by and large approached the music with great respect for the existing fiddle tradition. Those who play melody instruments like saxophone, flute, and even in some cases the more traditional clarinet and accordion have consistently cited the need to study fiddle bowing to play folk music well; with the air stream or bellows conceived as a substitute for the bow. Sten Källman, the preeminent player of Swedish folk saxophone, makes this argument:

> You're borrowing a genre where fiddlers are your primary predecessors, and the fiddle is still what carries the swing of the music and the dance. It's point-less to try to talk it away, that's just the way it is. It's not the bagpipe, if you're going to think "what other instruments are there in Sweden? Okay, bagpipe." I don't have any idea how bagpipes might have sounded in polska, since they don't have anything that approaches the swing of the bow. Phrasing. Rhythm. And that's why you go to the fiddle and the bow to get information. That's how it's always been.[59]

Hanna Wiskari, a student of Källman's, makes similar statements and cites him as her source when it comes to this approach. She says that "there is no folk music saxophone school, because it's based on the premise that you're supposed to sound like a fiddle."[60] This paradoxical statement (because of the nature of the school, there is no school) illustrates beautifully the ideology of the new tradition of folk music saxophone players and their reluctance to make themselves independent of their parent fiddle tradition. This, again, is part of the folk music balancing act. The weight of playing a new instrument must be counterbalanced by explicit identification with an older one. The folk music saxophone tradition can only develop by locking itself to the development of the fiddle tradition. Otherwise it risks evolving too far from home.

Non-melody players often make similar statements about the lack of schools or traditions for their instruments, despite the fact that many of those instruments too have now been used in folk music spheres for thirty years or more. Unlike melody instrument players, however, they cannot model their playing on that of the fiddle, because their musical roles are too different. Instead, most of these musicians relate having to develop a personal solution, often involving a difficult process of trial and error, for accompanying a music that has developed without the need for, and without leaving much space for, separate harmony and rhythm parts. While most of these musicians relate having had to develop personal styles without the support of a previous tradition, the solutions they reach seem to have much in common. Most critically, they almost all discuss a need to avoid the easy trap of locking the melody part into a strict metrical frame, though some have reached this conclusion only after years of playing. Sten Källman, who as a multi-instrumentalist in the group Filarfolket was essential to the early development of Swedish folk percussion as well as saxophone styles, describes the evolution of his attitudes toward percussion accompaniment in polska:

> Mostly we developed ideas around the drums and how you could play them, which had to do with my background and experience within Haitian music. . . . When it came to percussion, you could take 6/8 music which was [*vocalizes 12/8 ostinato pattern: 2 + 2 + 1 + 2 + 2 + 2 + 1*] and you redid it: [*changes pattern to 9/8: 2 + 2 + 1 + 2 + 2*]. . . . If you cropped the last three, the result was that you got nine, and it became the polska's triplet subdivision. . . . But the problem with this that I discovered, and I'm sure others realized this too, was that it became very static. It was just a little stiff, with this kind of drum accompaniment figure. You forced the tunes into this [*drumming in strict 9/8*]. And they're not like that. They're not so determined. They haven't chosen sides between triplets and straight eighth notes. . . . So suddenly the tambourine and the talking drum came, and these soft drums; they become more interesting. Björn Tollin in Hedningarna, his way of playing tambourine, I thought "wow, this way might have more possibilities."[61]

Though solutions do vary from player to player, everyone does end up answering the same question of how to support the melody without dominating or displacing it in any way. As players of non-traditional melody instruments subordinate themselves to the fiddle, so do players of non-melody instruments subordinate themselves to the melody.

In part due to the respect and humility players of non-traditional instruments tend to show toward the older traditions, and in part due to a general Swedish ideology of egalitarianism, explicit statements criticizing the use of non-traditional instruments today seem in my experience to be limited almost exclusively to musicians of the cultural preservationist camp. While my position as an ethnographer and a flutist may inhibit some from speaking their mind on this issue, my interviews with other players of non-traditional instruments suggest that few have experienced any friction because of it. Where the issue does come up, it tends to be over how such an instrument is played—whether or not it leaves proper space for the melody in the case of a supporting instrument, or respects the fiddle tradition in the case of a melody instrument—rather than the non-traditional nature of the instrument itself.

To say that the question of traditional vs. non-traditional instruments is a non-issue, however, would be overreaching. I would rather argue that the presence of non-traditional instruments in today's Swedish folk music sphere becomes yet another potent expression of the mutual reinforcement of innovation and tradition. Joar Skorpen relates that many people register surprise that he would, as a fairly conservative fiddler, perform with saxophonist Hanna Wiskari. He says that he does so because she has the right attitude toward and respect for the music. This utterance has the dual effect of showing that Skorpen is open to the kind of change the saxophone represents, while simultaneously validating the older tradition by demonstrating its value to an extended group of musicians and its ability to accommodate their instruments.[62] Newer instruments can thus contribute positively to the folk music movement's need for simultaneity of tradition and innovation, of Swedish heritage and cross-cultural inclusiveness.

This may go to explain the anger generated among some Swedish folk musicians at attempts by folk music organizations to draw official defining lines between traditional and non-traditional instruments. When this happens, the logical inconsistency built into a "tradition" concept constructed over decades by a sequence of people with varying motivations and ideologies becomes the strongest weapon for those who argue for inclusiveness. The result of such a process is that every boundary can be shown to be arbitrary.

Most arguments I have heard decrying artificial dividing lines between traditional and non-traditional instruments regard the criteria for determining what kind of instrumentalists are considered eligible for the riksspelman title. The example I choose to examine here is slightly different, however. I choose it because it is one case where the specific reasons for using that dividing line are brought into the debate.

In the summer of 1999, visitors to the Ransäter spelman gathering were greeted by the following sign at the entrance:

> Statute regarding free entry during the Ransäter gathering enacted by the board 6/24/98. The Ransäter gathering shall be a stimulus for traditional Swedish folk music. Therefore those spelmän who play fiddle, nyckelharpa, clarinet, bagpipe, and accordion are granted free entry upon presentation of any of these instruments. In addition, riksspelmän have free entry upon presentation of their instrument along with the Zorn badge in silver or gold. Other spelmän are wel-

come, but shall pay the entrance fee like everyone else. Buy a weekend pass
and support the Ransäter gathering.
    – The board of the Ransäter gathering association[63]

The ensuing debate entered print with the publication of two editorials in *Spel-mannen*, the quarterly periodical of SSR. The first was written by Gothenburg-area recorder player Lars-Gunnar Franzén, who reacted strongly against the posting of the statute.[64] Published with this letter was a response by Gert Ohls-son, the chair of the Ransäter gathering association, defending its use.[65] The debate continued into the next issue of *Spelmannen*, on the radio show *Mitt i Musiken*, and on the online svenskfolkmusik Yahoo discussion group, where it lasted twenty-five days and saw over a hundred postings, doubling the average monthly volume for the list.[66]

    Franzén argued that the statute was alienating to that segment of Sweden's folk music community who did not play one of the five legitimated instruments, effectively making them into second-class citizens. Much of his editorial was also dedicated to decrying the arbitrariness of selecting these five specific in-struments. The harmonica was as old as the accordion, the southern Swedish flute tradition was as well-documented as that of the bagpipe, and the chromatic nyckelharpa was a twentieth-century invention. Franzén concluded by suggest-ing various solutions to the economic problems of the gathering, including re-duced or voluntary admission for all.

    Gert Ohlsson responded that an economic issue did need to be addressed, but that the board wished to find a solution that would allow the tradition to flourish. The line was drawn where it was simply because it needed to be drawn somewhere. Ohlsson did make some attempts also at answering Franzén's criti-cism of the selection of these instruments, by noting for instance that the chro-matic nyckelharpa was the newer form of an older instrument. But he admitted also that one of the main motivating factors behind the statute was that people had been getting out of paying admission by displaying cheap plastic recorders and harmonicas at the entry.

    Dan Olsson, who plays regularly in a duo with Lars-Gunnar Franzén at Ransäter and elsewhere, leveled the most devastating argument against Ohls-son's side as the debate in its online form was drawing to a close:

It seems that the debate about the Ransäter gathering entry fee is nearing its end. Unfortunately. A little summation:
    As everyone has probably understood, the discussion is about two com-pletely different things. The gathering's official reason for the entrance fee is that they want to nurture traditional Swedish folk music; the real reason is that they want to solve a problem. It would of course have been better if the board had stated the case as it was, instead of hiding behind preservationist empty rhetoric and in defining traditional instruments furthermore appearing more his-torically ignorant than they really are. Instruments hundreds of years older than the fiddle do not fall within the tradition concept because they're too easy to fit in your pocket. Now they're forced into a debate they never meant to start and

the more they defend themselves the dumber they will appear—if they don't put the REAL reason in focus.[67]

Though the political motivations behind the gerrymandering of tradition are rarely so clear as Olsson points them out to be in this case, external factors guiding the conceptualization of tradition are always at play, if under normal circumstances more buried in layers of history. Thus, the persistent existence of exceptions to every rule, like the laundry list in Franzén's original letter, will typically support the argument for inclusiveness and against the creation of strict boundaries.

The problem is, however, that the romantic and conservative nineteenth-century notion of tradition remains at the core of the folk music concept, and possesses currency that cannot reasonably be abandoned. This dilemma becomes one of the only weapons available in such debates to those who do wish to enforce boundaries. Their strategy must then become the forcing of inclusivist arguments to an extreme, creating a situation in which, to adapt a phrase from Douglas Adams, Swedish folk music must simply vanish in a puff of logic.

In 2002, the Ransäter debate flared up again when Bengt Lindroth employed that very tactic in a *Spelmannen* editorial entitled "Swedish Spelman Music—Does it Exist?"[68] In this article he accused certain unnamed users of the svenskfolkmusik online discussion group of trying to analyze Swedish folk music into non-existence. He cited "what has happened with the Ransäter gathering"—probably referring to the fact that admission was now being charged to all—as evidence that their attempts were succeeding.[69] He concluded the editorial by ironically suggesting that "folk music" be renamed "people music," giving us "the perfect borderless and lucrative form where everyone will be happy."[70]

The editorial page of the following issue of *Spelmannen* featured a response entitled "Untruths and Conspiracy Theories" by Dan Olsson, who identified himself as one of the anonymously paraphrased targets of Lindroth's attack.[71] With characteristic acuity, Olsson used most of the article to pick apart Lindroth's factual errors and hypothesize about the sour grapes behind the editorial. He accused Lindroth of only being able to see in black and white, unable to envision a Swedish folk music that was and had always been subject to foreign influence. Significant, however, was the absence of any real argument directly countering the central implication of Lindroth's editorial, that critical analysis of the folk music concept, taken to its logical extreme, denies its legitimacy. Instead, Olsson defended himself by noting the improbability that someone who had "dedicated most of his life to traditional folk music (played, studied, taught, been president of a spelman organization, etc.)" should be plotting its downfall.[72]

Olsson's defense here is typical against this kind of argument, or against the post-modern angst than can result from the fluidity of boundaries even without the stimulus of an outside attack. When faced with the essential contestedness of the folk music concept, the best way to confirm solid ground is to stop talking and start playing, singing, dancing.[73] In a textual forum like the svenskfolkmusik discussion group or the *Spelmannen* editorial page, the practical realm can only be cited, as Olsson does. But in the context of face-to-face interaction, that move can be very real. When I met ethnomusicologist Owe Ronström at the 2002 Korrö Folk Music Festival and told him the subject of my work, he related that he and his friends used to spend whole nights arguing about the folk music concept. "Now we just play." Even online this solution is occasionally simulated: when the debate over entrance fees to Ransäter drew to its close, it was capped by the following exchange:

Thomas Fahlander: "Give me an A"
Daniel Höglund: "440"
Daniel Höglund: "441"
Thomas Fahlander: "thanks"[74]

Notes

1. For a discussion of the ascendancy of the work concept, see Lydia Goehr, *The Imaginary Museum of Musical Works: An Essay in the Philosophy of Music* (Oxford: Clarendon Press, 1992).
2. Not until the folk music revival of the 1970s would an aesthetic of stylistic distance from art music be firmly established within the genre. And the principle of selective collection work has only recently begun to be challenged in any serious way; see, e.g., Annika Nordström, *Syskonen Svensson: Sångerna och livet. En folklig repertoar i 1900–talets Göteborg* (Gothenburg: Göteborgs Stadsmuseum, 2002), 20–21.
3. For a comparative discussion of range in female vocalists as recorded in the twentieth century vs. transcribed in the nineteenth, see, e.g., Margareta Jersild and Märta Ramsten, "Grundpuls och lågt röstläge—Två parametrar i folkligt sångsätt," *Sumlen* 1987: 143–146.
4. By the 1920s, other forms brought by the gramophone began to overshadow that previous layer of accordion music. For a while, Swedish folk parks held simultaneous events, with one floor hosting "modern" dances like foxtrot and tango, while the other featured accordion-based old-time dance, or "gammeldans." Both of these terms remain in current usage.
5. The term "spelman" (pl. spelmän) is probably closest to the English "fiddler," though not necessarily specific to a particular instrument. Village spelmän had been playing at Skansen, Stockholm's outdoor folklife museum, starting in the early 1890s (see page 46 and 69n). Not until the twentieth century, however, did the rescuers of folk music come to establish institutions whereby village musicians themselves would become the agents of preservation.
6. For more on these contests, see Gunnar Ternhag, "Spelmanstävlingarna: Tävlandets och musikens sammanhang," in *Det stora uppdraget: Perspektiv på Folkmusikkommissionen i Sverige 1908–2008*, ed. Mathias Boström, Dan Lundberg, and Märta Ramsten (Stockholm: Nordiska museets förlag, 2010), 69–83.

7. At first, this gold badge was given as a kind of lifetime achievement award for services to the cause, open to champions and performers of Swedish folk music alike. In 1956, the criteria were revised to base the honor purely on musicianship. In practice, however, the gold badge does tend to go to musicians who have served the folk music community well. As such, it is still commonly perceived as an award for a lifetime of service.

8. For a more detailed discussion of the Zorn trials and the discourse surrounding them, see my own "The Zorn Trials and the Jante Law: On Shining Musically in the Land of Moderation," *Yearbook for Traditional Music* 39 (2007).

9. As early as a 1907 contest for Finland-Swedish folk musicians in Helsinki, collector Otto Andersson assembled all the participants on stage for a mutually agreed-upon tune, a practice now known as "allspel"; see Ville Roempke, "'Ett nyår för folkmusik': Om spelmansrörelsen," in *Folkmusikboken*, ed. Jan Ling, Gunnar Ternhag, and Märta Ramsten (Stockholm: Prisma, 1980), 266.

10. Jan Ling, *Svensk folkmusik* (Stockholm: Prisma, 1964), 7.

11. Ling argues vehemently against the kind of romanticization that insists on cultural purity, and for an understanding of folk music as a product of cultural contact between various strata of society in Jan Ling, "Folkmusik—En brygd," *Fataburen* (1979): 9, 32–33. He argues that the Swedish nyckelharpa was able to survive because of the willingness of its makers to change its construction as new foreign building techniques became available in "Folk Music Revival in Sweden: The Lilla Edet Fiddle Club," *Yearbook of the International Folk Music Council* 43 (1986): 1. And in "Groupa and Ransäterspôjker'a, Folk Music Ensembles in Transition," *Studia Instrumentorum Musicae Popularis* 10 (1992), he argues that insistence on cultural purity is what caused the demise of the group Ransäterspôjker'a, and that the embracing of innovative practices is what has allowed Groupa to survive (39–40). Other articles in which Ling has made variations on these innovation-as-tradition arguments include "'O tysta ensamhet'—Från känslosam stil till hembygdsnostalgi," *Sumlen* 1978: 50–58; "'Upp, bröder, kring bildningens fana': Om folkmusikens historia och ideologi," in *Folkmusikboken*, ed. Jan Ling, Gunnar Ternhag and Märta Ramsten, (Stockholm: Prisma, 1980), 11; "Folk Music Revival: A Case Study of Swedish Folk Music Today Focused on the Keyed Fiddle Club of Lilla Edet (Historical background)," in *Tradition in den Musikkulturen, heute und morgen*, ed. Günter Mayer (Leipzig: VEB Deutscher Verlag für Musik, 1985), 53; "Folk Song from Gärdeby: A Case of Musical Emigration and Immigration," in *Trends and Perspectives in Musicology: Proceedings of the 1983 World Music Conference of the International Music Council*, ed. Sven Wilson (Stockholm: Kungliga Musikaliska Akademien, 1985), 154; "Folk Music and Popular Music in Sweden," in *Tradition and Modern Society* (Stockholm: Almqvist & Wiksell, 1989); and "Nyckelharpan: Dialog mellan nutid och dåtid," in *Nyckelharpan nu och då*, ed. Birgit Kjellström (Stockholm: Musikmuseet, 1991), 7–9. Several collaborative articles between Jan Ling and Märta Ramsten build upon similar arguments: "Gärdebylåten: En musikalisk ut- och invandrare," *Sumlen* 1984: 37–39, 65; "The Gärdeby Folk Melody—A Musical Migrant," in *Analytica: Studies in the Description and Analysis of Music*, ed. Anders Lönn and Erik Kjellberg (Stockholm: Almqvist & Wiksell, 1985), 311–321; and "Tradition och förnyelse i svensk folkmusik: Leksandsspelet förr och nu," in *Musik och Kultur*, ed. Owe Ronström (Lund: Studentlitteratur, 1990), 214.

12. Ling, "Folkmusik—En brygd," 32–33.

13. Ling, "Upp, bröder," 20, 27–31; "Folkmusik—En brygd," 20–23.

14. One might consider me remiss in omitting the major paradigm shift that came with Eric Hobsbawm and Terence Ranger's *The Invention of Tradition* (Cambridge: Cambridge University Press, 1983). I choose not to dwell on this development here simply because it had little or no effect on Swedish folk music scholarship and practice. This may be due in part to the fact that it reached the realm of Swedish folk music rather late in the revival, allowing the inventions of its initiators in the late sixties and early seventies to have been safely obscured by time. Moreover, theorization about the nature of tradition among Swedish scholars and revivalists may have progressed to a point where the invented tradition model would have seemed unnecessarily primitive, not yet having been honed by the nuance of its later critics, e.g. Peter Burke, "Popular Culture between History and Ethnology," *Ethnologia Europaea* 14 (1984): 7; "We, the People: Popular Culture and Popular Identity in Modern Europe," in *Modernity & Identity*, ed. Scott Lash and Jonathan Friedman (Oxford: Blackwell, 1992), 29; and Carolyn Hamilton, *Terrific Majesty: The Powers of Shaka Zulu and the Limits of Historical Invention* (Cambridge: Harvard University Press, 1998), 26–32. I believe, however, that the main reason this model lacked influence was that its focus on fabrication would deny currency to folk music as a cultural practice. The power of the reinvented (as opposed to entirely invented) tradition came from its ability to challenge entrenched notions of tradition without sacrificing their cultural capital.

15. Albert Lord, *The Singer of Tales* (Cambridge: Harvard University Press, 1960), xiii.

16. For examples, see, e.g., Henry Glassie, "Tradition," *Journal of American Folklore* 108 (1995): 395; Sandra K. D. Stahl, "The Personal Narrative as Folklore," *Journal of the Folklore Institute* 14 (1977): 10; J.H. Kwabena Nketia, "African Traditions of Folklore," in *Jahrbuch: Internationale Gesellschaft fur Urheberrecht E.V.*, vol. 4 (Vienna: Manzsche Verlags- und Universitatsbuchhandlung, 1979), 225; Edward Shils, *Tradition* (Chicago: University of Chicago Press, 1981), 240–286; Mats Nilsson, *Dans— Kontinuitet i förändring* (Gothenburg: Etnologiska Föreningen, 1998), 46; Nordström, *Syskonen Svensson*, 23; and Nils-Arvid Bringéus, *Människan som kulturvarelse*, ed. Nils-Arvid Bringéus, Sven B. Ek and Anna Birgitta Rooth (Lund: LiberLäromedel, 1981), 129–130.

17. See, e.g., Nketia, "African traditions," 222.

18. Helen Myers, "Ethnomusicology," in *Ethnomusicology: An Introduction*, ed. Helen Myers (New York: W.W. Norton & Co, 1992), 11.

19. Frank Harrison, "Tradition and Acculturation: A View of Some Musical Processes," in *Essays on Music for Charles Warren Fox*, ed. Jerald C. Graue (Rochester: Eastman School of Music Press, 1979), 114–115.

20. See, e.g., Nilsson, *Dans*, 45; also, this volume.

21. For examples, see, e.g., Olle Edström, *Schlager i Sverige 1910–1940* (Gothenburg: Novum Grafiska, 1989), 295–297; Nordström, *Syskonen Svensson*, 20–21; Ling, "Lilla Edet Fiddle Club," 6–7; "Folkmusik—En brygd," 10.

22. See, e.g., Jan Ling, "O tysta ensamhet," 55–58; "Folkmusik—En brygd," 32–33; "Groupa and Ransäterspôjker'a," 39–40.

23. Riksförbundet för Folkmusik och Dans, or RFoD.

24. "Concerts Sweden," *Rikskonserter*, was a state foundation for live music in Sweden. It has been dismantled as of January 2011.

25. Based on a word search for the root "autent," including all permutations.

26. Based on a word search for "genuin," including all permutations.

27. Based on word searches (whole word only) for "äkta" and "äkthet." One side effect of using a language with letters like "å," "ä," and "ö" is the increased exposure to possibilities of mangled spellings upon travel to countries with languages not so endowed. The folk music group Väsen (meaning Essence, Spirit, Creature, Noise, or Racket) has complained of this problem in their onstage patter, where they bemoan the loss of a good deal of cool whenever their name is changed to "Vasen" (The Vase). Occasionally the group is exposed to hypercorrection as well, as in the case of the liner notes of the Dervish album *Live in Palma*, in which their guitarist was unfortunately rechristened "Röger" (1997, Kells KM-9516, 2 compact discs). Far more unusual are similar mistakes made when foreign music groups come to Sweden. The only case with which I am familiar is that of the Swedish-descended, Minneapolis-based "Äkta Spelmän," who when visiting the 2004 Bingsjö spelman gathering in central Sweden were somehow in all the festival publicity renamed "Akta Spelmän." I do not know all the circumstances of the case, but can imagine that some of the confusion had to do with the likely fact that no one in Sweden would ever consider naming a group "Genuine Spelmän." The alternate name, "Beware of Spelmän," would seem far less out-of-place.

28. Based on a word search for "tradition," including all permutations and compounds.

29. Ingrid Åkesson has coined a similar set of terms for describing differing attitudes toward tradition and innovation among Swedish folk singers: re-creation, re-shaping, and renewal, in her "Recreation, Reshaping, and Renewal among Contemporary Swedish Folk Singers: Attitudes toward Tradition in Vocal Folk Music Revitalization," *STM Online* 9 (2006).

30. Considerable scholarship has been done on the revivals of these instruments; see, e.g., Gunnar Ternhag, "Playing and Handling Bagpipes: Two Swedish Cases," *STM Online* 7 (2004); "The Story of the Mora-Harp: Museumization and De-museumization," *STM Online* 9 (2006); Owe Ronström, "Making Use of History—Revival of the Bagpipe in Sweden in the 1980s," *Yearbook for Traditional Music* 21 (1989): 95–108; Per-Ulf Allmo, *Säckpipan i Norden* (Stockholm: Allwin, 1990), 145–196; Per-Ulf Allmo and Jan Winter, *Lirans hemligheter: En studie i nordisk instrumenthistoria* (Stockholm: Ordfront, 1985), 125–136; and Per Gudmundson, "Djäwul'ns blåsbeöl'e: Om säckpipans uppgång, fall, och återuppståelse," in *Musik och Kultur*, ed. Owe Ronström (Lund: Studentlitteratur, 1990), 247–290.

31. Greger Siljebo, interview by author, December 3, 2001.

32. Anders Waernelius, interview by author, January 18, 2002.

33. The *hardingfela*, or hardanger fiddle, is a Norwegian folk instrument, slightly smaller and brighter than a violin, with sympathetic strings and a flatter bridge so as to facilitate play on multiple strings. For information on this instrument see, e.g., Pandora Hopkins, *Aural Thinking in Norway: Performance and Communication with the Hardingfele* (New York: Human Sciences Press, 1986).

34. Joar Skorpen, interview by author, November 18, 2001.

35. Joar Skorpen, interview by author, November 18, 2001. This quote is actually taken from Skorpen's answer to the question of how to define folk music generally, but summarizes perfectly our discussion earlier in the interview regarding his approach to learning the music of Bohuslän.

36. Joar Skorpen, interview by author, November 18, 2001.

37. For more information on the strictures of Norwegian folk music classification, see, e.g., Chris Goertzen, *Fiddling for Norway: Revival and Identity* (Chicago: University

of Chicago Press, 1997); "The Norwegian Folk Revival and the Gammeldans Controversy," *Ethnomusicology* 24, no. 1 (1998): 99–127.

38. Joar Skorpen, interview by author, November 18, 2001.

39. An inverted reading might also suggest that Sweden and Norway actually act as counterbalances to Skorpen's shifting positions, thus affording him the opportunity to personally occupy a greater range along the time axis.

40. "Sax" Mats Nilsson, interview by author, January 9, 2002.

41. In 2001 RÅmantik also gained a part-time fourth group member, fiddler/vocalist Louise Wanselius (nee Schultz).

42. "Sax" Mats Nilsson, interview by author, January 9, 2002.

43. "Sax" Mats Nilsson, interview by author, January 9, 2002.

44. "Sax" Mats Nilsson, interview by author, January 9, 2002.

45. "Sax" Mats Nilsson, interview by author, January 9, 2002.

46. The position of the accordion and its relationship to the folk music concept in Sweden is discussed at length in Chapter Four, pages 83–89.

47. Magnus Ek, interview by author, April 2, 2002.

48. Märta Ramsten, "De nya spelmännen: Trender och ideal i 70-talets spelmansmusik," in *Folkmusikvågen*, ed. Lena Roth (Stockholm: Rikskonserter, 1985), 67.

49. Ramsten, "De nya spelmännen," 67.

50. Ramsten, "De nya spelmännen," 72.

51. Ramsten, "De nya spelmännen," 57–59. The historical relationship between the various deep-past-oriented developments of the Swedish folk music revival on the one hand and early music movement on the other deserves a study that is beyond the scope of this dissertation. Harald Pettersson, who has been a key figure in the development of Swedish bagpipe and hurdy-gurdy styles, has long had feet in both early music and folk music camps. Pettersson's present membership in the folk music group Raun (see chapter 7) came via his association with lead singer Helena Ek, who knew both him and fellow band mate Göran Månsson from early music circles. Connections between Swedish folk music and early music movements have also been cultivated in the past decade by scholar and fiddler Magnus Gustafsson, who has been the driving force behind a set of recordings by folk and early musicians interpreting seventeenth- and eighteenth-century Swedish manuscripts (Höökensemblen, *Höök! Musik bland stadsmusikanter, krigsfångar och mästertjuvar*, 1995, Drone DROCD007, compact disc; *Polski Dantz: 1600-talsmel-odier på vandring*, 2002, Drone DROCD026, compact disc; Sågskära, *Krook! Musik bland trumslagare, bröllopsspelmän och bergtagna kvinnor*, 1997, Drone DROCD010, compact disc).

52. Finnish singers Sanna Kurki-Suonio and Tellu Paulasto joined in time for the group's second album (*Kaksi!*, 1992, Silence SRSCD 4717, compact disc). Saami yoiker Wimme Saari joined in time for their third (*Trä*, 1994, Silence SRSCD 4721, compact disc).

53. See, e.g., Hedningarna's *Hippjokk*, 1997, Northside NSD6003, compact disc.

54. Lars Nylin, "Kaksi!," liner notes from Hedningarna, *Kaksi!*, 1992, Silence SRSCD 4717, compact disc, emphasis in original.

55. See, e.g., Ernst Emsheimer, "Tollabössa och videpipa: Två traditionella folkliga ljudinstrument hos barn," *Sumlen* 1984: 9.

56. The voice is the only instrument that spans all three of these domains: ballads and lullabies in the home, *trall* or vocable singing for dancing, and herding calls for the forest. Dance instrumentalists and singers of domestic songs also often used the same melodies, though they did not typically perform together before the revival; see, e.g.

Margareta Jersild, "Om förhållandet mellan vokalt och instrumentalt i svensk folkmusik," *Svensk Tidskrift för Musikforskning* 58, no. 2 (1976): 53–66.

57. For an expanded and somewhat more nuanced discussion of gender in Swedish folk song, see, e.g., Ingrid Åkesson, *Med rösten som instrument: Perspektiv på nutida svensk vokalmusik* (Stockholm: Svenskt visarkiv, 2007), 69–73.

58. For a discussion of how the Swedish Folk Music Commission reified the standard forms for instrumental Swedish folk music through *Svenska låtar*, see Dan Lundberg, "Folkmusik—En definitionsfråga," in *Det stora uppdraget: Perspektiv på Folkmusikkommissionen i Sverige 1908–2008*, ed. Mathias Boström, Dan Lundberg, and Märta Ramsten (Stockholm: Nordiska museets förlag, 2010), 225–238.

59. Sten Källman, interview by author, January 9, 2002.

60. Hanna Wiskari, interview by author, December 28, 2001.

61. Sten Källman, interview by author, January 9, 2002.

62. By way of comparison, arguments that Bach's "universality" manifests itself in non-traditional adaptations by the likes of Wendy Carlos and others may fulfill a similar validating function.

63. Quoted in Lars-Gunnar Franzén, "Märklig stadga på Ransätersstämman," *Spelmannen* 1999, no. 3 (1999): 12.

64. Franzén, "Märklig stadga på Ransätersstämman," 12.

65. Gert Ohlsson, "Lysande stadga!," *Spelmannen* 1999, no. 3 (1999):12–13.

66. The *Mitt i musiken* debate aired on October 25, 1999. The online discussion lasted from October 14 to November 7, 1999.

67. Dan Olsson, "Officiella och verkliga orsaker," October 15, 1999, http://uk.groups.yahoo.com/group/svenskfolkmusik/message/497 (accessed August 20, 2011).

68. Bengt Lindroth, "Svensk spelmansmusik—finns den?," *Spelmannen* 2002, no. 4 (2002): 11.

69. A second Ransäter debate had erupted over the svenskfolkmusik list with the decision to charge general admission in 2000. Bengt Lindroth was one of those to protest most vehemently.

70. Lindroth, "Svensk spelmansmusik—finns den?," 11.

71. Dan Olsson, "Osanningar och konspirationsteorier," *Spelmannen* 2003, no. 1 (2003):11.

72. Olsson, "Osanningar och konspirationsteorier," 11.

73. One might read North American college world music performance groups as fulfilling a similar function within ethnomusicology today. As epistemological concerns threaten to destabilize the discipline, its theorists may find safer ground in the world of practice. Jeff Todd Titon suggests that the ascendancy of world music performance on college campuses was part of a broader disciplinary move from an epistemology of "explanation" to "understanding" in his "Knowing Fieldwork," in *Shadows in the Field: New Perspectives for Fieldwork in Ethnomusicology*, ed. Gregory F. Barz and Timothy J. Cooley (New York: Oxford University Press, 1997), 91–92.

74. Thomas Fahlander and Daniel Höglund, "a," "SV: a," "SV: a," "SV: a," October 28, 1999, http://uk.groups.yahoo.com/group/svenskfolkmusik/message/556 through 559 (accessed August 20, 2011).

CHAPTER 3

—⁓—

Geographical Boundaries
(and their Limits)

In his introduction to *Texter om svensk folkmusik*, Owe Ronström suggests that "few phenomena are so international as nationalism."[1] He cites ethnologist Orvar Löfgren to "describe nationalism as a kind of language with a well-developed vocabulary and grammar," noting "that in other countries they use the same language, with the same basic cultural vocabulary and grammar."[2] However, the Swedish nationalist project can be considered quite distinct from that of its neighbors to the east and west, both of which in the nineteenth century were contending with a recent independence coming out of a long period of colonial rule.[3] The modern Swedish state was born as a constitutional monarchy in 1809, in the aftermath of its military loss of Finland to Russia.[4] Fed by no history of foreign colonial occupation, Swedish nationalism has never been quite so intense as that of Finland or Norway. Today many Swedes identify themselves more willingly with their villages of personal or ancestral origin than with the nation itself. Accordingly, as Ronström points out later in that same introduction, "[i]n Sweden much of the nationalist rhetoric has been transformed to the regional level."[5] The terms for discussing geographical units of identity thus become compatible both across space (nation to nation, region to region) and at different levels of scale (nation to region to parish to village). This adaptable terminology has in turn allowed folk music, with its historical ties to the nationalist project, to gain identification not only with nations, but also with smaller provinces and villages, and more recently with international culture spheres. Where the previous chapter dealt with the continuous tension between the preservationism at the root of the folk music concept and the innovationism that serves as its constant foil, this chapter will deal with the nationalism at the root of the concept and the persistent challenges to it by local, regional, and international group identifications.

The regionalist approach to folklife in Sweden finds its origins in the mid-nineteenth century. A society for the history of Skåne was founded in 1844, leading folk music collector and impresario Richard Dybeck to call for the formation of similar organizations in other provinces.[6] Over a decade would pass, however, before the formation of the next organization for provincial history, the Association for the Collection and Organization of Nerike's Folk Languages and Ancient Artifacts, in 1856.[7] Its founders saw this as the beginning of a national network of similar institutions, a cultural equivalent, perhaps, to the inauguration of the first Swedish railroad, which took place in the same year and city of Örebro.[8] Historian Kerstin Arcadius has demonstrated that the Swedish county museums in general, of which this was the first, were imagined both by their local founders and national press and government as parts of a national whole.[9] The organized collection efforts that would come about through these museums could form a complete picture of Swedish folk culture.

In 1891, Artur Hazelius founded Skansen, Stockholm's outdoor museum for Swedish folklife.[10] Skansen was to be a Sweden in miniature, hosting transported and replicated village houses, farmyards, and churches, each representing the folk art and architecture of its own province.[11] For the first time, in other words, Sweden could actually be visualized as a whole in its provincial parts, easily accessible to that considerable portion of the populace that either inhabited or visited its largest city. Skansen thus became the greatest manifestation to date of the sort of provincialist nationalism Kerstin Arcadius describes.[12] Within a decade of its inauguration the outdoor museum had hosted the first celebration of Sweden's flag day, June sixth, in 1893, and contests for the creation of a national anthem in 1895 and 1899.[13] Skansen was also critical to Swedish folk music history in that it presented the first major tourist venue for folk music as performed by actual village musicians. Hazelius thus initiated the active participation of spelmän in the performance of folklore in the early 1890s, with the employment of fiddler Skölds Anders Hedblom from Leksand, Dalarna.[14]

The province-centered mapping of folk music Sweden has its foundations in the collection work of the late nineteenth century. Particularly influential in this regard was the work of Nils Andersson, who spent decades collecting and compiling the tunes for his 24-volume *Svenska låtar*. This work, eventually published between 1922 and 1940, is now the definitive collection of Swedish folk tunes. Although its province-based scheme of organization has seen some critics, *Svenska låtar* has by and large institutionalized that system of classification.[15] This drawing of Sweden's folk music map was further confirmed and entrenched by the foundation of provincial spelman organizations beginning in 1925, and their eventual confederation under the National Organization of Swedish Spelmän (SSR), founded in 1947. It would also prove to be of considerable significance to the folk music and dance revivals of the 1970s and 1980s.

The Polska Dance Revival

The primary impetus for the dance revival came from within (and as a reaction against) an established Swedish tradition of amateur folk dance groups called *folkdanslag*. Most of these groups were confederated under a national organization known as the Swedish Youth Ring.[16] They shared a nation-wide core repertoire consisting largely of choreographies that were originally composed for folklife plays in the mid-nineteenth century.[17] The dance revival came about in the wake of the folk music revival, in part as a result of a growing awareness that this existing "folk dance" repertoire did not accurately represent the dance culture of pre-industrial Swedish village society.

Following the example of the folk music revival, the primary genre of the dance revival would be the polska, a triple-meter promenade-and-turn couple dance. The polska can be divided into two broad types. The older slängpolskor hold to a single spot on the floor, at least during the turning phase; while the younger round polskor follow a counterclockwise "waltz track" around the room. Slängpolska today is commonly danced in one of two or three variants. The round polska, on the other hand, manifests in a myriad regional styles.[18]

Based upon this revived couple dance repertoire, two easily discernible dance cultures have emerged. The first of these, a group I'll call social polska dancers, have associated themselves closely with the folk music subculture, adding a kinesthetic dimension to folk music gatherings, clubs, and concert events. These social dancers may deprioritize expertise on specific regional variations in favor of a generalized polska style. Those with greater experience may know some variations, but are also likely to value technique, grace, and musicality over regionalist knowledge. At these events, the polskor are generally interspersed with various gammeldans forms, primarily schottische and waltz.[19]

The second group, whom I'll call the Polska Dancers, have essentially retained the folk dance group format but replaced the old repertoire with scores of regional polska variants. This group may be said to construct a Swedish identity based on the "county museum" model, from a collection of regional puzzle-pieces. The origins and mission of one Polska Dance group in Gothenburg is here described by its founder, Lennart Mellgren:

Mellgren: [W]hen the Youth Ring was going to have their 75th anniversary, when could it have been? '95 or '96. We thought we should play polskor, so that people who came from different provinces would feel at home. And we formed Mellgrens blandning. . . . Our mission is to play polskor from different provinces in Sweden. And we're trying to expand our repertoire. We're playing polskor from Dalarna, Värmland, Uppland, then there's Småland, Västergöt-land, Skåne, Halland also, and Bohuslän.
Kaminsky: Why polskor specifically?

Mellgren: Well, polskor have characteristics that allow them to be identifed by province. You can't do that with ordinary tunes, with schottisches and waltzes.[20]

The status of the polska as Swedish folk music and dance form *par excellence* is very much tied up with its perceived nature as a national music and dance form with identifiable regional variations. Embedded in the polska concept is something of the complementary relationship between the regional and the national in Swedish folk music. Mellgren established his group out of a desire to be nationally inclusive, and found polska to be the appropriate medium precisely because of its special characteristic of regional variation. He could just as easily have motivated his selection of the polska on the strength of its being both older and more uniquely Swedish than his counterexamples, schottische and waltz. The polska's credentials as especially Traditional and National do, of course, play a part in elevating it to the status of primary musical signifier of Swedish folk music. The fact that Mellgren cites its provincial specificity first, however, demonstrates something of the significance of regionalism in constructing national identity.[21]

Regional style variation in polska is of considerable interest in most branches of the Swedish folk music world, for dancers and musicians, preservationists, neotraditionalists, and innovationists alike. A common theme in arguments from all these corners is that the novice mistake of not paying attention to regional style variations dilutes the polska in some way; it may become less musically interesting, less within the bounds of traditional folk music and dance, or both. This argument also tends to require certain rigor of study, practice, and knowledge to become a "real" spelman or dancer. It thus finds its counter in the popular notion of a folk music open to all regardless of skill or previous experience.[22]

The neotraditionalist argument for paying careful attention to regional details tends to ground itself simultaneously in factors of provincial identity and musical interest, as expressed here by Joar Skorpen:

> That's what I find lacking in Sweden. Sometimes it's more about "well, that was a nice tune, we'll play it no matter where it comes from." In the worst case you don't even know where it comes from at all, or what it is. And I think that's too bad. Which isn't to say, of course you should play what you think is good; just make sure to keep the dialect in the tune. I find it a little sad when the tune starts to move around from one area to the next, because in the end you're just left standing with the melody. And like I said, the melody isn't the most important thing, because for me what's great about folk music is everything else that's on the side. When you get to a point where the melodic material is all you have left, well of course then it's very simple. Yeah, for me there isn't much left at that point.[23]

Innovationist arguments usually lie along similar lines, but tend to focus more upon musical interest, underplaying the cultural significance of regional identity. "Sax" Mats Nilsson explains a revelation he had on this subject during a conversation with band mate Sverker Pettersson:

Sverker said "you have to emphasize one and three." And that's the normal way of describing it. But just when he said that, I realized that that's exactly wrong. Because the whole point of these different types of polska and their rhythmic phrasing, it's where we place the two. . . . [I]f you play a short one, or a long one, if you emphasize the two strongly or weakly, if you generally trill on the two [sings example] you get a completely different feel. And so on and so forth. So when you're describing the differences between the different polskor, it's all about where you put the two.[24]

For Nilsson as well as for Skorpen, what brings musical interest to the tune is not a commonality with all other Swedish polskor, but rather that which distinguishes it as separate from other types—here the idiosyncrasies of the second beat.

Similar discussions of regional style variation can be heard in the dance world. Two schools of thought regarding how to teach beginning polska may be discerned, associated with the two main branches of the polska revival. The social dance instructor teaches a basic non-regionally specific version, in order that beginners can begin dancing in the world of polska clubs and spelman gatherings as quickly and as smoothly as possible. Polska Dance instructors, on the other hand, insist on specific regional identification for all the dances they teach.

The Gothenburg Polska Dancers' group Skjortor och Särkar (SoS) has multiple teachers in each category. My first interaction with SoS was at an all-day beginner's workshop meant to bring new people into the group. The class was taught by Anders Dahlgren and Peter Nordqvist, both of whom fell into that first category of social dance instructors who teach a generalized basic round polska. Anders and Peter made their approach very explicit to the class. They felt it better that we should be able to get around the floor and have fun than that we should worry about putting our feet in exactly the right place.

Because the generic polska is not generally conceived as a formalized dance with a right and wrong way of doing things, it has no standardized form, and much variation can be found in how different teachers teach it. Often the dance is based on the polska from the village of Bingsjö, but with more relaxed rules about foot placement and up-and-down motion or svikt (Bingsjö polska is otherwise danced entirely level). Some dance teachers will explain, when asked, that they are teaching the women steps from one area and the men steps from another. In the case of SoS's beginner polska workshop, Nordqvist told the class that "in all honesty the polska we've been dancing is pretty close to [the Norwegian] rørospols. But the counterclockwise turn [bakmes] is some kind of Värmland variant."[25] I later asked Dahlgren about their reasons for teaching the dance in this way:

Kaminsky: I'm a little interested in that there's this, especially in the course on Sunday, that Sunday course, that you teach a polska that isn't, it's almost a polska that doesn't exist.

50 CHAPTER 3

Dahlgren: Yeah, I understand what you mean. We've called it "round polska," but we don't specify Bingsjö, Orsa, or whatever. I actually think there's a point to that. In a lot of places where you dance polskor, both Allégården and especially the summer spelman gatherings, musicians don't usually say what kind of polska they're playing or where it's from. You just listen and dance what you know. And I don't think you should need a specialist's education in a bunch of different polskor to be part of the dance. What's more, when you're at a spelman gathering you're asking strangers to dance, so you need a standard polska that you can use in every situation, even if you don't know exactly the kind that's being played. And that's actually the most common polska variant at the spelman gathering. You feel it out and find a polska that goes with the music and your partner, and then it's usually the round polska that we've taught.

Kaminsky: Is there any standardization of this polska, or is it—

Dahlgren: Not transcribed or described in any book anywhere, but it builds a lot on the Bingsjö polska. Although I think a living tradition has come about in our circles. And that's where the spelman gatherings have a lot of significance also, in that a dance tradition is being developed there. I don't think the polskor should be museum pieces, something that absolutely has to be preserved. Polska should be usable as a social dance, and a way to meet people.[26]

My experiences as a dancer at gatherings and the Folk Music Café generally confirm Dahlgren's statements. The most common practice at gatherings does seem to be to dance some version of basic polska, rather than a specific regional variant, especially when the dancers are first-time partners and the musicians do not announce the tune type.

However, Dahlgren's habit of using the term "normal" polska (as opposed to Bingsjö, for instance) in the more formalized environment of Skjortor och Särkar rehearsals does not sit well with all the dancers there. The following exchanges have occurred at different times when Dahlgren was leading the group in the presence of sometime teacher and founding member Ulla Bergsten:

Dahlgren (to the group): I'm going to put on some normal polskor, and we can continue to warm up in pairs.
Bergsten (aside): The question is, what are normal polskor?[27]

And:

Dahlgren (to the group): Let's start with a normal polska.
Bergsten (aside): I'm sure it will be a Bingsjö.[28]

In an interview with Ulla and her husband Anders Bergsten, they explain their position:

Kaminsky: [I]t's pretty standard in polska courses that they teach something called "polska," and not Bingsjö or Boda or something specific. Why do they do that?

Ulla Bergsten: Basic polska? Yeah, you might ask them. Because—
Anders Bersten: That's not our ambition.
Ulla Bergsten: No. Hans and me, we've had beginning courses, and we've taught Bingsjö then. I still don't have an understanding of what basic polska is, as opposed to Bingsjö. So that—
Anders Bergsten: It's another way of sneaking out of—
Ulla Bergsten: Yeah.
Anders Bergsten: —if you don't dance Bingsjö completely correctly then you can still say that it's polska you're dancing, right? If you say you're dancing Bingsjö, you have other demands placed upon you. It's the same thing with musicians. I often feel that they don't want to tell you what they're playing. If they say "now I'll play a Bingsjö polska," the audience might think, "this doesn't sound at all like Bingsjö." It's sort of the same thing.[29]

As Anders Bergsten's argument slides over from dance and dancers to music and musicians, its parallels to those presented by Joar Skorpen become more apparent. The absence of regional specificity in both song and dance is a mark of dilution, lack of the knowledge and/or skill necessary to execute them properly. This again relates directly to the tendency to place emphasis on the province, rather than the nation, as primary Swedish culture area.

As Anders Dahlgren's earlier statement suggests, one counter to the argument for clarity of regional boundaries in dance styles is that it requires an expertise that, if insisted upon, might preclude the development of a living tradition both by cutting off the flow of beginning dancers and formalizing the culture to death. Åsa Grogarn Sol credits her easy entry into Swedish folk music and dance in part to the fact that she was never held to such high standards:

I came into completely new circles, people who liked this stuff and who were familiar with it, and who were also very magnanimous and tolerant. I didn't experience anything of what I've heard and read about, people saying "you put your foot in the wrong place, and this tune doesn't go that way, and that ornament wasn't Särna [style]." It wasn't like that at all. I felt very welcome.[30]

The fundamental flaw with this kind of inclusivism, on the place just as on the time axis, reveals itself when the argument is brought to its logical extreme. When all the boundaries are erased, so are the idiosyncrasies that define the music and dance and make it interesting. In music the innovationist solution to this problem is typically the explicit privileging of regional variation as essential to the music, rather than to provincial identity *per se*. Regional style variations thus become necessary tools for musical expression without being overly restricted by their attachment to cultural heritage.

Dancers Urban Lind and Emma Rydberg relate similar ideas about regional style variations in dance. Rydberg expresses a direct correlation between knowledge of various regional traditions she has gained from Mellgrens blandning, and her increased capacity for innovation: "I've tried dancing a bunch of different types of polskor, different steps, and due to the fact that you get more tools for the dance you can also experiment a lot more."[31] Lind demonstrates a similar attitude toward the dance in his explanation of the difference between dancing in Mellgrens blandning and the social dancing he engages in at gatherings and the Folk Music Café:

> *Lind*: [Mellgrens blandning] is very much the traditional Polska school. You dance different polska variants and look a lot at what's particular to this or that variant, what are the steps, and so forth. And in some sense you're starting a little bit at the wrong end, but it's fun anyway because there's often some connection to the music.
>
> *Kaminsky*: The wrong end in what way?
>
> *Lind*: Well, in some sense it feels more natural to begin dancing like you want, and then you listen to the music, and you try to adapt yourself to the music. Something along those lines. Here you start a little more with the solution right away, and then the music goes along with it. . . .
>
> *Kaminsky*: In what contexts, what contexts are there where you take it from the right direction, so to speak?
>
> *Lind*: Well, I guess when you dance a whole night in Ransäter or Bingsjö or whatever.
>
> *Kaminsky*: Has it influenced the way, or does it influence the way you dance more freely when you know the different variants, or how—
>
> *Lind*: It can work both ways. Many people have experienced that in the beginning you get pretty locked in, when you start to know a few variants but don't have that many. Because then you try to listen to the music and say "what is this?" And you decide that this is Boda, and you try to dance Boda, and it immediately becomes pretty strange. You wind up thinking a lot about the details. Then hopefully, and for many people it works out this way, when you know enough, you can free yourself from that and take a little from here and there. Then it becomes more of a repertoire that you can mix yourself, so you're not particularly locked in.[32]

Here the dance becomes a vehicle for individual expression and enjoyment, something that can be enhanced and enriched by a knowledge of regional variations, as soon as that knowledge is broad enough and internalized to such a degree that it can come naturally and without too much concentration. That knowledge becomes a means to an end, and not an end in itself, its internalization an intermediate stage in an individual's development between novice and expert.

The mastery of regional styles that can be summoned and mixed at command might be considered a perfectly embodied expression of the unification of individual and Swedish identity, one that can be simultaneously provincial and national. The polska becomes a pan-Swedish dance that can only be mastered through an understanding of its multiple regional variations. For the expert it can become an entirely personal expression of Swedish identity, and a source of innovation grounded in tradition.

Nation vs. Province

Up until the revival, folk music insiders generally imagined the provinces as unproblematic pieces of a larger map of Sweden, following the conceptual precedent set by the county museum project. Skansen, *Svenska låtar*, SSR, all represented an image of the nation as a whole in provincial parts.[33] With the folk music revival of the seventies, however, came a qualitative shift in attitudes about regional identity. The counterculture movement, of which the international folk revival was an element, sought to distance folk culture from the large-scale power structures of statehood and the global market. "Dig where you stand" became a popular motto of the revival, placing the local in opposition to the national. This motto spoke especially to revivalists outside of central Sweden, who sought to counteract the hegemony of Dalarna and Hälsingland in favor of the music of their home provinces. This in turn bled easily into the general reaction against the previous folk music generation, which had so heavily favored the central provinces in constructing a monolithic Swedish folk music tradition. Along with that generational break came a strong sense of skepticism against the existing national institutions for folk music and dance in Sweden, with their associations of cultural conservatism and national romanticism.

At the same time, however, the revival built upon those institutions. Revivalists problematized, yet participated in the Zorn trials; critiqued, yet joined SSR and the Youth Ring; challenged, yet adopted institutions like the spelman group, folk dance group, and spelman gathering.[34] Furthermore, this largely leftist movement was forced to grapple with the dilemma that, then as now, the cultural currency tied to folk music was also bound to its past, to tradition—in short, to all its conservative ideological baggage. Compounding this problem was the need to maintain respect for tradition bearers while questioning the institutions that had historically supported them.[35]

In my view, the primary strategy that was implemented in solving these problems was the disentanglement of Nation from the remaining three ways of understanding folk music.[36] The nationalist aspect is, to insiders, the most obviously conservative element of the Swedish folk music concept. Most Swedes meet overt expressions of nationalism with distrust, perceiving them to coincide with the xenophobia of the far right.[37] In recent years the appropriation of the Swedish flag by right-wing anti-immigrant groups, for instance, has caused many Swedes to shy away from this key symbol.[38] The general mistrust of nationalist sentiment also manifests itself in the debate within the Swedish folk music community over whether or not the nyckelharpa should be made the official national instrument of Sweden. In this debate the opposition camp frequently goes so far as to suppose direct (and even causal) links between the creation of national symbols and increased anti-immigrant sentiment.[39] Critical to the attack on Nationalism as an aspect of folk music was the fact that it could be carried out without threatening the status of the individual tradition bearer. The tradition bearer's connection was never so directly to Sweden as a whole as

much as it was to ideas of Tradition, the Folk, and the Natural. Put simply, revivalists revised the existing narrative of cultural provincialism, making it an
alternative to (rather than an element of) nationalist folklore.[40]

The National as a way of conceiving folk music can never be entirely abandoned, however, as Dan Lundberg and Gunnar Ternhag note in the introduction
to their 1996 survey *Folkmusik i Sverige*:

> If several elements distinguish our book from those of our older colleagues, we
> still have a fundamental characteristic in common in that we all proceed from
> the Swedish nation as a descriptive unit. The tradition from the first days of the
> folk music concept seems to be inescapable, no matter how internationalized
> we imagine ourselves to be today. Folk music is described once and for all na-
> tion by nation. Swedish folk music is something of its own, Norwegian folk
> music something else, not to speak of the Danish . . .
>   This debatable point of departure is something the reader must come to
> live with in the coming pages. It is compensated to a certain extent by the sec-
> tions on Saami music and music in multicultural Sweden, as well as by our re-
> current looking out over folk music outside the country's borders.[41]

Lundberg and Ternhag's problematization of this issue does reflect a self-
conscious effort to shift away from the idea of a single national ethnic identity.
The very choice of title for their book—*Folk Music in Sweden*, and not *Swedish
Folk Music*—is a manifestation of their desire to stress the disconnect between
cultural and national boundaries. This choice furthermore reflects a broader
trend in which the namers of newer survey texts and national institutions for
folk music have generally abandoned use of the once-ubiquitous "Swedish" or
"Sweden's" as a modifier.[42] However, separating out the National and distancing it from folk music is both difficult and imperfect as a politically progressive
project. It is difficult because of Nation's fundamental inherence to the concept,
and it is imperfect because the remaining three ways of understanding folk music also bear the mark of their culturally conservative beginnings. The above
citation from *Folkmusik i Sverige*, beyond describing (the first part of) this problem, exemplifies its discursive mitigation, made possible by the power of discourse to move more quickly, flexibly, and farther than the reality it constitutes.[43] Lundberg and Ternhag can work to disarm the nation concept by arguing
that it is a fiction, all the while knowing and even acknowledging that the power
of that fiction could never be dissipated by any argument they make. Jan Ling in
several contexts engages a similar strategy to solve the second part of this dilemma, problematizing all aspects of the national-romantic view of folk music
as reactionary throwbacks. He challenges all four established ways of understanding folk music at once, in favor of simply hearing it as pure music on its
own terms.[44] Yet never could anyone expect that baggage, that currency, to actually be abandoned in any real sense.

The Norwegian Connection

Along with and supporting the political and institutional factors that favor the province as the primary geographical unit for folk music, musical factors also play a role. Sweden is too large and too varied a musical area to truly be considered unitary, and no single musical factor can be said to be both uniquely and ubiquitously Swedish. Musical areas along the western Swedish border have far more in common with eastern Norwegian musics than they do with those of eastern Sweden; the music of northeastern Sweden has more in common with northwestern Finnish music than it does with that of southern Sweden, and so forth. The province too may be an arbitrary unit for partitioning regional dialects, but naturally has less internal variation than the nation due to its smaller size.

Joar Skorpen goes so far as to argue that, with regard to the folk music dialect map, provincial boundaries are more culturally significant even than national ones:

> *Kaminsky*: What do you think of it when, if you take these local differences between music and dialect and the like, and the border that goes between Sweden and Norway?
> *Skorpen*: It's completely nonexistent. National borders are very often completely nonexistent in that respect. The old provincial boundaries are really more relevant. And—
> *Kaminsky*: Do they also go along the border, or not?
> *Skorpen*: Well, yes, they do. But if you think internally in the country, they're more relevant, because then they tied together the areas that were bound to one another. The county boundaries are completely irrelevant. [*laugh*] Because they're administrative units that have to do with population density; they pay no attention to village culture and old main roads. . . .
> *Kaminsky*: Can you talk about a Swedish, or does it become problematic to talk about a Swedish folk music and a Norwegian folk music?
> *Skorpen*: Yeah, in the border areas there's no point, really, because it's both. This isn't my area, but if you take western Värmland and the Finnskog, it's all exactly the same, tradition and tunes and playing technique, really. And the same upwards, if you go from Røros over to western Dalarna. So I think that if you see any difference there, it's tied directly to the fact that people who live on the Norwegian side went to *kappleikar*, and those who live on the Swedish side went to spelman gatherings. That's the difference. In olden times I don't think there would have been any differences at all there.[45]

In acknowledging music culture areas that cross the border between Sweden and Norway, Skorpen validates the age of that Tradition by suggesting that it predates the modern idea of nationhood, and emphasizes its connection to the Folk by disconnecting it from top-down political structures. The validation of the provincial boundary over the county one is also intimately related to its connection with Nature: Skorpen repeatedly gives the example of mountains in Norway and Sweden as the source of these real cultural boundaries. In other words, in challenging the legitimacy of the Nation, Skorpen intensifies the realities of Tradition, the Folk, and the Natural.

The two border areas mentioned by Skorpen in the above quote are especially well-known for their porousness. One of the most significant developments in recent years in the world of polska dance is the reconstruction of the Swedish/Norwegian "finnskogspols." Fiddler Mats Berglund (on the Swedish side) has been a central actor in the creation of a style of playing and dancing based on Einar Övergaard's transcriptions from western Värmland and research done by Norwegian fiddlers and dancers on the other side of the border.[46] The resulting "finnskogspols" has in recent years become a popular music and dance form, generally conceived as a border tradition, neither entirely Swedish nor Norwegian.

An album of finnskogspols from 2002, *24 polsdanser frå finnskogen*, features Mats Berglund and other fiddlers from both Norway and Sweden.[47] A similarly bi-national album, *Suède • Norvège*, was released ten years earlier by French radio, representing music from Dalarna/Härjedalen in Sweden and Setesdal/Telemark in Norway.[48] Both albums primarily feature tracks with musicians from one side of the border or the other, not both.[49] In other words, the National boundary is undermined in some sense on the cover, yet remains as a subtle reality in the fine print. This phenomenon, too, may be read in multiple ways: The abandonment or challenge of any single way of understanding folk music may always be necessarily incomplete. Or musicians may simply be more likely to play with others of their own nationality, for reasons of language, tradition, or proximity.

Skorpen and others have pointed out that folk music on the Norwegian side of the border, for reasons of its higher status in that country, and because of the relatively late and less all-encompassing process of urbanization, has been more continuous in tradition there than on the Swedish side. Mats Berglund's tactic of reviving Swedish traditions by looking at nearby Norwegian ones has also been applied in other situations. One specific example involves the recent Swedish interest in reviving the halling, an acrobatic male solo dance traditionally associated primarily with Norway, but with a historical presence in western Sweden as well. During the summer of 2003, for instance, festival organizers brought Norwegian halling champion Martin Myhr to lead workshops at the Öckerö spelman gathering and Uddevalla folk music festival for the purpose of reviving Bohuslän's lost halling dance tradition.

The fact that social activities involving music and dance do not always have to involve explicit discussion can further advance the conceptual blurring of the Norwegian/Swedish border. This can apply in any Swedish folk music and dance venue, not only in border areas. At a gathering, musicians may simply play a finnskogspols or two, and people will dance them before moving on to the next more nationally specific tune and dance type. When a Norwegian *rørospols* is played, some people may do the "right" steps, while others dance a basic polska, or perhaps some Värmland or Western Dala variant close in feel to the Røros dance. In other words, distinctions between the Swedish and Norwegian may simply be forgotten or made insignificant by the fact that they are mixed together in such a way that to unravel them would take more time and energy than most would care to dedicate to the project in a social music and dance milieu.

On the other hand, sometimes the close connections between Swedish and Norwegian music, and the ease with which they translate over the border, can power an explicitly stated political position. Much of the Swedish left has opposed the initial entry into and later the displacement of power to the European Union. Reasons generally given include its undemocratic nature, ties to globalization and delocalization of power, and specific to Sweden, the dismantling of the welfare state, restrictions on immigration, and the death of Swedish neutrality. The first two times I saw saxophonist Sten Källman perform in Gothenburg, he used the opportunity for banter between tunes to criticize the European Union's message that they increase the international free trade not only of products, but also ideas. He pointed to the borrowing of ideas across the Swedish/Norwegian border (specifically his interest in playing tunes associated with Norwegian fiddler Hans W. Brimi) as counterevidence, given that Norway never entered the European Union. He explains in an interview:

> [E]ven if the border is closed, it's never been that way when it comes to folk music. I'm trying to point out that the EU doesn't change everything. People form their lives according to their own minds, and always have. Of course, we are subordinate to events and sociopolitical structures. It's not that I'm claiming those things are unimportant, it's just nice to know that the musical exchange between Norway and Sweden is completely independent of their membership or non-membership. So the idea is to point out that the EU doesn't mean everything.[50]

Källman's argument here, though specific to the instance of the European Union, parallels that of Skorpen in suggesting an inverse relationship between the political vs. cultural significance of the Swedish/Norwegian border. Both operate on the principle that moving away from the political realities of the nation-state brings focus to the local grassroots.

The North Atlantic Connection

The border between Sweden and Norway runs entirely to the north of Gothenburg. The city itself is far enough south to lie on the ocean, where it falls within a second international music culture sphere, that of the North Atlantic. This overseas connection has especially in recent years become quite important in the folk music life of the region, due much to the efforts of Bohuslän fiddlers Göran Premberg and Svante Mannervik.

The province of Bohuslän is known especially for the "engelska" dance, whose music, choreography, and name all betray kinship with the reels of Britain and Ireland. Göran Premberg has sought to revive the engelska music tradition by rescuing it from Swedish folk dance atrophy:

> [T]he engelska is a kind of music that's mainly been used for staging folk dances. And often what winds up being central to the stage dances is the costumes. So what's been prioritized in these folk dance group engelskor is their usefulness in performance, because there are some moves that are very visual, and the skirts have to have time to flutter, and so on. And so, once again, the attitude has been that the music that's used in those contexts has to occupy a position of low-level servitude to the dance and the skirts. Which means of course that if you're going to have an opinion on Swedish folk music as a spelman and a musician, and you hear that kind of engelska, you're going to think "what the hell is this, it's 'uppa tuppa tuppa tu,' this isn't music." And I agree with that. But when I listen to this these old recordings, when they play, when I hear vocable singers, when I hear Axel Abrahamsson sing an engelska, it's full of life and feeling; the music is really complete.[51]

Premberg has created his own style of playing engelskor, based upon the techniques of older spelmän he has played with on the island of Orust, recordings of an even older generation of Bohus spelmän, and last but not least, musical traditions of Britain and Ireland. He explains to his fiddle workshop at the 2003 Ransäter gathering:

> David Andersson who I play with, he uses this bowing.[52] Backwards, like this. And Jeff Bowen from Yorkshire, one of my English playing buddies, he sent me a letter. He'd just found this in England in tune books from Newcastle. Let me put on my glasses. It reads something like "the third style is rather more difficult of acquirement than the second, and may be named 'the sand dance style.' As it produce a very short and distinct articulation of every note and is very effective when playing pianissimo, as the music is generally wanted in a sand dance, in which every touch and slide of the feet on the sand stage must be heard."[53] So in these instructions from 1889 or thereabouts, they talk about three different playing styles of hornpipe in Yorkshire: there's "Newcastle style" that Ernst Abrahamsson plays in Skaftölandet. . . .[54]

Premberg also sees fit to include newer North Atlantic musical idioms in his engelska playing, which he also teaches at Ransäter and describes in an earlier interview:

> [T]here was a band that played in Gothenburg together with one of my bands. It was one of these groups made up of Irishmen and Scots who travel around the world. "Four Man and a Dog" they're called. And the way they played, I haven't heard anything better, before or since. It was such a fantastic listening experience. There was never a dull moment. And they did things, before you knew it, I didn't understand how, but they'd "CHO ke che CHO ke che CHO,

CHO" and they'd keep going. I think it was a speciality that they had invented, inserting those things into the music. And I've run into it sometimes; Scotland's best-known and most-respected living spelman is Alasdair Fraser. I met him in Aberdeen. I was at a master class with him, and what was funny was that he did it too. . . . And I did it myself [*plays a short melody with the same 3+3+2 accent pattern*]. So maybe that's also a little connection we have over the North Atlantic.[55]

The strategy employed by Premberg here is not altogether different from that of Mats Berglund, who in his reconstruction of the finnskogspols crossed the border into Norway, another nation with greater continuity in its folk music traditions. The effect that this has in deemphasizing the national boundary is even more pronounced with Premberg, however, because he makes the argument explicit:

[B]ecause I've studied history and have an interest in it, I look in the long term at the question of "what is a nation state?" And unlike a lot of other people I get less and less Swedish every year. Soon the only thing that's going to be left of Sweden is the national soccer team, and ice hockey, the world of sports. What I see is that in the future according to the EU ideology or paradigm, what is Sweden? Well, it's some kind of organization, but what's basic to us here is our own region and the threads it has out over the sea. What we have in common both with Norway and the British Isles.[56]

Thus can provincialism link directly to international connections at the expense of national ones.

This occurs, nevertheless, within the formalized structures of the modern Swedish folk music subculture, the gathering circuit and so forth, which do, as Joar Skorpen points out, operate within Sweden on a national level. In some sense the reality of that national system and the political security of the border are the very factors that allow that boundary to be safely challenged in discourse on heritage. Further, provincialism can also be seen as a reinforcer of nationalism, most obviously in a work like *Svenska låtar* or in the system of county museums as explored by Kerstin Arcadius.[57] Competitiveness between provinces may be read less as a challenge to that national identity, and more as evidence that expressions of national unity and pride are entirely unnecessary within the intranational contexts in which such competition occurs.

When provinces vie for legitimacy and space in that national folk music arena, local international connections can become valuable markers of provincial uniqueness and sources of cultural currency. This principle is especially well-demonstrated when the relatively obscure folk music province of Bohuslän is placed up against the model Swedish folk music province of Dalarna. This occurred in a very real way in 2000, when Bohuslän was featured as guest province at Dalarna's Falun Folk Festival. Göran Premberg brought his band "The Atlantic Orchestra," and performed as a soloist. Svante Mannervik created the all-Bohuslän spelman group "Ranrike spelmän" for the venture; here he describes the results:

> [I]t was a wild success up there. We had asked Märta Ramsten to present the music of Bohuslän, but she thought we were the ones who knew it best. The concert went very well; it was broadcast over the radio several times. And Ranrike acquitted themselves honorably. There was a bit of a to-do, because no one had heard a spelman group play that type of music and in the way we do. And then the Atlantic Orchestra was a complete surprise for the audience. Just before they went on, it wasn't the Wrigley Sisters, but it was some other girls from Scotland or Shetland or the Faeroe islands who were very good. And it had been completely packed, so when the Atlantic Orchestra went on I wasn't sure how the atmosphere would be, but it was really a success.[58]

Implicit in Mannervik's statement is that the measure of achievement for the Atlantic Orchestra was to successfully follow the foreign north Atlantic act that preceded it. This legitimated the group as being of international caliber, and a real part of that north Atlantic culture sphere.

The currency of the Falun Festival was related to its international status, its ability to make an otherwise marginal Sweden into a temporary center for world music. The festival was dominated by acts from outside of Sweden, and at the same time Sweden was the individual nation most represented, placing it at the center of an international folk music community. In 2000 Bohuslän was able as guest province to occupy a similar status on a smaller scale among the Swedish acts, challenging Dalarna's position as center within Sweden. The difficulty of confronting Dalarna in that way on its home turf, doubtless outnumbered by Dala acts, required a challenge to the very right to those international connections claimed by Dalarna via the Falun Festival. The performance by the Atlantic Orchestra represented a claim to those connections for Bohuslän, based on historical cultural exchange over the Atlantic that Dalarna could not legitimately own.

Göran Premberg thus reacts with some territorial ire when Swedish musicians unaffiliated with Bohuslän or the west coast begin experimenting with Swedish/Celtic fusion:

> There's a strange thing that's happening today. Just a couple of months ago Ale Möller put out a record with Aly Bain, who's a Shetland spelman. And on that album and in its publicity they start talking about the similarities here and what commonalities there are between Swedish folk music and Shetland music. And there are other groups like SWÅP that have started to do similar things. But from my perspective, with my tunes, with my repertoire, and what I know, I say that's bullshit. I've only heard one or two tracks off that album, so I don't know, but how the hell, you can't have a common Swedish folk music repertoire with Shetland music without involving music from Bohuslän. . . . [J]ust generally you can't say that there are common features in Swedish folk music, that is all of polska Sweden, and Shetland music. On the other hand I know that

my tunes, or those Bohuslän tunes, they go hand in hand with the ones out there.[59]

Politically at stake here is a certain cultural capital and popularity ascribed to music of Britain and Ireland, which may outweigh that of Swedish folk music even within Sweden. For people like Ale Möller and the members of SWÅP, the claim to that currency comes from the kind of world music internationalism typified by the Falun Festival. Their collaborations are ambassadorial, a meeting of the Swedish and British, where provincial identity is only marginally significant. In this context the foreign music is "Celtic," a highly visible and marketable genre whose cultural (and economic) currency may rub off on the more obscure Swedish music when these musicians meet as equal partners.[60]

For someone like Göran Premberg, however, dedicated to a relatively unknown regional tradition with demonstrable connections to Britain and Ireland, the connections he has made with musicians from the Shetlands have the potential to validate his province and make it special. Premberg does not call the music "Celtic," presumably because Celtic music has no Swedish roots.[61] Instead it is "North Atlantic," belonging to a culture area that includes Bohuslän but not Dalarna. When musicians from other areas claim a Celtic connection for Swedish music generally, Premberg thus sees it as a threat to the special value of the tradition he stands for.

Folk Music Ambassadors

The kind of internationalism represented by the Falun Festival, that self-consciously political meeting-of-the-nations, is intimately connected to Swedish world music and its patron saint, Ale Möller. In 2000 Ale Möller was given a three-year commission by the Falun Festival to be the center of a "world music tent" made up of expatriate musicians from around the globe, to perform at the festival through 2002.[62] The group became more formalized as the "World Music Orchestra," had a nationally telecast concert from Stockholm in 2001, and became the festival's most popular attraction during that time. The project was touted generally as a vehicle for multicultural understanding and cooperation.

Ironically, though perhaps not surprisingly, this self-consciously internationalist project, and others of its ilk, have both musically and emblematically reified national difference and essentialized national identity to a much greater extent than modern Swedish intra-national folk music projects tend to. This may be read as an obvious effect of pan-national style mixing. The crossing of the border, in some sense, is what makes it real. A slightly different angle of interpretation would suggest that the Nation as an element of folk music remains hidden (for now-familiar political reasons), until such time as its identity is actually threatened by the potential creation of international musical styles. In any case, the aesthetic valuation of this sort of world music fusion by members of the Swedish folk music community tends to reinforce the musicians' efforts at retaining separate audible national identities in the music. Positive statements generally involve the musicians' unwillingness to compromise their own identities, whereas negative ones lament the musics' devolution into, in the words of Jan Ling, a "gray soup of it all."[63] These valuations regarding the relationship between national and international are isomorphic with those discussed earlier in terms of the regional/national dynamic—in both cases, the loss of the idiomatic musical identity of the smaller area in blending with the larger becomes aesthetically displeasing.

In the case of Ale Möller's recent projects, the musicians most susceptible to the calcification of their national identities have been not native Swedes, but immigrants. The native Swedish players in these groups, first of all, represent the place where the mixing takes place, a modern multi-ethnic nation, to be contrasted with the "traditional" societies the international musicians can be assumed to represent. Unlike their multi-national band mates the Swedes wear no iconic national garb when performing, but rather hold to the subtly and ambiguously ethnic clothing common within some corners of the post-revival folk music community. Their individual regional musics may also be familiar to an enlightened Swedish audience, counterbalancing the weight of their identities as national musicians. The international musicians can expect no such detailed knowledge of music from their own nations, and thus become general musical ambassadors representing Greece, India, Senegal (or perhaps Africa), and so forth.[64]

This is not to suggest that Swedish musicians in this context are not also national musical ambassadors; their role as such is simply more nuanced due to the factors I have described above, coupled with the obfuscating effects of Swedes' ambivalence regarding their own nationalism. The ambassadorial role played by the Swedish musician in this sort of self-consciously mixed world music context is perhaps more obvious, however, in the case of the duo formed by Swedish fiddler Ellika Frisell and Senegalese kora griot Solo Cissokho. Here Urban Lind introduces their act at the Folk Music Café:

> [T]onight we will be party to a very exciting meeting between Africa and Sweden, between Senegal and Bingsjö, between fiddle and kora, and we will partake of ancient traditions that have grown up separately and which are braided together and in some strange sense seem to belong together.[65]

Much about this introduction should seem familiar from my discussion of Möller's World Music Orchestra. Lind's braid metaphor affirms the independence of the two cultural strands: they are mutually complementary when joined, and yet they retain their distinctive identities. Ellika's village is contrasted to Solo's nation, her nation to his continent. When they come out on stage her garb is casual, perhaps vaguely invoking a simplified male Swedish folk costume in cut, while his is decidedly traditional.[66]

At the same time, several factors bring Frisell's status as a representative Swedish spelman to the fore, more even than for Ale Möller—arguably Sweden's highest-profile folk musician—in his World Music Orchestra. Möller masters multiple instruments, but is known primarily as a player of the bouzouki, easily trumped by Frisell's fiddle as a symbol of Swedish folk music. The simple binarism of Ellika and Solo's relationship also favors her here, where the multiple Swedish musicians in the World Music Orchestra might inspire thoughts of provincial differentiation, or in the case of Sebastian Åberg, confuse the matter further by playing tabla. Even Frisell's musical association with the village of Bingsjö, invoked in Lind's introduction, favors her in this regard. Bingsjö was home to Hjort Anders, the iconic Swedish spelman whose image is the logo for the Falun Folk Festival. It is the location of Dalarna's largest and best-known spelman gathering, and generally imagined as cultural dead center for Swedish folk music.[67] The folk music of this village thus has the credibility to stand for general Swedishness more than that of any other place in the country. The focus is also widened to the national and continental by Ellika's platinum-blond hair and Solo's blackness, as well as their distant geographic origins, compared to the more densely populated World Music Orchestra and its sliding melanin scale.

In the summer of 2004 Ellika and Solo were guests at the tenth anniversary Urkult (Ur-Cult) folk festival in northern Sweden, one of the nation's largest world music festivals. The Urkult grounds are located in the village of Näsåker, near the pre-historic rock carvings on the bank of the river Nämsforsen in Ångermanland province. Romanticized pre-history, environmentalism, various leftist and peace movements, and of course world music, are all unofficial themes of the festival; bonfires, drumming, and fire dancing are its signatures.

The quasi-ritual "fire night" that traditionally opens the festival on Thursday at midnight was particularly extravagant in this its tenth year, with an estimated audience of twelve to fourteen thousand. The forty-eight-minute show was dominated by mud-caked ur-people dancing to a series of musical performances by various guest acts of the festival, framed at the beginning and end with overtone-heavy pulsating rhythms of djembe and didgeridoo. During Ellika and Solo's segment the duo were doubled on the proscenium by two young girls, one Swedish, the other from a visiting African troupe, who joined hands in dance. The white girl's long blond hair brought me to wonder whether or not some other Swedish child (perhaps with shorter dark hair, maybe of middle-eastern or African descent) did not get that job. The answer to that question is of less importance, I think, than its implication. In this festival celebrating international peace and cooperation, through the vision of a mythic time before national boundaries existed, the symbolic representation of that sentiment cannot but force the essentialization and racialization of national identities.[68]

Dala Dominance

The right of Ellika Frisell's dancing avatar to stand for Sweden, while certainly a function of her racial identity, does not rest upon any overt declaration to that effect ("I am white and blonde, and may therefore represent you"). Similarly, Ellika Frisell's Dala repertoire grants her status as an iconic Swedish fiddler, without requiring her to make any explicit claims to such a status. For every other province that needs to prove itself a tradition area, Dalarna is the model and benchmark. Thus its representatives have no need to engage in the kind of activity that would validate themselves to those from other provinces. Provincialism may be said to be least overt in Dalarna, then, because it lacks this need to prove itself. The situation is analogous to that of Sweden's relatively low level of explicit nationalism compared to Norway and Finland, simply due to the fact that Sweden has never had to fight for validation through independence.

At the same time, just as Swedish nationalism is a real force, but tends to take on forms other than overt pride, so can provincialism be understood as a force to be reckoned with, even in Dalarna.[69] Consider the following event, which took place during the early hours of the 2003 Svabensverk spelman gathering, an unofficial leg of the week-long *Musik vid Siljan* folk music circuit.[70] I and Jeanette Eriksson, a young fiddler from Skåne in southern Sweden, were playing some mutual tunes from fiddler Hans Kennemark's repertoire. We drew a small crowd, and soon an older man came over to take some pictures. When we finished playing a tune he started to ask us some questions:

> *Reporter*: I'm writing a story for a local paper. Could I get your names?
> *Eriksson*: I'm Jeanette Eriksson, from Helsingborg, and I'm Sweden's youngest riksspelman. I'm seventeen now, but I was sixteen when I got it.
> *Kaminsky*: I'm David Kaminsky; I'm an American studying Swedish folk music.
> *Reporter*: How long have you played together?
> *Eriksson*: I don't think we've played together before now; we're not a group or anything.
> *Kaminsky*: I think we might have played together once or twice, but never just the two of us.
> *Reporter*: Are you the youngest riksspelman ever?
> *Eriksson*: There have been a few others; one was fifteen.
> *Kaminsky*: Åsa Jinder and Marie Stensby, maybe.
> *Reporter*: How did you get interested in folk music, living in Helsingborg?
> *Eriksson*: There's folk music there too; it's not just in Dalarna.
> *Reporter*: But aren't you supposed to be from Dalarna to be a riksspelman?
> *Eriksson*: No.
> *Kaminsky*: Åsa Jinder isn't from Dalarna.[71]
> *Reporter*: Maybe you'll be the next Åsa Jinder.
> *Eriksson*: I'm going to be the next Jeanette Eriksson.[72]

The reporter was probably not particularly involved in the Swedish folk music subculture, or he would most likely have known that most riksspelmän do not come from Dalarna.[73] But for an individual to make such an assumption is not at all surprising, due to the typical conflation of Swedish folk music with the music of that province. The provincialism at work here is perhaps more subtle than the explicit Bohuslän-centrism of Göran Premberg, but it is no less powerful—more powerful, perhaps, due to its tacitness. The defensive provincialism of Göran Premberg is, of course, also a direct reaction against this often unspoken conflation of Dala and Swedish culture.

For better or worse, folk musicians outside of Dalarna must deal with that province as the model for Swedish folk music. Some accept and embrace this. When asked for an example of a "typical" Swedish tune in Norway, for example, Västgöta fiddler Billy Lätt will happily play a Dala tune. When I asked Västgöta spelman Annelie Westerlund what musical example she would give to describe Swedish folk music to someone who had never heard it, she responded:

Westerlund: Marked polska in minor, I suppose.
Kaminsky: From where?
Westerlund: Since I'm from Västergötland it would be Västergötland. You thought I was going to answer "Dalarna." But I actually don't. . . . The fact that I would give an example from Västergötland is mostly just out of obstinacy, mostly stubbornness, because I think we're so neglected, the west coast in general, and our music isn't any worse than anyone else's.
Kaminsky: Why did you think I would—
Westerlund: Because everybody thinks that.[74]

Whether or not a Dala tune is used as an example of "typical" Swedish folk music, most players are aware of the expectation. Tellingly, even Westerlund does not subvert that expectation completely. By selecting a minor-mode tune, she appeals to the iconic Dala sound. The archetypal Västgöta polska is in major.

The construction of Dalarna as model Swedish province has been described most effectively by Owe Ronström:

In the last part of the 19th century, Dalarna was established as the most authentic and traditional region in Sweden, although it in many respects was one of the most atypical. Due to special historical, demographic and economical circumstances, peasants in the lake Siljan area lived in big and densely populated villages with a rather egalitarian structure and highly developed social control. Lacking fertile soil they were forced into seasonal labour migration on a large scale (Rosander 1976, 1985). They became known all over Sweden as a special type of people, highly conservative and traditional in their ways of living, with their dialect, colourful folk costumes and peculiar songs and fiddle tunes as distinctive "ethnic" markers. The villages around lake Siljan were the models from which people like Artur Hazelius, the founder of Nordiska muséet and Skansen (the big open air museum in Stockholm) created the picture of the *Typical Swedish Peasant Society*. This was supposed to be a society without class struggles, where people were proud to stick to the traditions of the old days, obviously a suitable model for the bourgeoisie in their struggle for economical and political power at the turn of the century (Frykman & Löfgren 1979).

In this truly anachronistic model, explicitly manifested in the permanent exhibitions at Skansen, the Dalecarlian was equated with the Swedish, the very specific with the most typical. This model was taken over by the people from Dalarna themselves and used as a platform for a type of provincial nationalism which tried to re-establish the medieval administrative unit, *landskapet* (the landscape), as the basic unit of identification (Löfgren 1987: 6). From the beginning of this century love for the mother country and love for *hembygden* (the home-region) was impressed upon the coming generations as two sides of the same coin (Alsmark 1982: 34).[75]

Those aspects of late nineteenth-century Dalarna that allowed its people to represent the Folk were thus not so much a function of their being a representative sampling of Swedish popular culture. Rather it was their dedication to Tradition, their possession of a material culture that could be mined for National symbols, and their connection to a rural, Natural life.

The Forgotten City

The connection to Nature and the rural is not specific to Dalarna, but an imagined feature of Swedish provinces in general. As revealed in the above citation, the secondary (and literal) meaning of the Swedish term "landskap" is actually landscape. The establishment of the province as a locus for cultural heritage in the late nineteenth century was intimately tied to this association with nature. All of this was occurring during a time in which the rural was developing as a key symbol in the construction of Swedish identity, out of the crises of urbanization and industrialization.[76]

In the context of my fieldwork in the urban folk music subculture of Gothenburg, I have found that many individuals identify strongly with the rural heritage of some specific region in Sweden. That identification may be rooted as the place of their own youth, but may be just as strong among people born in the city, and for whom summer cottage vacations (perhaps in regions once farmed by their grandparents) formed that sense of regional identity, or "home village feeling" (*hembygdskänsla*).[77] The connections between summer vacation, rural life, and folk music culture are further reinforced by the litany of spelman gatherings and festivals that take place in rural settings during the summer months.[78]

A city like Gothenburg, though its folk music scene is certainly more active than that of most rural areas, thus occupies something of a marginal position on the Swedish folk music map. In a Swedish nation made up of cultural provinces, a major city like Gothenburg simply does not exist. Which is to say that Bohuslän, Västergötland, and Halland, the provinces that together contain the Gothenburg greater metropolitan area, are like all Swedish provinces imagined as rural areas. Spelmän who live in Gothenburg and who associate themselves with specific geographic traditions most often link themselves to one or more of these provinces (Värmland is also common here), and never specifically with the city itself. Though they may live in the city, their music-making and their original compositions conventionally fall into the regional traditions with which they are associated.

The province-centered mapping of Sweden's cultural geography is only one of several associated factors that marginalize the city in the world of folk music. This cartographic peripheralization is bound up with the conception of Swedish culture as being specifically rural, and the popular notion that urbanization, emigration, industrialization, and internationalization all bespoke an abandonment of that culture. Thus, at no point does the music of the city, or of the industrial working class, become a generally accepted branch of the tradition.[79]

In recent years, some scholars of urban culture have come to challenge this rural-centricity in Swedish folkloric studies. Olle Edström, for instance, is a musicologist who has focused much of his scholarly attention on the popular music culture of early-to-mid twentieth-century Sweden. He proclaims in his book *Schlager i Sverige* that "schlager," the popular music of that era, is the new Swedish folk music. Edström argues that if popularity is an index, what is currently called *folkmusik* cannot legitimately lay claim to the term.[80] He explains his motivations in an interview:

> [T]hey had a huge year to celebrate Swedish folk music, 1990. And in that context I occasionally felt a kind of historical falsification, actually, I will go so far as to use that word. Because they made it look like Swedish folk music from Floda or Hamburgsund or whatever had been a significant undercurrent in Swedish music culture all along. And I don't think that's true. I think it's just a construction that could be retold—not by land-owning farmers and nationalists, like in the 1920s, only strangely enough more by people who politically and ideologically are grouped toward the left, and who hold important positions in Stockholm, and have contacts in radio, television, in political networks. . . . But since I had spent so much time and research on this, my sense was that it was really Ernst Rolf, and Sven-Olof Sandberg, and Ulla Billquist and all those schlager artists, whose songs the people had sung. There was a clear discrepancy between the construction of the life-force of Swedish folk music during the twentieth century in relation to what I considered to be the truth. And "folk music" had a positive charge, for art musicians too, you could arrange it if you wanted, elevate it to legitimize it in that way. Folk music had always had currency among the academic and political elite, during the entire twentieth century, and from the nineteenth century as well. But of course schlager, which is born as a concept in the 1910s and goes out of use more or less in the sixties I would think, that's still half a century, there hadn't been those positive connotations to the term at all. Only it was just a kind of lower-class music in some way.[81]

It is to this question of folk music and its relationship to popular culture that the following chapter is dedicated.

Notes

1. Owe Ronström, "Inledning," in *Texter om svensk folkmusik—Från Haeffner till Ling*, ed. Owe Ronström and Gunnar Ternhag (Stockholm: Kungliga Musikaliska Akademien, 1994), 16.

2. Ronström, "Inledning," 16; cf. Orvar Löfgren, "Nationella arenor," in *Försvenskningen av Sverige: Det nationellas förvandlingar*, ed. Billy Ehn, Jonas Frykman, and Orvar Löfgren (Stockholm: Natur och Kultur, 1993), 23.

3. Orvar Löfgren, "Kring nationalkänslans kulturella organisation," *Nord-Nytt* 25 (1985): 80.

4. Åke Ohlmarks and Nils Erik Bæhrendtz, *Svensk kulturhistoria: Svenska krönikan* (Borås: Forum, 1993).

5. Ronström, "Inledning," 20.

6. The type of regional unit with primary significance to folk music and dance style area classification is the Swedish province (landskap), a medieval administrative entity that for centuries has lacked official legal significance. Certain provinces also share their names and boundaries with counties (län), territories established in the seventeenth century that remain official government units to this day.

7. Kerstin Arcadius, *Museum på svenska: Länsmuseerna och kulturhistorien* (Stockholm: Nordiska museets förlag, 1997), 32, 279n.

8. Arcadius, *Museum på svenska*, 25, 279n.

9. Arcadius, *Museum på svenska*, 32–34.

10. See Nils Erik Baehrendtz, "Artur Hazelius och Skansen," in *Boken om Skansen*, ed. Nils Erik Baehrendtz (Höganäs: Bra Böcker, 1980), 12; Ingemar Liman, "Folkdans," in *Boken om Skansen*, ed. Nils Erik Baehrendtz (Höganäs: Bra Böcker, 1980), 134.

11. See Ingemar Liman, "Vårt Sverige i miniatyr," in *Boken om Skansen*, ed. Nils Erik Baehrendtz (Höganäs: Bra Böcker, 1980), 76; Arne Biörnstad, "Flytta hus," in *Boken om Skansen*, ed. Nils Erik Baehrendtz (Höganäs: Bra Böcker, 1980), 118; Baehrendtz, "Hazelius," 12; Jonas Berg, "Folkmusikens första början på Skansen och Skansens ordinarie spelmän 1891–1930," *Noterat* 6 (1998): 5.

12. Arcadius, *Museum på svenska*, 16–18, 32–34.

13. Arne Biörnstad, "Svenska flaggans dag," in *Boken om Skansen*, ed. Nils Erik Baehrendtz (Höganäs: Bra Böcker, 1980), 96; Anna Ivarsdotter-Johnson and Märta Ramsten, "Folkmusiken som nationell och provinsiell symbol," in *Musiken i Sverige III: Den nationella identiteten 1810–1920*, ed. Leif Jonsson and Martin Tegen (Stockholm: Fischer & Co, 1992), 240. Few of the entries were considered viable in either year. Richard Dybeck's "Du gamla du fria" was finally selected, essentially by default (240). Dybeck had set the hastily-written text to a tune from Västmanland collected by his assistant Rosa Vretman, as a last-minute addition to a concert of Nordic folk music in 1844. He considered the words mediocre at best, and never intended them to be printed or disseminated beyond that event (Gunnar Ternhag, "'Att rädda några dyrbara lemningar af fordna tiders musik': Om folkmusikens källor," in *Folkmusikboken*, ed. Jan Ling, Gunnar Ternhag, and Märta Ramsten (Stockholm: Prisma, 1980), 53–54; Anna Ivarsdotter-Johnson, "Upptäckten av folkmusiken," in *Musiken i Sverige III: Den nationella identiteten 1810–1920*, ed. Leif Jonsson and Martin Tegen (Stockholm: Fischer & Co, 1992), 68). June sixth has never held anything like the significance of the American Fourth of July, or

Norway's Syttende Mai. It was only in 1983 that it became the official flag day and national day of Sweden, and not until 2005 would it become a bank holiday.

14. Ivarsdotter-Johnson and Ramsten write that Hedblom performed at the opening in 1891 in "Folkmusiken," 239–240. Jonas Berg writes that he was employed initially as a laborer in 1891, and that his first documented performances were in 1893 in "Folkmusikens första början," 9. Stefan Bohman writes in one place that Hedblom began performing at Skansen in 1891, and in another that he came to Skansen that year, and started playing "regularly" in 1893; see Stefan Bohman, "Folkmusiken," in *Boken om Skansen*, ed. Nils Erik Baehrendtz (Höganäs: Bra Böcker, 1980); "Folkmusiken på Skansen," *Fataburen*, 1979: 38. Tommy Sjöberg has in his comments to a draft of this book pointed me to an earlier source, Gustaf Upmark's "Skansen 25 år," *Fataburen*, 1916. Upmark writes: "*Skölds Anders* from Rättvik [sic], who was employed at the museum already in 1891, has since 1893 played fiddle at Skansen, partly at the dance hall for the folk dance groups, partly in the cottages" (160, italics in original).

15. For an in-depth discussion of the role of *Svenska låtar* in reifying the provincial map of folk music Sweden, see Mathias Boström, Dan Lundberg, and Märta Ramsten, "Förord," in *Det stora uppdraget: Perspektiv på Folkmusikkommissionen i Sverige 1908–2008*, ed. Mathias Boström, Dan Lundberg, and Märta Ramsten (Stockholm: Nordiska museets förlag, 2010), 7. For a critical response to that system of classification, see, e.g., Ronström, "Inledning," 22.

16. The official full name of the organization was The Swedish Youth Ring for Village Culture (*Svenska Ungdomsringen för Bygdekultur*). The original name in 1920 had been The Swedish Folk Dance Ring (*Svenska Folkdansringen*). The organization renamed itself "The Youth Ring" in 1922, then reverted back to "The Folk Dance Ring" in 2005. In this work I use "The Youth Ring" throughout, in order to avoid confusion.

17. For a slightly more detailed discussion of folk dance groups and their origins, see page 76.

18. For a detailed discussion of the polska and its history, see Märta Ramsten, ed., *The Polish Dance in Scandinavia and Poland: Ethnomusicological Studies* (Stockholm: Svenskt Visarkiv, 2003). The promenade phase in polska is usually characterized by an open position and footsteps on beats one and three, or on all three beats. In the turning phase that follows, the partners lock together and turn as a unit, generally using some iteration of the the repeating foot pattern left—right—right. The round polskor developed in the wake of the early nineteenth-century introduction of the waltz to Sweden; these follow a counterclockwise path around the floor, with a full clockwise rotation every measure in the turning phase. A dizzying array of regional round polska variants are known, in some cases with differences as subtle as minor variations in the basic turning step. These minor variations may involve slight differences in foot placement, weight distribution, and degree and timing of *svikt*, or up-and-down motion. Some variants may also include slower (six-beat) turns as an additional element of the dance, either clockwise (*polkettering*) or counterclockwise (*bakmes*). The footwork in these slower turns may vary, but tends to betray some morphological similarities to waltz and polka.

19. For a more in-depth discussion of the social polska dancing scene, see my own "Gender and Sexuality in the Polska: Swedish Couple Dancing and the Challenge of Egalitarian Flirtation," *Ethnomusicology Forum* 20, no. 2 (2011), 123–141.

20. Lennart Mellgren, interview by author, August 4, 2002.

21. cf. Arcadius, *Museum på Svenska*, 16.

22. For a discussion of issues pertaining to folk music and accessibility, see also chapter 4.

70 CHAPTER 3

23. Joar Skorpen, interview by author, November 18, 2001.
24. "Sax" Mats Nilsson, interview by author, January 9, 2002.
25. Peter Nordqvist, author's fieldnotes, February 3, 2002.
26. Anders Dahlgren, interview by author, February 21, 2002.
27. Anders Dahlgren and Ulla Bergsten, author's fieldnotes, February 20, 2002.
28. Anders Dahlgren and Ulla Bergsten, author's fieldnotes, February 20, 2002.
29. Anders and Ulla Bergsten, interview by author, May 22, 2002.
30. Åsa Grogarn Sol, interview by author, October 5, 2001.
31. Urban Lind, interview by author, March 13, 2002.
32. Urban Lind, interview by author, June 27, 2002.
33. It may be enlightening to consider why the province, rather than the county, should hold this significance. Both are historically established administrative units covering areas of similar size. Often they share boundaries and names. The province is no doubt favored in part due to its greater age as a category. Perhaps more important, however, is that only the county remains in use as a governing unit. The province, on the other hand, was resurrected in the nineteenth century to serve symbolic purposes, and has since been conceived as a locus for cultural heritage (Owe Ronström, "Making Use of History—Revival of the Bagpipe in Sweden in the 1980s," *Yearbook for Traditional Music* 21 (1989): 101; Arcadius, *Museum på Svenska*, 32–36). Its lack of association with the present-day Swedish system of government also allows its boundaries to be imagined as bottom-up cultural divisions, as opposed to the county's artificial and arbitrary top-down political borders. Perhaps most significantly, the county boundaries are still meaningful with regard to government structure, and can thus be changed based on population flows and other factors, whereas provincial boundaries are locked in place.
34. See, e.g., Märta Ramsten, "De nya spelmännen: Trender och ideal i 70-talets spelmansmusik," in *Folkmusikvågen*, ed. Lena Roth (Stockholm: Rikskonserter, 1985), 46; "Med rötter i medeltiden—mönster och ideal hos 1960- och 1970-talets balladsångare," in *Återklang: Svensk folkmusik i förändring 1950–1980* (Stockholm: Svenskt Visarkiv, 1992), 105–106, 129; "Folkmusiken," in *Musiken i Sverige IV: Konstmusik, folkmusik, populärmusik 1920–1990*, ed. Leif Jonsson and Hans Åstrand (Stockholm: Fischer & Co, 1994), 298.
35. For a discussion of the importance of the "tradition bearer" concept within the revival, see Gunnar Ternhag, *Hjort Anders Olsson: Spelman, artist* (Hedemora: Gidlunds, 1992), 19.
36. For a discussion of the Swedish left and its uneasiness with regard to nationalism, see Lars Lilliestam, "Nordman och 'det svenska,'" *Noterat* 4 (1997): 41.
37. This association has been well borne-out in the political rhetoric of the anti-immigrant Sweden Democrat party; see Postscript.
38. See, e.g., Billy Ehn, Jonas Frykman, and Orvar Löfgren, *Försvenskningen av Sverige: Det nationellas förvandlingar* (Stockholm: Natur och Kultur, 1993), 9, 11.
39. Stefan Bohman and Lars Faragó, "Nationalinstrument—Splittrar mer än förenar," *Svenska Dagbladet* (March 17, 2002).
40. Divisions of folk music Sweden may occur in areas larger or smaller than the province as well. "Western Sweden" is a concept used much in Gothenburg's folk music sphere, and people commonly make reference to northern, southern, and eastern Sweden as well. On the opposite end of scale, in a folk music center like Dalarna, individual villages may be conceived as separate style areas. In cases both large and small, however, the province remains a primary referent—when people define western Sweden, they define it in terms what provinces it includes, and Dala villages tend to be classified accord-

ing to their location (east vs. west) within Dalarna. Individual spelmän today are also generally associated with a single province, even if they are familiar with the music of several. When they specialize more locally, the province usually remains the named referent, generally modified by a directional (e.g. western Värmland, southern Bohuslän).

41. Dan Lundberg and Gunnar Ternhag, *Folkmusik i Sverige* (Smedjebacken: Gidlunds, 1996), 16, ellipsis in original.

42. The first general survey of Swedish folk music was Tobias Norlind's *Svensk folkmusik och folkdans* (Stockholm: Natur och Kultur, 1930); and the second Jan Ling's *Svensk folkmusik* (Stockholm: Prisma, 1964). Revival-era texts include Bo i Ransätt Isaksson's *Folkmusiken i Sverige* (Motala: Borgströms Tryckeri, 1979), which is a shorter work for laypeople; the collaborative tome *Folkmusikboken*, ed. Jan Ling, Gunnar Ternhag, and Märta Ramsten (Stockholm: Prisma, 1980); and eventually Dan Lundberg and Gunnar Ternhag's *Folkmusik i Sverige* in 1996. In terms of national folk music institutions, Riksförbundet för Folkmusik och Dans (lit. The National Organization for Folk Music and Dance) was founded in 1981, sometimes conceived as a more culturally progressive answer to the pre-revival Swedish Youth Ring (1920) and National Organization of Swedish Spelmän (1947).

43. cf. Slavoj Žižek, *The Plague of Fantasies* (New York: Verso, 1997), 18.

44. Jan Ling, "'O tysta ensamhet'—Från känslosam stil till hembygdsnostalgi," *Sumlen*, 1978: 55–58; "Folkmusik—En brygd," *Fataburen* (1979): 32–33.

45. Joar Skorpen, interview by author, November 18, 2001.

46. Bjørn Sverre Hol Haugen, "Polsdans frå finnskogen," liner notes from Various Artists, *24 Polsdanser frå finnskogen*, 2002, Finnskogen Kulturverksted FiKCD 1960, compact disc. The major Norwegian contributors to this reconstruction have been fiddler Atle Lien Jenssen and dancers Bjørn Sverre Hol Haugen and Veslemøy Nordset Bjerke.

47. Mats Berglund, Göran Håkansson, Atle Lien Jenssen, and Olav Sæta, *24 Polsdanser frå finnskogen*, 2002, Finnskogen Kulturverksted FiKCD 1960, compact disc.

48. Lena Willemark, Kirsten Bråten-Berg, Per Gudmundson, Gunnar Stubseid, and Ale Möller, *Suède • Norvège: Musiques des vallées scandinaves*, 1993, Ocora C 560008, compact disc.

49. Twenty-three of *Suède • Norvège*'s 31 tracks and all of *24 polsdanser frå finnskogen*'s 24 tracks involve musicians from only one side of the border or the other.

50. Sten Källman, interview by author, January 9, 2002.

51. Göran Premberg, interview by author, May 16, 2002.

52. David Andersson is an old spelman from the island of Orust in Bohuslän.

53. Quoted (verbatim, believe it or not) from William Crawford Honeyman, *Strathspey, Reel and Hornpipe Tutor* (Blyth: Dragonfly Music, 1898), 38.

54. Göran Premberg, field recording by author, June 8, 2003.

55. Göran Premberg, interview by author, May 16, 2002.

56. Göran Premberg, interview by author, May 16, 2002.

57. Arcadius, *Museum på svenska*, 16.

58. Svante Mannervik, interview by author, June 25, 2003.

59. Göran Premberg, interview by author, May 16, 2002.

60. Both the Ale Möller/Aly Bain collaboration and SWÅP have been marketed internationally as Celtic/Swedish fusion. For an analysis of the commercial viability and success of "Celtic music" in the world music market, see Shannon Thornton, "Reading the Record Bins: The Commercial Construction of Celtic Music," in *New Directions in Celtic Studies*, ed. Amy Hale and Philip Payton (Exeter: University of Exeter Press, 2000), 19–29.

61. The "Celtic" has been constructed, problematically as some have pointed out, as a simultaneously linguistic and biological category; see for instance, Amy Hale and Philip Payton, "Introduction," in *New Directions in Celtic Studies*, ed. Amy Hale and Philip Payton (Exeter: University of Exeter Press, 2000), 5. "Celtic music" has been linked to specific geographical regions that exclude Scandinavia: Brittany, Cornwall, Ireland, the Isle of Man, Scotland (including Shetland), and sometimes Galicia; see Thornton, "Reading the Record Bins," 20.

62. The project was in some sense a continuation of Ale Möller's "Stockholm Folk Big Band," formed in 1998. By the end of its commission the world music tent had been formalized as the thirteen-member "World Music Orchestra"; it has since lived on in somewhat pared-down form as the six-piece "Ale Möller Band."

63. Jan Ling, interview by author, May 23, 2002.

64. The exception here is French-Canadian bassist Sebastian Dubé, whose generalizable instrument (and perhaps also his whiteness) allows him to avoid being ethnic-musically marked according to his nationality.

65. Urban Lind, field recording by author, March 1, 2002.

66. The liner notes to Ellika & Solo's first album, *Tretakt takissaba*, include seven pages of photographs of the pair of them (2002, Xource XOUCD 133, compact disc). Solo's traditional Senegalese dress is prominent, whereas it is quite difficult to ascertain what Ellika is wearing.

67. To be specific: Bingsjö is a small village in the parish of Rättvik, in the area off lake Siljan, in eastern Dalarna. Each of these four successively larger geographic areas are generally thought of as centers for Swedish folk music, as is Dalarna generally. Tina Ramnarine has mapped the village of Kaustinen in Finland at the center of a similar folk music bullseye in *Ilmatar's Inspirations: Nationalism, Globalization, and the Changing Soundscapes of Finnish Folk Music* (Chicago: University of Chicago Press, 2003), 169.

68. For a discussion of white identity as national identity (the British case), see, e.g., Simon Clarke and Steve Garner, *White Identities: A Critical Sociological Approach* (New York: PlutoPress, 2010), 60–84.

69. For a discussion of covert expressions of Swedish nationalism, see, e.g., Löfgren, "Nationella arenor," 27–28.

70. Musik vid Siljan is a week-long series of folk, classical, and popular music events in early July, concentrated around lake Siljan in eastern Dalarna. Each day people choose between multiple different types of events to attend. Polska Dancers may struggle to decide between spelman gatherings and bystugedanser (village dance halls), and listeners may be torn between numerous competing concerts. For most folk music insiders, however, the gathering pathway is well-marked: Svabensverk on Monday, Bingsjö on Tuesday and Wednesday, Östbjörka on Thursday, and Boda on Friday. The obscurity of this pathway to outsiders is strong evidence as to the tendency among hard-core enthusiasts to keep their world hidden. Only the Bingsjö gathering on Wednesday is truly public, the centerpiece of the week's events, with little or no competing programming. Östbjörka on Thursday is advertised simply as one of a number of competing bystugedanser. The remaining events (Svabensverk, Bingsjö pre-gathering, and Boda) have no official connection to Musik vid Siljan, and go completely unadvertised in the program.

71. Neither, for that matter, is Marie Stensby.

72. Author's fieldnotes, June 30, 2003.

73. However, Dalarna is certainly overrepresented compared to other provinces in terms of the number of riksspelmän it can claim.

74. Annelie Westerlund, interview by author, April 26, 2002.

75. Ronström, "Making Use of History," 100–101, italics in original.

76. Orvar Löfgren has mapped shifting perceptions of the countryside that came out of this process in "The Nature Lovers," in *Culture Builders: A Historical Anthropology of Middle-Class Life*, ed. Jonas Frykman and Orvar Löfgren (New Brunswick: Rutgers University Press, 1987). Here I summarize his argument briefly (page numbers are given for English translation and Swedish original, respectively):

The countryside of nineteenth-century Swedish peasant society was a landscape of production, a set of areas defined by their economic possibilities as farmland, fishing waters, timber forests, and the like (43–47/46–50). This landscape was also populated and controlled by supernatural creatures who reinforced societal norms by rewarding those who followed them, and enforced taboos by punishing those who violated them (47–50/50–52). With industrialization, the countryside came more under human control and was increasingly distanced from human life; the supernatural creatures that populated it were generally dismissed as superstition (50–51/52–53). As a corollary to this process, a nostalgic Rousseauian view of nature arose among the bourgeoisie. At first, the nature here worshipped was not the rural or agrarian, but the exotic mountains and rivers of a non-productive wilderness, pure and untouched by humanity (51–57/52–56). But during the last century (from the 1890s), as nature came to stand for the genuine, simple, and natural, the focus shifted from the majestic onto the rural, in opposition to an urban unnatural. At first even this nature was one isolated and untouched, but it soon became populated by the old peasant society. That bygone social world came to be represented specifically by the area of eastern Dalarna, whose comparatively egalitarian village social structure was highly atypical within Sweden's broader peasant society, but fit very well with bourgeois images of that lost utopia supposedly untouched by modern class hierarchy. This mystification of nature and peasant society became the grounding for Swedish folklore studies, also born in the last decade of the nineteenth century (57–63/56–61). The popular Swedish connection to nature became reified throughout the twentieth century with the institution of the summer vacation. Summer vacation became idealized as an opportunity for people to find themselves and become whole, fleeing regularly into a natural, rural landscape to escape the stresses of urban life (64–68/61–65). The division of dehumanizing work time and humanizing free time created conceptual connections between those elements associated with free time: nature, home life, and the female sphere. The resulting sentimental attachment to nature became naturalized as a human universal, though in reality the strict distinction between free time and work time applied at first only to a select bourgeois minority, only with time and economic development becoming a reality for the general working class as well. Thus did the recently developed bourgeois view of nature become generalized to the broader Swedish populace (68–75/65–69). In the twentieth century this attachment to nature has been increasingly used to commercial gain both in the market created by vacation culture and in advertising (this section is cut from English translation, and replaced by extended section on pets/69–71).

77. The functions of "home village feeling" in Swedish society may well be considered analogous to those of Japanese *furusato* as described by Marilyn Ivy, *Discourses of the Vanishing: Modernity, Phantasm, and Japan* (Chicago: University of Chicago Press, 1995).

78. Tellingly, the only three major non-summer events I know of are all urban—the Linköping Festival and Uppsala gathering in October, and the Umeå Folk Festival in February.

79. The striking differences between Swedish and American "folk musics" can be mapped back to the 1930s, when the concept served the right in Sweden, and the left in

74 CHAPTER 3

the United States. While Woody Guthrie, Charles Seeger, and Alan Lomax were redefining American folk music to include the songs of the workers' movement and including black as well as white music under its rubric, the bourgeois champions of Swedish folk music were engaging it as a bulwark against the degenerate jazz-influenced tastes of the urban working class; see, e.g., William G. Roy, *Reds, Whites, and Blues: Social Movements, Folk Music, and Race in the United States* (Princeton: Princeton University Press, 2010), 100–125; Jan Ling, "'Upp, bröder, kring bildningens fana': Om folkmusikens historia och ideologi," in *Folkmusikboken*, ed. Jan Ling, Gunnar Ternhag, and Märta Ramsten, (Stockholm: Prisma, 1980), 27–31.

80. Olle Edström, *Schlager i Sverige 1910–1940* (Gothenburg: Novum Grafiska, 1989), 295–297.

81. Olle Edström, interview by author, March 27, 2002.

CHAPTER 4

—⁓—

Folk Music and the Public Eye

On November 16, 2001, a seven-page spread ambitiously titled "The Genres of Music" in the Gothenburg newspaper offered its readership an overview of more than forty different kinds of music.[1] The article made no mention of folk music, nor was it included under some other name, or as a subcategory of another genre.[2] Swedish folk music is simply not an overt element of the country's mass-mediated musical soundscape. The genre's obscurity to the general public has proven the primary stumbling block for my consultants as they have attempted to define the term for me in interviews. It is to this issue of folk music's relationship to the populace at large—the commonality axis—that this chapter is dedicated.

The history behind the current hiddenness of Swedish folk music has not been a subject for much debate within the community. Historically, what is now called folk music pertained to functions of a pre-industrial village culture which, with modernization, urbanization, and industrialization, have become generally obsolete. In addition, international influences, at first European, and over the course of the twentieth century, increasingly American, have dominated Swedish music culture more and more. The prognostications of early folk music collectors about a vanishing heritage have thus in a broad sense proven to be entirely correct. Some modern practitioners will counter that, with the revival of the seventies and the country's progressive music education system, the number of skilled practitioners of instrumental folk music in Sweden has never been higher than it is today. Many also argue against the alarmist notion that the slightest relaxation of vigilance with regard to the preservation of traditional musics will cause them to be forever lost. They note the vibrant, if for most of Sweden entirely invisible, folk music subculture as evidence that such a problem is not so imminent. Some are optimistic and point to an increasing knowledge among the general populace about what Swedish folk music is. But none

75

would argue that folk music, in any real way, is today a music "of the people" in the sense that it might have been in the eighteenth and nineteenth centuries.

The situation, despite some disagreements, is thus rather simple. The complexity comes with the question of how one can justify applying the term "folk music" to a music that is currently so obscure. This dilemma will perhaps be less obvious to native English speakers, whose language distinguishes between folk and popular cultures. In Swedish usage, the distinction is not so clear.

Folk vs. Popular: A Swedish Grammar

The initial uses of "folk" terminology with regard to Swedish music and dance were similar grammatically to the German usage, and to the English. Swedish, like German, allows for compound nouns, so that *folk* may be joined with *musik*, *dans*, and *sång* to form *folkmusik*, *folkdans*, and *folksång*. These three concepts all arose in the early nineteenth century, and all still connote a connection to "the folk" in the sense of a pre-industrial peasant class.

In addition, however, Swedish has a distinct adjective, *folklig*, allowing for a duplicate terminology: *folklig musik*, *folklig dans*, *folklig sång*. As such, when the authenticity of those early nineteenth-century genres comes into question, the language leaves an opening for an alternate usage. To the best of my knowledge, the first person to engage one of these adjective-modified terms as a conscious challenge to the earlier compound noun forms was Ernst Klein, writing on folk dance in 1927. In his article *Folkdans och folklig dans* he noted that the repertoire of Swedish "folk dance" groups consisted by and large of choreographies originally composed by ballet master Anders Selinder for the Stockholm Opera in the mid-nineteenth century.[3] They extended via Selinder's students to the first folk dance group, Philochoros, around 1881, to the second, Svenska folkdansens vänner, in 1893, and across the country as the movement spread in the early twentieth century. To counter the disingenuousness of the term *folkdans*, Klein proposed the term *folklig dans*, establishing a distinction between Selinder's stage forms and the authentic peasant dances that preceded them.[4]

Half a century would pass before this challenge was widely heard and acted upon, when dance master Henry Sjöberg began to adopt and spread Klein's terminology. Henry Sjöberg was a seminal figure in the dance revival of the seventies and eighties. Today, both scholars and teachers of what is now called Swedish *folklig dans* trace their intellectual and pedagogical lineages back to him. Moreover, some of Sjöberg's direct heirs have expanded the concept beyond that originally intended by Ernst Klein, extending it to include so-called modern dance (e.g., foxtrot, bugg, charleston).[5] Andreas Berchtold and Ingrid Frykmo, both students of Henry Sjöberg and teachers at the Eric Sahlström Institute, have gone so far as to integrate "modern dance" into their *folklig dans* pedagogy program.

Folklig dans as a term has not entered into the common parlance, but is used primarily by professional dance scholars and pedagogues. It also means different things in definition and usage. In theory, *folklig dans* now signifies "popular dance," or as Mats Nilsson's ethnographic subjects call it, "normal dance."[6] In usage, however, it generally does not extend to today's club dancing. Nor does it cover the current international dance class repertoire (salsa, tango, lindy hop, belly dancing, contact improvisation, etc.). In practice, the term has come to signify those repertoires that were danced socially by a large portion of the Swedish populace during any period that is now considered historical. It is still used primarily to refer to the dances associated with the folk music revival, and continues to exclude the staged dances of the folk dance group. In effect, the usage reflects a superimposition of two definitions, one from the 1920s and the other from the last decades of the twentieth century.[7]

The terminology becomes even trickier outside the scholarly realm. Social dancers may avoid the term "folk dance" in order to distance themselves from the world of folk dance groups. On the other hand, those who engage in both stage dancing and social dancing may consciously use "folk dance" to refer to both, in order to erase those boundaries and challenge the stigma attached to stage dances among social dancers. Likewise, outsiders and others who are unfamiliar with Ernst Klein's *folk/folklig* distinction are likely to use "folk dance" as a catch-all.

Even among social dancers, the term *folklig dans* is rarely used in practice. "Polska" may be used as a general term, much in the way that "tango" can refer to tango, vals cruzado, and milonga, or "salsa" to salsa, bachata, and merengue. The potential ambiguity here goes beyond that question of narrow vs. broad definitions, however, to potentially erase the important boundary between social dancers and those Polska Dancers who dedicate themselves to learning scores of polska variants within the folk dance group context.[8] Another solution has been to refer to "folk music and dance" (*folkmusik och dans*). This usage is unambiguous, and also stresses the essential and functional interconnectedness of dance to music, a critical ideological tenet of the post-revival subculture. Unfortunately, sometimes people want to refer to the dance without referring directly to the music, and so again this construction falls short. In terms of everyday usage, probably one of the most common solutions is simply to refer explicitly to the context in which these dances are danced—"Allégården," "Skeppis," "gatherings," "Ransäter," or "Bingsjö."

On the musical side, people tend to be less concerned with establishing terminological distinctions between camps. While people often discuss folk music as a problematic concept, in practice people use it with far less hesitation than the analogous dance terms. For most people, *folklig musik* and *folklig sång* are simply synonyms for *folkmusik* and *folksång*.

However, the *folk-/folklig* distinction has proven useful for some scholars of urban music. Annika Nordström is an ethnologist whose dissertation focuses on the song repertoire of three elderly sisters from Gothenburg: "I myself have, without closer definition than that it has to do with everyday singing, used the terms *folklig sång & musik.* . . . That has also been intended to lead thoughts away from folk songs, folk music, and large stages, and into people's everyday lives."[9] She cites folklorist Reimund Kvideland as her source for this specific terminology and usage.[10] Ernst Klein's dance-related terminology is also an obvious influence here, especially given Nordström's reference to "large stages," and the fact that she has worked with Mats Nilsson.[11] Her usage here implies, both in terms of how she frames it and in its parallels to Klein's terms, that the *folklig musik* she studies possesses the very connection to the people that folk music claims (with less legitimacy) as its source of cultural currency. The argument is less explicit, but operates much like Klein's suggestion that *folklig dans* is the "true" folk dance, or Olle Edström's suggestion that schlager is the "real" folk music.[12]

Nordström also distinguishes between her methodology and that of most folk music scholars. She distances herself from recent definitions of folk music that classify it as a genre, rather than the music of a specific group of people:

> The concept of folk music still manifests—in general usage and within musi-cological circles—with a point of departure in the music itself, as a genre cate-gory for an often aurally transmitted music with roots in the preindustrial soci-ety. . . . I have not limited my study according to the origins of the material, but instead tried to examine the siblings' entire song repertoire.[13]

Nordström's statement that she has not limited her study according to the ori-gins of the material distinguishes it not only from the folk music scholarship of the present, but also from the entire history of that scholarship, which from its very origins in collection work examined repertoire selectively according to its perceived age. In doing so she brings into focus one of the primary criticisms that scholars of folk music have directed against their own intellectual history, while neatly sidestepping it in her own work. Nordström self-consciously avoids the kind of manipulation of her field of study that has been the source of many of the intrinsic conflicts of the folk music concept. She does what many folk music scholars agree everyone should have been doing all along, that is, accepts the entire repertoire of every person she studies as significant. Nordström avoids the trap of mediating the tradition for the purpose of improving its authenticity. In so doing, she grants that tradition a working-class cultural currency less available to a folk music estranged from its proletarian roots by constant defini-tion and redefinition by ivory tower and political ideologues. Implicitly, she duplicates Ernst Klein's argument in the musical realm, with the folk music collector's selectivity functioning as an analogue for Selinder's choreography.[14]

Nordström's implied argument is effective in part because the realities of modernization have created an incompatibility between the Traditional and Natural on the one hand, and the increasingly urbanized Folk on the other. Put another way, the people of Sweden are less and less the villagers of Dalarna. Nordström takes the opportunity to rearrange the conceptual terrain: She proceeds from the territory of the Folk and reinvents Tradition as continuous change, and Nature as lack of mediation by the scholar. Because she does not have to commit to ruralness, her music can become more of what folk music claims to be with regard to its other markers: an unself-conscious, non-commercial, living tradition unfiltered by any history of scholarly ideologies.

Popular Culture as the Lowest Common Denominator

The same factors that allow Nordström to funnel cultural currency to her subject of study tend to make life difficult for those folk music enthusiasts who wish to retain that currency. Karin Eriksson puts it in the barest terms: "Folk music has never been *folkligt*. It's a huge myth that folk music is *folkligt*, I think. If you need to say that something is folk music, it isn't *folkligt* any more. That's the big myth we carry from the nineteenth century."[15] Åsa Grogarn Sol further explains the dilemma inherent to the *folklighet* concept that forces folklore and common-ality to struggle for dominance of its conceptual terrain:

> But what is *folkligt*? It's dance band music, right? Or dancing to dance band music, because that's what people [*folk*] do. Hundreds of thousands of people do that, at least. But not nearly as many dance polskor to old peasant music. Or what's *folkligt*? It's singing in a choir, and most of the great number of choirs that exist in Sweden don't sing folk music; they'll sing anything at all. But the actual phenomenon of singing in a choir, it's extremely *folkligt*, particularly for Swedes. So I mean, what's *folkligt*? It's watching Bingolotto, because that's something anyone can do, and it speaks to the ordinary person. You do it on Saturday night, and everybody does it.[16]

The terms "*folkligt*" and "*folklighet*" are closest to the English "common" and "commonality" in their connotations of both mass appeal and unremarkable-ness.[17] They also suggest "in-commonness," in that they usually apply to dis-tinctively and definitively Swedish things. Furthermore, these terms are often applied to phenomena that are generally considered cultureless, mass-mediated, of a "lowest common denominator."[18] In the United States the terms might be applied to reality television, for instance, as an example of something that oper-ates in the popular imagination as a manifestation of hollow mass culture.

In Sweden the most common metonymic signifier of this type of soulless *folklighet* is the television show Bingolotto, to which Sol refers above. Bin-golotto is a regular Saturday night program, a combined variety show, lottery drawing, and call-in game show. Classically, much of Sweden gathers around television sets on Saturday nights to watch the program. My sense is that Bin-golotto operates as an ideal case example of *folklighet* for several reasons. It is both exclusively and pan-Swedish, it operates within a kind of apolitical haze that shrouds it from the real world and thus allows it to be seen as a kind of opi-ate for the masses, and it focuses unabashedly upon material things. Nor is this negative view of Bingolotto and its sister program, Färgfemman, necessarily restricted to the Swedish folk music subculture. The familiarity of that image in the national mass consciousness is perhaps best exemplified in the 1998 Swedish blockbuster movie *Fucking Åmål*, in which the watching of such programs functions as a signifier of zombie-like conformity.[19]

Part of the *folklighet* of Bingolotto also involves its status as "world-famous within Sweden," a common and self-ironizing label for things every Swede knows, yet few outside the country have heard of. Bingolotto functions as a kind of in-joke that binds Sweden as a nation in the know when, for example, it appears in the video for Madonna's "Ray of Light," directed by Stockholm native Jonas Åkerlund. Thus it becomes a symbol of *folklighet* where, for instance, Baywatch never did; because Baywatch, though quite popular in Sweden in its day, was not uniquely Swedish. This *folklighet* relates to nationally specific phenomena that show clear influence from extra-national sources, and lack any relationship to or influence from pre-industrial rural Swedish culture.

Parallel phenomena may be found in the musical realm as well. In this case that which receives this implicitly pejorative *folklighet* label is neither "folk music" nor the most popular pop—Britney Spears, Rihanna, or even internationally known Swedish stars like Robyn or ABBA. Rather, what becomes emblematically *folkligt* in the realm of music, again mentioned by Sol in the above quote, is the genre known as dance band, sometimes described as a diluted Swedish answer to American country.[20] What qualifies it primarily for that position, in my view, is the fact that it is the most popular musical genre produced by and specifically for Swedes, with almost no international target audience. A secondary qualification is its common perception as musically and culturally vapid, another symbol of an impoverished and hollow national mass culture.

The remaining example Sol gives of typical Swedish *folklighet*, that of choir singing, is different from the first two in that it does not generally connote this kind of shallowness. It is also a far less commonly expressed example, and Sol's choice of it likely relates to the fact that she herself is a choir director. It does reveal, however, the possibility of a modern *folklighet* without negative connotations, especially in cases where the person who uses the term has some connection to the emblematic activity.

While an etymological study of the Swedish folk concept is beyond the scope of this work, I proceed from the assumption that the above-described *folk/folklighet* schism followed the process of industrialization and urbanization that changed the identity of most Swedes from peasant to industrial laborer. Other scholars have suggested that the symbolic importance of the rural peasantry to the bourgeoisie during industrialization was bound up with a nostalgia for an older caste system in response to the new urban working class and their burgeoning socialism.[21] Attacks by the bourgeois guardians of folk music on the newer musical forms popular among industrial workers were thus in some sense also a reaction against the threat posed by those laborers to existing economic and class hierarchies. Writings in The Youth Ring's journal *Hembygden* during its first decades often lamented the corruption of the folk to modern and international influences.[22] Even if the secondary and implicitly pejorative meaning of *"folklighet"* was not yet in play, some of its conceptual roots do seem to show at this point in history.

In my experience, the schism in the folk concept is rarely if ever discussed in Swedish folk music circles. Nevertheless, I read the use of these terms to describe both older idealized cultural practices and newer impoverished ones as bespeaking a nostalgia for an abandoned Swedish cultural life. This is especially apparent in the way that *folklighet* can describe phenomena that signify the cultural vacuum of the modern era, at the root of a national identity crisis. An internal irony and pessimism marks the present usage of the term, in that it points to an emptiness at the supposed base of the nation.

The question of how to bring folk music more into the public eye, to make it truly *folkligt*, is a common one, especially among professional musicians and people who dedicate time to the organization of events and management of venues. Reasons for wanting to introduce Swedish folk music to the Swedish populace are many and varied. For professional musicians, economic considerations may be primary. Some people appeal to the need to reintroduce Swedes to their cultural heritage, implicitly or explicitly summoning the image of an empty present-day *folklighet*.[23] The task has proven difficult, however, for a number of reasons.

The Hidden Pathway

Today, the primary force that folk music insiders see to be preventing a resurgence of interest in their music is the economic bottom line that informs mass media in general and the music industry in particular. People are loath to blame anyone in the private sector in particular for denying a place for folk music. The argument simply goes that folk music is not marketable. Two reasons for this commercial non-viability are generally cited: first, there is no reason for the music industry to take the risk of promoting music that is not already popular. Second, folk music is an experience that goes beyond sound, something that to be experienced fully must be part of a broader context—dance perhaps, or social interaction between musicians. Greger Siljebo explains:

> Folk music has been a functional music for so many years and generations. Let's say you take a trip, for simplicity's sake we'll say you travel to Dalarna, and you wind up in some spelman's kitchen. You can smell the open fire, and coffee brewing, and it's a fantastic summer night, and other spelmän come, and there's atmosphere, and they play and they dance in the kitchen, and it's a wonderful time. That experience becomes genuine and it becomes strong. And it's very, very difficult to move to a concert stage. I think that's the core of the problem. In the sixties and seventies, and even the eighties, they tried to trans-

fer exactly that genuine feeling directly from the kitchen to the stage. And the stage in this case can be radio or television or the concert stage. But out to the general populace. Only they don't have any idea about the kitchen, and the genuine experience. They just hear it directly. It's as if I were going to come out on stage with an injured hand and the stomach flu to boot, and play very poorly. If you know the circumstances, maybe you can see an incredibly strong achievement, that I even went through with the concert. Given the fact that he's hurt in the hand and has the stomach flu, it was a fantastic achievement. But your neighbor in the chair next to you, he's just heard about Greger Siljebo the spelman, that it's supposed to be good. He doesn't know I have an injured hand, he doesn't know I have the stomach flu. He thinks it's crap.[24]

A small minority of my interview subjects also suggest that part of the reason folk music remains obscure is that the people who tread that inner pathway (to borrow Ruth Finnegan's terminology) are not interested in making it too public.[25] Karl Malbert presents this as a point of internal conflict among members of the folk music subculture:

> I feel like people who do folk music might complain about there being so few people doing it, but at the same time it feels like they aren't so interested in other people doing it either, because then they'd have to open the codes a little to let in ordinary people. And they don't want to do that.[26]

Guitarist and singer Johan Hogenäs admits to feeling two ways about it, much in the way Malbert describes: "And I think it's too bad, at the same time as there's something cool about it too, of course, to be part of a little select subculture that knows the secrets. There's an appeal to that too. Who knows, maybe I wouldn't be doing it if everyone was doing it."[27]

The secret world to which Hogenäs refers is one I would describe as only one of the musical pathways in a larger network which together make up folk music Sweden. This pathway has no agreed-upon name, but is sometimes referred to as "polska Sweden"; occasionally also the term "folk music Sweden" is used to signify only this smaller arena. More commonly the pathway is referenced metonymically by its venues—gatherings generally or Ransäter specifically, folk music and dance clubs in general or (in Gothenburg) Allégården in particular. Its defining characteristics are a focus on polska music and dance, the elevation of music to a status equal to or greater than those of dance and heritage, and the privileging of the social aspect, resulting in a general lack of interest in performing for outsiders in other-than-professional contexts.

To give one example of how this concealment operates, consider the 2002 midsummer celebration at Nääs outside Gothenburg, probably the largest such event in the city's greater metropolitan area, with attendance in the thousands. A typical midsummer's festival, the day's main events were choreographed to a large extent by the Skallsjö folk dance group, to music by its ancillary players, among whom I was a temporary appendage. The music we were to play was determined by the dance leaders, and went, predictably, with their standard folk dance fare. I was not the only polska musician in the group however—the lead fiddler, Håkan Lindberg, led that double life, as did one of the younger musicians, Jenny Svensson. In between sets and away from the microphones, inside an empty hall near the main event, Svensson was taking the time to teach polskor to Lindberg. At the other end of the field, concealed behind another building, two young fiddlers (one of them Lindberg's son) played their own polskor before an audience of passers-by you could count on your hand. The two hidden sessions were separated by a field of a few hundred paces and a crowd of thousands if not tens of thousands.

In the Nääs case the concealment of the polska sessions may be considered at least in part an effect of their incompatibility with the traditional midsummer dancing. During the central Swedish gatherings on the other hand, polska sessions are very much compatible with the dance, and exactly what much of the interested audience has come to see. It may be of interest to consider, therefore, the motivations behind musicians who seek to hide from public eyes in these contexts. Here even finding an out-of-the-way place may not suffice; the locations are often too compact and the crowds too big. Instead, musicians may prioritize the nighttime as an appropriate time to enter the public area and play, after the crowds have died down. At the 2004 Bingsjö gathering, for instance, fiddle pedagogue Pelle Gustafsson arranged a jam session to start at 2 am that then went on into the early morning hours. Later in the week at the Boda gathering, after the 3 am closing of the indoor dance floor moved the dancers to the grassy area around an outdoor session, Gustafsson shouted: "Yes! Now the Boda gathering begins."

A large part of this privileging of the nighttime, I think, involves moving out of the public eye, evading the local press that attends these central Swedish events during the day, and operating beyond the post meridiem hours of the gathering during which an official order of events is prescribed and an outsider audience is still in attendance. The hidden subculture can operate without contributing to whatever picture outsiders may hold of folk music, with whatever connotations the music may have of national romanticism or quaintness. The suggestion some of my interview subjects have made regarding the inner circle's unwillingness to open the subculture completely to a wider populace seems to be born out in these nighttime events in central Sweden, where the wider populace (during this week of the year at least) actually seems to have taken a genuine interest.

The Visible Periphery: Accordion Crimes

In other cases it is not the outsiders' gaze that drives polska musicians to hide, but rather another group of musicians. At the 2003 Hällesåker spelman gathering I noticed that fiddlers occasionally hid from accordionists in order to play polskor in peace. A common difficulty with accordion players is that they are accustomed to playing gammeldans, and thus that their left-hand rhythmic accompaniment figures tend to homogenize all regional polska variations into standard hambo. The etiquette of the spelman gathering is generally such that any musician can essentially join any session. The loudness of the accordion combined with its tendency to erase the rhythmic subtleties of polskor can thus make life difficult for polska fiddlers at gatherings, who may thus be driven to hide in out-of-the-way places.

Those accordionists who play polska music acknowledge this problem, and speak to the level of difficulty and effort it takes to learn to play with polska fiddlers in such a way as to enhance, rather than detract from, the rhythmic and harmonic subtleties of the music. This issue came to a head in a debate in *Spelmannen* in 2001, initiated by some complaints regarding the accordion nuisance. The first writer, Björn Sandberg, wrote:

> I don't know if they consciously sabotage for other spelmän with softer instruments or if it's ample self-righteousness or just ignorant stupidity, but the fact is they are successful in doing so. Without consideration they stand in huge groups and shovel out decibels in places where they can be heard far away.
>
> If the accordionists themselves don't have the sense to understand that they disturb and destroy—and make themselves quite unpopular—by doing what is certainly the right thing but in the wrong place, I would like to see an organizer who had the authority to arrange separate playing spaces for accordions, or at least accordion-free zones for strings and winds.[28]

A second writer, Bengt Enqvist, wrote about his experience as a listener trying to enjoy music at a nyckelharpa gathering where a bumbling accordionist ruined it for everyone.[29]

Ingvar Strömblad, a Gothenburg accordionist, responded to the charges:

> I agree with most of what you're saying, except for one *critical* point, which is that it doesn't apply to *everyone* who plays accordion at a spelman gathering, which you write. At least that's how I understand your meaning.
>
> Unfortunately there are many, maybe too many, who behave in the way you describe. But it's *important* not to generalize and single out *all* accordionists as disturbers of the peace. A propos disturbers of the peace, it's not particularly pleasant to hear a fiddle player playing loudly and *out of tune*, or are these *exempt* from the concept disturbers of the peace, no matter how it sounds, just because they play with a bow?[30]

In the title to his opinion piece Strömblad distinguishes between "accordionists" and "spelmän who play accordion." As I interpret it, the first term describes someone within a tradition of accordion music just close enough to older folk music in its forms that he or she can apply the rules of the former to mangle the latter. The spelman who plays accordion, on the other hand, actually dedicates time and energy to learning the rules of folk music, and in so doing takes on great challenges on several fronts. One such challenge, as Strömblad suggests in his article, is the defensive social barrier erected against accordionists of the first variety, and occasionally applied indiscriminately against those of the second. Another is the design of the instrument itself, whose left hand is generally built according to principles of Western tonality—rows of roots, thirds, triads, and seventh chords, ordered in columns according to the circle of fifths—in ordinary circumstances used to generate accompaniment figures that would be very much out of place in polska music.

As a result, "spelmän who play accordion" must find their own way with the instrument, creating new left-hand techniques unimagined by the instrument's designers, in order to fit more readily within polska structures. The two Gothenburg-area accordionists I have interviewed, Ingvar Strömblad and Per Sandberg, report similar experiences regarding this personal voyage. The trek is difficult and requires an individualistic sense of musical discovery. Once it is made, however, the accordion actually becomes ideally suited to the music, as Per Sandberg describes here:

> It's a lot of fun trying to interpret it on the accordion. It's damn hard, really. Damn hard. Partly because with the fiddle you can create any note you want. You can't do that on the accordion. Plus in Swedish folk music you slur the notes a lot. And that's very difficult to do on the accordion. . . . [T]he instrument is really a fantastic instrument. It's really one of the most complicated instruments human beings have invented. And it has everything folk music needs. You can play a drone. You can form your notes to a certain extent, by working with the bellows. You could say it's like a voice. It's fantastic for working with fifths. I mean a normal accordion has a bass tuned in fifths. And the fifth for me is very much folk music, because that's the open interval. It's the most open interval I know. So I work a lot with fifths, and that's very easy to do on the accordion, because if you play a C in the bass, you have the G right next to it.[31]

In other words, Sandberg exploits a design aspect of the accordion in a way un-intended by its creators. The innermost two rows of buttons in the left hand are single notes, arranged according to the circle of fifths in order to facilitate harmonic motion to the dominant and subdominant. Sandberg uses them instead to generate open intervals, and not for their intended function of harmonizing tonally conceived music. This is only one example of how a voyage of personal discovery—Sandberg has no formal training on the accordion—can allow the accordionist into the polska realm.

For this reason, the accordionists who do enter this world tend to fit in well with that general category of folk musicians who do not play bowed instruments, and who as a rule have beaten out their own musical paths into polska. In their left hand spelmän-who-play-accordion stand with guitarists and percussionists, noting the difficulty of finding a space for accompaniment parts in the music. In the right they stand with flutists and saxophonists, citing the need to manipulate the air stream as a substitute for the bow. Strömblad's written counter-attack against the marginalization of his instrument is thus fairly typical for polska accordionists in taking the tone of standard innovationist arguments: How you play is more important than what you play.

Strömblad began his musical career in a house full of fiddlers, learning the chromatic accordion because his family members encouraged that variety. At the time he experienced no differentiation in status between accordion and fiddle, nor did his family distinguish between everyday popular music and tunes he would later learn were elevated as folk material. In his interview he revels in the logical inconsistencies inherent to preservationist attempts at delegitimizing the accordion. The chromatic accordion, he says, dates back to the nineteenth century, around the same time the diatonic accordion swept through Sweden, much to the chagrin of that day's cultural conservatives. Yet his instrument, which can do anything a fiddle can do except play microtones, is considered by the Zorn jury to be less a folk music instrument than that very diatonic accordion once reviled by preservationists. Likewise the chromatic nyckelharpa, no more than sixty years old, enjoys acceptance, while his older instrument does not. He blames outside academics who have come into the folk music world and thought to understand it, to draw dividing lines that for real spelmän were completely foreign.[32]

The question Strömblad poses about the relative legitimacy of the diatonic and chromatic accordions is worthy of consideration. At one time the "durspel" (diatonic accordion) was indeed the primary symbol of folk music's imminent downfall.[33] Its scalar limitations brought with it a repertoire that threatened to replace older village forms.[34] Cheaper and louder than the fiddle, and far easier to learn, it was well-suited to the developing dance hall culture of the late nineteenth and early twentieth centuries.[35] As a foreign factory-made instrument it also functioned well as a symbol of industrialization, homogenization, and internationalization.[36]

The durspel was quickly surpassed as a symbol of all the above threats to folk music, however, by the gramophone and the "jazz" it played, further adding miscegenation and corruption to the list.[37] It would not be long either before the diatonic accordion's obsolescence to the chromatic, which has since that time retained its status and visibility as a popular instrument via genres like gammel-dans, schlager, and dance band.[38] This consignment of durspel music to history, the apparent threat of its extinction just as it once threatened fiddle music, may have been the primary factor in its later legitimation as a folk music instrument. Its extremely limited range, which of course also contributed to its obsolescence, may be another contributing factor, connoting a primitivism that might place it in a similar category to the cow horn or willow flute. Finally, and ironically, perhaps because of its very significance to folk music as a past threat, the durspel's candidacy may have been elevated by simple principle of historical association. None of the above factors would be likely to be cited officially by the Zorn jury as a justification for legitimizing the diatonic accordion over the chromatic, however. The durspel's candidacy should in theory be a function of its being more popular than the chromatic accordion, not less. Nevertheless, while the official qualification for any instrument to be traditional is typically its constant use through a given period of time, it does seem that the durspel's folk currency is actually increased by a disconnect from modern practice.

Conversely, what bars the chromatic accordion from status as a true folk music instrument is very much its continued presence in broader Swedish musical life. The chromatic accordion represents an uncomfortable bridge between the world of polska and those of gammeldans and schlager. It still threatens to tonalize and dilute the fiddle tradition just as the durspel did when it came on the scene.

The situation is exacerbated by the fact, observed by many within the folk music subculture, that outsiders often think of Swedish folk music as primarily exemplified by accordion. This idea of a false front for folk music, a popularized veneer, is brought up for example by Ulf Kinding as a phenomenon that goes well beyond Sweden's borders:

> We were in Ireland with the folk dancers, and I was going to buy a record. We were in a shop looking at records, and I asked the shopkeeper "what's the deal with the Irish music—is it all accordion and mandolin?" Because that's what it seemed like. And he said "so you want the real thing?" He took out a record from under the counter.
> *Kaminsky*: What was the record?
> *Kinding*: What?
> *Kaminsky*: What was the—
> *Kinding*: Well, it was bagpipes and fiddles and so on, but it was the kind of thing that wasn't selling much, only it has to be electric guitar and accordion even in Ireland. But I guess of course, that's what makes money.[39]

The fact that the accordion is in fact a more popular instrument is an added irritation here, given the supposed connection between folk music and the Folk.

Part of the chromatic accordion's threat to the fiddle is posed by its greater musical accessibility, a function of its modern technological features. The instrument lacks the flexibility to allow serious intonation problems, is never scratchy, boasting a full bass, mid-, and treble range, and possesses the ability to play melody and accompaniment with familiar tonal underpinnings. It lacks the idiosyncrasies that make fiddle music less like other musics, and grant Swedish folk music both its characteristic flavors and general obscurity to the public. The listener does not have to be initiated into any kind of special world in order to acquire a taste for accordion music. In a sense, the chromatic accordion can thus represent the potential fear among folk music insiders that the popularization of folk music might force its alteration by aesthetic ideals that inform more popular musics—tonality, cleanness of tone, equal temperament, and so forth.

That fear is exacerbated, again, by the fact that public perceptions place folk music and accordion music in the same category. By association this puts Swedish folk music that much closer to the increasingly mass-cultural musical forms with which the accordion has been associated. At the same time, defenders of these popular genres, like Olle Edström, have not generally separated out the accordion as a topic for discussion, nor attempted to grant it status as a folk music instrument on the grounds of its *folklighet*.

Likely due primarily to their popular music associations, chromatic accordions in spelman groups have often been subject to a certain degree of camouflage. Still today in the Gothenburg spelman group Göteborgs spelmansförbund, for instance, these instruments occupy a liminal status, as noted by Ulf Kinding:

> *Kaminsky*: What instruments to you have in Göteborgs spelmansförbund? Is it—
> *Kinding*: We have fiddles and nyckelharpa, and two-rowed accordions. We have a clarinet too. And you can say that all those instruments are *folklig*, they've been a part of it since the olden days. But every now and then a guitarist comes, and of course he can be a part of the rehearsals, because it's always good to have a little accompaniment. But you shouldn't have that at a performance, or a music listening event. If you're playing for a dance it's okay, of course, there we have both a bass and a larger accordion and so on. But then it's not folk music any more. Not genuine, anyway.[40]

Ingvar Strömblad has remarked on this sort of attitude toward chromatic accordions and other accompanying instruments, which he notes has had significant historical precedent:

> Almost all the great spelmän had a playing buddy who played the accordion, when they were out at their wedding gigs and dances and all that. But when these academic know-it-alls started writing about them, we just disappeared systematically into thin air. Before they got a hold of Hjort Anders—he's done a lot of good, they're a bunch of fine tunes and everything—but before he got so scholarly and the upper crust got a hold of him, he was very taken with [accordionist] Calle Jularbo. But if you said that to him in later days he would have taken great offense, because that wasn't refined. . . . In almost all spelman groups, the accordionist can come along if they're going to have a dance performance; it supports the whole thing. And the bassist has lived the same life. Basses have been a part of this since time immemorial. Well not really, but a long time anyway. So it's kind of a funny thing—I've seen a really old photo of a small spelman group. I know they had an accordionist, and he wasn't in the official photo. But they couldn't have completed a real performance if he wasn't along.[41]

In sum, the accordion is marginalized in folk music Sweden for the twofold threat it poses. First, it occupies a liminal position between folk and popular culture, and as such, threatens to erase the boundary between them. This problem is exacerbated by folk music insiders' ambivalence toward that boundary—on the one hand, erasing it would bring folk music back to the people; on the other, maintaining it allows folk music to retain its distinctiveness. Second, the accordion camouflages the "real" Swedish folk music by substituting for it in the national imagination. And in this obscuring role, it is not alone.

The Visible Periphery: Folk Costumes

Another major problem that insiders tend to point to as an explanation for the general obscurity of folk music is an attached stigma of *töntighet* (approx. "lameness" in the figurative sense). This perception is often blamed to a large extent on the public face of folk music and dance as presented by folk dance groups. Clarinetist Pers Nils Johansson describes an event that for him exemplifies the problem:

> [T]here are a lot of people who don't do folk music, who may not say anything if you say you do folk music, but if you say you play folk music, you mean something completely different than what they perceive it as. They have a completely different perception of folk music than I have myself. We had a national day celebration in Alingsås a few years back. I was playing in a brass band, and the people in that band aren't exactly folk music types. And there was a folk dance group there also; they were dancing a stage dance in folk costumes, and it felt like maybe the folk dance wasn't quite in its element there. You might say it was outside its everyday context. So it felt a little artificial. It wasn't the wild dancing that you might have at a gathering, where it's not about the stage dances. And the weather was bad, so the fiddlers couldn't tune their instruments either; the conditions they had to work with were pretty bad. And one of these guys in the brass band whispered to me: "Is that what you do?" And he laughed a little. So you get this sense about what people think about folk music. It doesn't quite do it justice.[42]

Folkloric stage dances are especially visible around Swedish summer celebrations like June sixth and especially midsummer, when folk dance groups are hired by communities to perform in parks and lead children's game songs. As such their public presence easily eclipses that of the core folk music scene, whose activities tend to be far more internally oriented.

Much of what folk dance groups represent, for themselves, to polska Sweden, and to the nation at large, is tied symbolically to their standard uniform of traditional folk costumes. Historically, this costume was a formal set of clothing meant for special occasions like church and weddings, and was not typically worn at informal social gatherings or dances. The folk costume was one of the primary objects of interest to the rescuers of folk culture, and has historically been tied especially to the Youth Ring. Regional style variation is of extreme import to those interested in these garments, with density of variation increasing in central Sweden due to a more continuous tradition there, much as in the case of the polska. Historical accuracy in production is often of great concern, including the question of whether or not to use modern materials or technology. Today, for those who wear it, folk costume tends to represent pride in cultural heritage, and often in local or regional culture given its geographic specificity. In some places it is still used as formalwear. Others who wear it tend either to be involved in performing folk dance or spelman groups. Those who own folk costumes may also wear them on midsummer.

In Swedish popular culture, folk costumes can also signify backwoods ruralness. The comic figure of the country bumpkin in Sweden has typically worn this uniform, which has thus held similar connotations (both positive and negative) to the barefoot Huck Finn overalls and straw hat ensemble in the United States. In particular, the knee tassel common to many of the men's costumes has become a popular metonymic signifier for folk-culture-associated lameness. These connotations, given that folk costumes also operate as symbols for Swedish cultural heritage and national identity, demonstrate some of the general skepticism that Swedes have toward their own nationalism.

The costume also, because it is such a visible marker of national identity, comes to represent something of how Swedes imagine themselves to be perceived by outsiders. For instance, during my high school year abroad in 1992 in Gothenburg, a classmate asked me if the common image of Swedes in America was that they walked around in folk costume all the time. Over a decade later, at the Delsbo spelman gatherings in Hälsingland, I told fellow attendee Maja Hjertberg that I had been seeing many Americans at the central Swedish gatherings; she suggested that their primary interest was probably pretty young girls dancing in costume. In both cases the people I was talking to miscalculated the cultural knowledge of Sweden among the Americans in question. Regarding my high school classmate's query, most of the United States would probably think "bikini team" before they thought "folk costume," or if they thought folk costume would likely imagine lederhosen.[43] Concerning the second example, that particular subset of Americans traveling the central Swedish gathering circuit were generally hard-core polska enthusiasts, more aural and kinesthetic pilgrims than visual tourists.

Nevertheless, Maja's conjecture does reflect an understanding of how Swedish women are sexualized in the international popular imagination. Whether manifested in the form of a busty beer-ad blondes in matching bikinis, or Jamie Lee Curtis in lederhosen, or young dancing girls in actual Swedish folk costumes, this sexualization is catalyzed and amplified by the uniform.[44] Those within the folk dance community can also be quite sensitive to this as a problem, as Ulla and Anders Bergsten suggest:

> *Ulla Bergsten*: When they have world championships here in track and field, the Youth Ring is called in to bear standards. Or placards, with folk costumes and so on, so it gets to be a little—
> *Anders Bergsten*: One time, the city of Gothenburg was organizing it, and they said they wanted "pretty young girls." They had worded it a little foolishly, so we basically objected to it on those grounds.[45]

Folk costume is thus also tied to a set of general anxieties about how Swedes are perceived by the rest of the world, an emblem of the dumb Swede and the dumb blonde, of simple-mindedness, rural myopia, and hypersexuality.

Of even greater concern to people within the polska community, however, is what folk costumes represent to the Swedish populace at large. Here "lameness" is only part of the picture. The highly visible costumes are also intimately tied to the world of amateur spelman and dance groups, where presentation of heritage often eclipses musical concerns, and where staged performances can obscure and divert attention from the world of polska and gathering. It also conjures a romanticized past where every peasant wore colorful formal dress in their everyday lives and danced elaborately choreographed group dances expressing their social utopia. The costume thus becomes a preservationist screen, obfuscating Sweden's view of its own core folk music subculture and living music-cultural traditions.

This is not to suggest that folk costumes are entirely absent within polska Sweden, given that pathway's connection to the worlds of spelman and folk dance groups. In areas in which those individual worlds are more distinct, the costumes are rare—they would almost never be seen today at Ransäter, Korrö, Urkult, or an urban folk music café, for instance. At the central Swedish gatherings, on the other hand, where the pathways overlap more and the core subculture is more visible to the outer world, folk costumes are worn by a significant minority of participants. The rural Hällesåker gathering on the southern outskirts of Gothenburg also sees a few attendees in full dress. At the now-defunct nearby Öckerö gathering, likewise, folk costume was quite common, given that the event revolved primarily around folk dance groups. All of these events see a fair amount of interaction between multiple pathways related to Swedish folk music.

At the 2002 Öckerö gathering, Urban Lind and Emma Rydberg wore clothing much simpler than that worn by most of the other dancers present, creating a look that Lind referred to in casual conversation as "half costume." For the first half of their performance, the male dancers of the folk dance group National's youth section, led by Rydberg and Lind, danced without vests, to similar effect.[46] In a later interview I asked him to explain:

> *Lind*: We did that for a reason. These folk costumes that we wear are a kind of formalwear, something people wore when they went to church. And you didn't dance in church; that was a different kind of occasion. When people went dancing, they didn't wear formal costumes. They wore ordinary clothing. So the point is to show that difference.
>
> *Kaminsky*: When you go in half costume, is it some kind of, do you take only a part of it, the whole costume, or do you wear something different? Do you see what I mean?
>
> *Lind*: Well we took away certain details, the men's vests, for example. Really we should have had other clothing, simpler clothing, but in practical terms we just couldn't. We didn't have time to change, and also not everyone has those clothes.[47]

This compromise between full costume and civilian garb is thus a self-conscious mitigation of the folk dance movement's romanticized historical revisionism as manifested in costume culture.

The removal of extraneous parts of the costume, furthermore, may also address another issue, the lameness associated with knee tassels and other gaudy ornaments. An even sharper example of this strategy of deaccessorization was the regular wardrobe of Gothenburg super-group Bäsk, who left off not only such ornaments, but also most of the rest of the costume. All they retained were the elegant overcoats, which they wore over simple dark clothing. The result was a half costume that avoided the normal busy and variegated elements altogether, leaving a two-tone simple and stylish, yet in some sense "traditional" dress.

The Visible Periphery: Fusion and the Foreign

The garb worn by Bäsk was in some sense a visual analogue to their music and that of many other professional Swedish folk groups. It represented a negotiation between the traditional and modern, local and international, folk and popular, hand-made and mass-produced. Fusion has been one of the most effective ways for professional musicians to sell their music. Today the market for Swedish folk music that includes no post-revival instruments is essentially limited to active participants in the culture.[48] Various forms of fusion, however, have the capacity to reach the market already claimed by the genre with which the folk music elements are combined—rock, jazz, world music, classical, and so on—to which folk music can then function as an added spice. The possibility of mixing musical styles and genres also creates a greater variety and wider palette, an advantage in the realm of commercial music that orients itself to listeners as opposed to dancers. Even more fortuitously, the fusion of Swedish folk music with other national or ethnic musics also generates that political advantage of undercutting any problematic nationalistic sentiments that one might otherwise interpret to be present in "pure" Swedish folk music.

This phenomenon is also one that tends to polarize people, especially with regard to that "world music" approach of mixing various national and ethnic traditions. Some people find this sort of fusion very exciting, a celebration of multiculturalism at its best. Amateur fiddler and folk music revivalist Inger Rydberg (Emma's mother) brings it up as a counter to the idea that folk music might be associated with right-wing nationalism, even arguing that cultural self-knowledge makes you more open to other cultures:

> I know that Jan Ling writes about that. Jan Ling was in our food group for a long time, so I know him well. He brought it up a bunch of times in our discussions, that you have to be very careful to make sure it doesn't turn into that. I don't really see it. I mean I realize it was used that way in the '20s and '30s, but the idea that you would be in some kind of danger because you like Swedish folk music, that it affects you, that you get high off it, that it would somehow make you really nationalistic, I don't understand that. Because it can also have the opposite effect, I mean it makes you open to other peoples' folk music also. You can see that when Ale Möller does his thing. I recently taped a show that was just wonderful.[49] And Ellika & Solo, for example, who we heard at Allégården, that's also really wonderful. It's just as powerful as when you hear a

Bingsjö musician, or someone like Pers Hans. But it's good that we're not stuck with the idea that there's some sort of national socialism in folk music.[50]

Others find it problematic that the public image of folk music should so consistently feature intercultural fusion. Singer and fiddler Annelie Westerlund remarks:

> Our folk music has never had sitars. It's never had those strange Chinese sticks, whatever they're called. I don't remember what they're called, but I heard it on the radio when I was driving just the other day. I wound up laughing really hard, because it sounded so weird. They were trying to play a waltz from somewhere in Dalarna on some kind of "pyoing"-sounding instrument. And that can be fun, to sit and jam if you're just doing it for fun. But that winds up being the image that everyone gets of folk music. I think that's too bad. Show what we really have instead of according everything that isn't Swedish a higher value.[51]

International fusion, for Westerlund, threatens to obscure the "true" Swedish folk music much in the same way that the accordion does for Ulf Kinding, or the folk dance group for Pers Nils Johansson. Westerlund also obliquely invokes the other sort of criticism directed at mixed musics, mentioned in the previous chapter, problematizing the de-prioritization of the music itself to petty ideological concerns. This sort of critique operates much in the same way as those against preservationist "museum" folk music. The attack is formulated not on cultural heritage directly, but rather on the reduced quality of a music subjugated to its restrictions.

This shift from a cultural argument to an aesthetic one is useful given the core dilemma with which Westerlund is forced to wrestle. The notion of a pure Swedish folk music may be too close for comfort to that of a pure Swedish cultural and racial identity. Moving the argument to the level of musical sound adds a buffer of distance from the concept's uncomfortable ideological history.

An even more effective strategy, as far as distancing the notion of a pure Swedish folk music from its reactionary roots, is that hinted at by Inger Rydberg in her above quotation. Turn the tables by positing that making Swedes aware and proud of their own cultural heritage will actually reduce xenophobia. Åsa Grogarn Sol relates that both she and her daughter have come to this conclusion independently:

> She's a punk and an anarchist and just under seventeen. And she agrees with me completely on this. She says that—especially where there's a lot of insecurity around your own roots and their value, and how worried you can get when people from another culture come with their experiences, and there can be a lot of tensions and uncertainties—she says that it's often because you don't have any idea about who you are, and where you come from. . . . She says that they should teach all young people polska dance and songs, because then Swedes would feel much more secure, and have a much easier time accepting other

people's values and cultures. . . . She's heard and seen enough to be able to have these opinions. And I haven't told her this, she's actually figured it out on her own.[52]

This argument operates as an effective counter to the connection often drawn between romanticized folk culture and reactionary nationalism.[53]

Understandably, folk music insiders become extremely defensive when people start asking questions about right-wing racist groups and their use of Swedish folk music and culture as a symbol. Consider the following example, in which folk music saxophonist Pär Moberg, responding to a commission by German radio to help with a program about recent trends in Swedish folk music, wrote to the Yahoo! Swedish folk music discussion group for advice regarding this issue:[54]

> One aspect I have been asked to illuminate is the extent to which it happens that Swedish folk music is used by young people in racist/fascist contexts, since this has begun to happen in Germany. My spontaneous reaction to that question would be no; it's certainly happened before (in the Youth Ring's brown past, etc.) but I haven't heard of it happening today. What do you say? Do any of you know of any such connections in modern times? The connection was made on television a while back between the nyckelharpa's potential status as national instrument and nationalist/racist tendencies, but that connection doesn't seem particularly serious I don't think; racist bands tend to advocate more aggressive rock music (blissfully unaware, it seems, that that music was created by blacks! But they don't have that many brain cells between them . . .). So, does anyone know White power polska?[55]

The first respondent to this query, Ethel Wieslander, argued both that personal cultural pride reduces xenophobia, and further that the government should do more to support Swedish folk music without the need for mixing in other elements:

> My immediate answer is also no! I think, quite the opposite, that increased knowledge about our own culture gives less negative views of other cultures. Racism and anti-immigration sentiment are built largely on fear. If I don't know anything about my own culture, I feel less worthy and more insecure compared to other groups with stronger cultural identity. Insecurity breeds fear. Furthermore, many immigrant groups have a greater necessity of expressing their cultural identity since they are strangers in a strange land—no more peculiar than that we like to play Skåne tunes in Dalarna, for example.
>   That is: the more we Swedes can be proud of our own culture, the more generous we can feel about other cultures!
>   This involves one other thing: If an ever-growing part of folk culture in Sweden becomes multicultural (that's the only thing you get funding for) the possibilities for us to strengthen our own identity as Swedes diminishes, and all the well-wishing multicultural endeavors I think can bring about some misdi-

rected effects. Sometimes I get the feeling that "just" Swedish folk music isn't
fine or trendy enough, and that's not good. For anyone.

   Support Swedish folk music! Make us proud, secure, and open to other
things!

   Good luck in Germany,
   Ethel[56]

This posting illustrates very well the difficulties of supporting Swedish folk
music without falling back on early twentieth-century racist traditions. Nowhere
is that dilemma better exemplified than in the question of how to address the
issue of immigrant and multicultural music projects absorbing public funding
that might otherwise support efforts at popularizing Swedish folk music. Given
the history of Swedish folk music as a concept, and its construction from the
very beginning as a musical tradition threatened by internationalization, Wieslander must cut off the argument from its obvious national-romantic roots to
avoid seeming xenophobic. The first paragraph here thus operates as a qualifier
for the second.

   Another form that the modern concern with internationalization takes regards the negative effects of American cultural imperialism. Vivi Nilsson re-
calls:

   We Swedes were spared the war. We had made it. And afterwards, when it
   opened up, we had buying power. So we bought all the American crap. Everything that was good and everything that was bad. We bought jazz; that was
   good. We bought silk stockings and so on. I mean, we bought their whole culture and killed our own. We stopped playing—this is generalizing, we didn't do
   this completely, but we became the most Americanized country in the whole
   world. . . . We were so open to everything, because we had possibilities. The
   others, who were bombed out and devastated, they didn't. We could, we were
   rich. Compared to others. We could buy everything. And so what was ours
   wasn't so valuable any more. We were supposed to forget about that. It became
   hickish and poor. I remember how it was a little bit. Not just with music, but
   with everything.[57]

Mass-mediated American culture is a common villain when it comes to the marginalization of Swedish folk music, far less politically sensitive to invoke than
immigration. Sweden, like the rest of the world, is highly influenced by American culture. American phrases pervade the language more and more, and
American films and television shows are the norm. For Nilsson, with her leftist
sensibilities, the abandonment of Swedish traditional culture is intimately tied
up with capitalism and the selling of the Swedish soul.

   Like Nilsson, Jan Ling also cites World War II as turning-point, though in
this case with regard to a shift in international loyalties. Ling points to a convergence of supposedly conflicting political ideologies, both of which lament the
loss of Swedish folk music and culture, and both of which see Americanization
as the culprit:

We were very German-friendly, not just before the war, but also during the war. There were strong forces for Nazism in Sweden, not least here in Gothenburg. And when we were to change to an Anglo-Saxon identity—symbolized by the fact that we weren't going to begin with German in school any more, and we were distancing ourselves from German culture—that was also a sign for jazz to come in and prepare for rock in a way that would have been difficult if we had still had that German culture. And that was also the anchor to folk music culture, since the exchange we had had with Germany was also very strong in the area of folk culture. So there was a shift in identity, from Germany to the United States. And these anti-American feelings that arose didn't only have to do with the US and the Vietnam war. They were also informed by a lot of unconscious ideological thoughts and currents, where there were these cultural roots that had suddenly been cut off.[58]

Thus, according to Ling, enmeshed in the argument that blames American influence for the decline of Swedish folk culture is the national memory of a painful separation from Germany. Ling here makes oblique reference to those early twentieth-century politically and culturally conservative writings that sought to protect the position of Swedish folk music from being usurped by African-American musics.[59] Looking back at Vivi Nilsson's quote, I think it would be reasonable to suggest that her explicit statement hailing jazz as one of the good things American influence brought was a necessary mitigation of the elements of her argument to which the right may have historically contributed. Like the whole first paragraph of Ethel Wieslander's posting about the position of immigrant musics in Sweden, Nilsson's little qualifier about jazz as a positive influence points to the carefulness needed when raising arguments that posit foreign influence as a threat to Swedish folk music.

The Politics of Romanticism

While the fused element in folk music fusion is key to the expansion of audience base, the cultural currency of the folk music element itself can also be drawn upon to marketable effect. Sten Källman notes that Hedningarna, one of Sweden's most successful folk fusion acts, appealed to its broad audience by using folk music as a signifier of romanticized cultural identity:

They've have had a large audience mostly due to the fact that they've stressed certain romantic markers. . . . There's a nostalgia and a romantic trip in larger audiences. I think it's different with the dancers. There's nothing nostalgic about being interested in dancing polska; the only reason to do that is if you think it's really fun. People wouldn't do it otherwise. Because the productions aren't that cool; the only cool thing about it is if you think it's cool to dance polska. I don't think Allégården is the most entertaining place in the world. But even so, there are people who like to go there to dance. So there's no nostalgia or romanticizing about it. There's no mythologizing, no drones going [*sings a soft and mysterious drone, and breaks it up with some snippets of polska in the middle*]. The music that evokes a mystical pine forest, for a city audience that's starved for history or their own roots, wondering in today's mass-mediated world "who I am, really?" When Hedningarna come on stage their music speaks to that audience. It's exactly the right thing to produce that experience in a group of people who are seeking their identity and history and origins.[60]

This sort of romanticizing strategy too has seen its critics within the Swedish folk music community. Jan Ling has been particularly apocalyptic about the perils of an overly mythologized folk music leading to the potential reinvigoration of national socialism. In his 1979 article "Folkmusik—En brygd" he takes Bo i Ransätt Isaksson's 1978 *Folkmusiken i Sverige* to task for waxing dangerously romantic:

> It is unfortunate that such preposterous ideas have begun to saturate parts of the ideology of Swedish folk music. The most treacherous part is that they show up in an otherwise so often well-documented and interesting text, and not rarely with well-played music. In their search for an alternative identity, a segment of young people within the folk music revival have thus come to embrace a national-romantic view of folk music, with its chauvinist and mythologizing ideology. It is in the deepest sense of the word reactionary, built on faulty analysis of what music is and can be, a false historiography that paves the way for a national-socialist understanding of folk music, which stands very close to that of 1930s' Germany.[61]

This issue came to a head in the early nineties, a period of some political turmoil in Sweden.[62] After the 1991 national elections the Social Democrats were removed from power for only the second time since 1936, and Swedish parliament was controlled by the center-right bloc, headed by the conservative Moderate party.[63] The new prime minister, Carl Bildt, promised to run the country on more of an American model, with lower taxes and cuts in social programs. A serial killer was targeting immigrants and making national news, and for the first (and only) time the New Democrats, an extreme-right racist political party had been granted seats in parliament with 6.7 percent of the national vote. Neo-Nazism was high on the popular consciousness, and Ultima Thule and other white power rock bands were enjoying increased popularity and notoriety.

The chart-topping Swedish band for the mid-nineties was a rock group called Nordman (lit. Norseman). Nordman was made up of gravel-voiced lead singer Håkan Hemlin and Mats Wester on the nyckelharpa, backed up by a number of musicians generally left out of any publicity, many of them high-profile names within Swedish folk music.[64] The group's use of mythologizing and romanticizing signifiers of Swedish folk culture, from the nyckelharpa, to Viking iconography, to the name "Nordman" itself resounded somewhat uncomfortably with many.[65] The 2002 documentary film *Nyckelfeber* posed the problem thusly:

[*Images and music of Ultima Thule and other white power bands*] White power music. Viking rock. Phenomena that will also cast their shadows over the nyckelharpa. And there is a band that shows up right then [*switch to images and music of Nordman*]. Why the Celtic cross? Why the necklace with the hammer of Thor? And why the shaved haircut that only skinheads have at that time? Why all of this at this particular time?[66]

This segment is followed by a Nordman concert with a massive attendance. Audience members sing along with a clear and intense dedication, and the scene—like that of any enormous rock concert where everyone knows the words—bears a striking resemblance to the fascist rally.

The mystique of the Nordic was a powerful aesthetic tool in the popularization of national socialism. When similar techniques are used to popularize folk music, then, alarm bells are sounded within the inner world of folk music Sweden, a mostly left-leaning subculture of a mostly left-leaning nation still sensitive about its historical connections to Germany. This represents a serious obstacle in the search for a truly popular Swedish folk music. Mystique and romance, perhaps the most formidable tools available to folk music groups who wish to gain popular appeal, carry a taint that grows in direct proportion to that appeal.

The flip side of this problem is an often exaggerated insistence that insiders within the Swedish folk music world are not susceptible to any romanticized sheen possessed by the culture. One example is the Sten Källman quote above, in which he suggests that people who come to Allégården to dance do so simply because they enjoy dancing, as opposed to Hedningarna fans, whose primary interest is trying to find themselves in a mythical past. Similarly, in an ethnographic article on the Lilla Edet nyckelharpa spelman group, Jan Ling writes of its membership that

> [m]ost of them were violinists who for one reason or another wanted to change to another instrument or to have a second instrument. The *sound* of the keyed fiddle was what, above all, decided their choice of this instrument. None of the fiddlers was driven by any kind of "village nostalgia."[67]

And later, about the nyckelharpa revival in general:

> The interest in the revival of the keyed fiddle is apparently a purely musical one, which has very little in common with the ideologies of "back to the good old peasant time," with its village nostalgia. However, when such an instrument seeks new functions in society, it can easily come to be associated with this sort of ideological movement. At that moment, a consciousness of tradition is established and a repertoire, playing style, and function is canonized as "folk music."[68]

Ling sets up a binary opposition between interest in folk music as music and as a romanticized object of heritage. To my mind he overstates the polarization between these two ends, both as part of his polemic against the use of folk music as a national romantic symbol, and no doubt out of respect for his consultants, whom he wishes to distance from this phenomenon. For any fan of Nordman, attraction to the music itself and to its romanticizing connotations would be impossible to separate and chart independently. Likewise, for folk music Sweden's insiders the primary interest may indeed be musical, but the trappings of heritage are also a constant and integral presence within that subculture, and of no little significance.

Ling establishes a similar dichotomy between different musical arrangements of a folk chorale in his article "O Tysta Ensamhet: From 'Empfindsamer Stil' to Village Nostalgia."[69] He argues that Jan Johansson, by approaching the material from a strictly musical standpoint as a jazz musician, creates an "ideologically neutral" version.[70] Hammond organist Merit Hemmingsson, on the other hand, draws upon and magnifies all available markers of village nostalgia, creating a much more dateable piece of music that will in all likeliness fail to stand the test of time.[71] He has since been proven accurate in that prediction — the Jan Johansson version has remained a classic, while Hemmingsson's has faded into obscurity. His suggestion that the Johansson version does not draw upon romanticized markers of Swedishness, however, I think is also something of an exaggeration. The sparseness with which Johansson treats the tunes on *Jazz på svenska* generally, and that first track particularly, stands in stark contrast to the variety and density of sound with which he approaches his straight jazz, or even the Russian folk tunes on his follow-up album *Jazz på ryska*. The general understated melancholy of *Jazz på svenska* is often cited as an expression of typically Swedish sentiment.[72] The types of minor-mode melodies Johansson selected for that album, likewise, belong to a category of tunes often cited by folk music insiders as expressing a stereotypically Swedish melancholy.

An analogous comparison to that between the music of Hemmingsson and Johansson can also be made between musics of Nordman and Hedningarna. I actually feel myself in a similar situation to that of Jan Ling in my personal reaction to these more recent groups, very much enjoying the music of Hedningarna, and feeling some ideological discomfort at that of Nordman. My sense is that, for Nordman, folk music was as much an emblematic ornament as Håkan Hemlin's hammer of Thor. Fundamentally the music was popular rock in its formal and rhythmic structures, with Mats Wester's nyckelharpa functioning in place of the lead guitar. The inclusion of recorder on many tracks also implied ancientness and regalness by blurring the timbral line between early and folk musics, one that would be unclear in any case to Nordman's broader audience.[73]

Hedningarna, on the other hand, approached their music from the opposite direction. Rather than ornamenting rock with folk, they undergirded the folk with rock, electrifying traditional instruments and rounding out the heavier sound with percussion. Their repertoire included polskor, waltzes, hallingar, marches and polkas, and as such had a more demonstrable connection to the inner Swedish folk music subculture, and less to modern popular forms. Thus, while they were quite popular compared to other folk music groups, they never drew audiences close to Nordman's, and their romantic image of folk culture became proportionally less alarming. Further, the mythology they invoked was qualitatively different from that of Nordman in its de-emphasis on markers of place, in favor of those of nature and ancientness. Where "Nordman" signifies the Nordic, the name Hedningarna (The Heathens) suggests pre-historic nature-worship. Where Nordman utilized the nyckelharpa as a clear icon of Swedishness, Hedningarna's wide instrumental palette was a virtual catalogue of the oldest reconstructable Scandinavian nyckelharpor, bow harps, simple flutes, hurdy-gurdies and bagpipes, signifying the primitive and ancient over the national. Beyond their stylized rock-carving logo, Hedningarna engaged few obvious visual icons of any kind, compared to Nordman's emphasis on symbols like the nyckelharpa in publicity, and back-up Swedish folk dancers in full costume in performance.

Nevertheless, while obvious place-references were underplayed by Hedningarna in comparison to Nordman, they could not be avoided altogether. Hedningarna's instrumental palette was clearly Nordic in character, as was their repertoire and language. On the other hand, counteracting the potentially problematic significations of their mythologized folk music was a clearly multi-ethnic character to their Nordicness. Though Hedningarna were originally a trio of Swedish instrumentalists, they did not achieve much fame until the release of their second album, and with it the introduction of two Finnish women singers to the group. By their third album they had been joined by Saami yoiker Wimme Saari, and much of the unique musical character of the group stemmed from its melding of distinct musical traditions. This multicultural aspect to Hedningarna's music ran generally counter to traditions of fascist rhetoric that have drawn upon the idea of a single and generalized ur-Nordic culture.

The Fiddle-Centric Aesthetic

Though they had musical connections to the inner Swedish folk music sphere, and as individual musicians the original core trio were very much a part of it, Hedningarna as a group did not play music that was truly representative of that world. The same can be said for any number of professional folk music groups, who—in creating forms appropriate to the concert stage and wide listening audiences—produce a music quite different from what is typically played at spelman gatherings for dance and in sessions. This is not to suggest that musical styles in concert, dance, and session settings do not exert influence on one another, but rather that each exhibits stylistic characteristics that mark their separate developmental histories.

As mentioned in chapter 3, one difference between "traditional" and "innovative" folk musics is that the latter usually makes use of the lower frequencies, where the former tends to be entirely melody-based. The prepondernace of fiddles in the "traditional" world (often to the exclusion of all other instruments) conspires to keep that sphere hidden from the wider public, for whom music without bass and middle range, or separate rhythm instruments, might seem aesthetically incomplete. The fiddle-only setup may also be associated in the public mind primarily with the music of folk dance groups, which tends to be ancillary to the dance and of limited intrinsic musical interest. The music of that inner folk music world thus lacks a certain potential for mass appeal.

A recurring tale among those who have come to the world of folk music late in life relates an initial contact with the music that was off-putting, and frames the process of coming to understand and enjoy the music as a kind of revelation or personal rite of passage. Fiddler Rose-Marie Landén Nord tells her version of this story:

> I went to Scandinavium for Nordlek, 23 or 24 years ago.[74] We went because we, my husband and I, had suddenly started dancing in a gammeldans class. And when I heard all this fiddle music, it was killing me. I'd never heard anything worse. I told him "I can't stand another minute. I don't want to be here." Anyway, I went home, and I thought about it: "Is this what I want to do in the future?" So I went to the folk dance group, because there they just had an accordionist. That didn't hurt my ears like a bunch of fiddles, which I thought was terrible. But then a guy named Gert came along, and he said "listen to this," and I started listening. And I thought it was really hard to hear the beat in polskor. But then, the next Monday, or the Monday after that, it was just like you said. Finally you think something is nice, right? You said that. You find something you like, and that's just the beginning. After that it gets better all the time. But you have to learn to like it, apparently. You don't just like this fiddle scratching from the outset; it's an acquired taste. In any case, that's how I got into it.[75]

The aesthetic difficulty of fiddle-only folk music may be one last explanation as to the willingness of the general populace to make the accordion their iconic "folk" instrument, or to prefer fusion to the "real thing." The roughness of that fiddle sound can also operate as a marker of authenticity to insiders, however. This is the final way of understanding folk music—as a function of the raw as opposed to the polished, the simple as opposed to arranged, the Natural as opposed to the cultured.

Notes

1. Ulf Johansson et al., " . . . och det blev . . . Musikens genrer," *Göteborgs-Posten* (November 16, 2001): 1–7.

2. Genres mentioned in the article were: Blues, soul, rhythm & blues, funk, ska, reggae, ragga, hip hop, gangsta rap, alternative rap, pop, Brit pop, top 40, boy bands, girl bands, disco, techno, house, electronica, synth, rock, blue collar rock, British wave, glam rock, psychedelica, hard rock, punk, hardcore punk, heavy metal, ska punk, grunge, death

metal, speed metal, thrash metal, jazz, free jazz, jazz fusion, rockabilly, country, singer/songwriter, americana, singer/songwriter rock, and female singer/songwriter.

3. Ernst Klein, "Folkdans och folklig dans," in *Om folkdans*, ed. Mats Rehnberg (Stockholm: LTs förlag, 1978 [1927]), 68.

4. Felix Hoerburger coined a similar English-language terminology in the 1960s, distinguishing between "first existence" and "second existence" folk dance in "Once Again: On the Concept of 'Folk Dance,'" *Journal of the International Folk Music Council* 20 (1968): 30–31.

5. See, e.g., Mats Nilsson, *Dans—Kontinuitet i förändring* (Gothenburg: Etnologiska Föreningen, 1998), 37–39.

6. Nilsson, *Dans*, 38–39.

7. For more on this issue see also this volume, pages 148–149.

8. One can distinguish between dancing "polska" (sing.) and dancing "polskor" (pl.), the latter of which more specifically signifies the Polska Dancers' context. The former, however, remains ambiguous.

9. Annika Nordström, *Syskonen Svensson: Sångerna och livet. En folklig repertoar i 1900-talets Göteborg* (Gothenburg: Göteborgs Stadsmuseum, 2002), 20, italics in original.

10. Reimund Kvideland, "Den folkelege songtradisjonens funksjonelle aspekt," in *Visa och visforskning*, ed. Ann-Mari Häggman (Helsingfors: Svenska litteratursällskapet i Finland, 1974) , 137–165.

11. Nordström and Nilsson have regularly co-taught a course called *Folklig visa och dans* at Gothenburg University.

12. The artificiality of the folk/popular split has been addressed by English-speaking scholars as well; see, e.g., Robin Kelley, "Notes on Deconstructing 'The Folk,'" *The American Historical Review* 97, no. 5 (1992): 1400.

13. Nordström, *Syskonen Svensson*, 20.

14. The parallel rings truer for the nineteenth century actually, when collectors arranged the music for piano, and on-stage folk music productions were entirely the province of art musicians. These productions were overshadowed very early in the twentieth century by contests and gatherings, which though they bore little social relation to the music-making world of pre-industrial Sweden, nevertheless represented its music with greater accuracy than the folk dancers did village dances.

15. Karin Eriksson, interview by author, January 5, 2002.

16. Åsa Grogarn Sol, interview by author, October 5, 2001.

17. There are actually fairly clear distinctions in usage between *folklig* on the one hand and *folkligt* and *folklighet* on the other. *Folklig* and *folkligt* are on paper the same adjective, the former gendered common, the latter neuter. Because most of the nouns that these terms modify are gendered common (song, music, dance, and crafts), *folklig* tends to be the modifying adjective. When a Swedish adjective is used without a modified noun, as Sol does in this quote, the gender of the adjective is neuter, here *folkligt*. As such, in general, *folklig* can be said to be the modifying adjective, and *folkligt* non-modifying. When this word is used as a modifier, the meaning can usually be translated as "folk;" when it's used a non-modifier, it's "common." Thus, *folklig* means "folk," while *folkligt* and *folklighet* mean "common" and "commonality," respectively. In effect, the problem is that this distinction in usage is not generally acknowledged—*folk, folklig, folkligt*, and *folklighet* are all understood to refer to the same concept.

18. The negative connotation in the term *folklighet* as applied to modern phenomena is generally implicit. That is to say, the term is not normally used in the pejorative, but its

classic exemplars (e.g. Bingolotto) do generally connote cultural impoverishment. One effect of this layered meaning of the term is to conceal something of the implicit elitism in its usage.

19. Lukas Moodyson, *Fucking Åmål* (Sweden: Memfis Film, 1998). This unpretentious little film famously rivaled *Titanic* at the Swedish box office, and thus on yet another level has come to signify the struggle against mass culture and its hypnotic effects. It was later released in the United States under the somewhat less daring title *Show Me Love*. The image of such television shows standing for hollow commercial culture is not uncommon in film and literature. Other examples include fictional programs hosted by Tristram Hazard in Angela Carter's *Wise Children* (London: Chatto & Windus, 1991), or Jim Broadbent's character in the movie *Time Bandits* (UK: Handmade Films, 1981).

20. Dan Lundberg, Krister Malm, and Owe Ronström, *Musik—Medier—Mångkultur: Förändringar i svenska musiklandskap* (Hedemora: Gidlunds, 2000), 178.

21. E.g., Ling, "Folkmusik—En brygd," 19.

22. Ling, "Folkmusik—En brygd," 21–25; "'Upp, bröder, kring bildningens fana': Om folkmusikens historia och ideologi," in *Folkmusikboken*, ed. Jan Ling, Gunnar Ternhag, and Märta Ramsten (Stockholm: Prisma, 1980), 28–35.

23. For instance, dancer and occasional Folk Music Café administrator Lilian Håkansson suggests that the Café functions as healthy alternative to modern club culture. The atmosphere is warm, people can talk and make real human connections since the music is unamplified, and nobody smokes or drinks. (My interview with Håkansson was conducted prior to the general Swedish smoking ban in bars, restaurants, and nightclubs.) Håkansson contrasts this description with one of typical party environments, which she associates with blaring music, smoking, drinking, and drugs. She suggests that her own youth could have been spared the latter if school had introduced her to the former: "I had music in school for nine years. And nobody ever presented these old spelmän to me. I feel like they let me down in school, because they had withheld something that actually belonged to me, that was part of our cultural heritage" (Lilian Håkansson, interview by author, October 26, 2001).

24. Greger Siljebo, interview by author, December 3, 2001.

25. See Ruth Finnegan, *The Hidden Musicians: Music-Making in an English Town* (Cambridge: Cambridge University Press, 1989).

26. Karl Malbert, interview by author, December 11, 2001.

27. Johan Hogenäs, interview by author, February 4, 2002.

28. Björn Sandberg, "Börja visa lite hänsyn, alla dragspelare!," *Spelmannen* 2001, no. 1 (2001): 13.

29. Bengt Enqvist, "Vart spel har sin plats," *Spelmannen*, 2001, no. 2 (2001): 12.

30. Ingvar Strömblad, "Det är skillnad på dragspelare och spelmän med dragspel," *Spelmannen*, 2001, no. 3 (2001): 11.

31. Per Sandberg, interview by author, December 28, 2001.

32. Ingvar Strömblad, interview by author, June 24, 2002.

33. Håkan Berglund, "Piglocka: Dragspelets införande och anpassning," *Sumlen*, 1987: 39.

34. Berglund, "Piglocka," 40.

35. Berglund, "Piglocka," 52, 60, 63.

36. Berglund, "Piglocka," 39.

37. Ling, "Folkmusik—En brygd," 18–22; Bohman, "Folkmusiken på Skansen," 56.

38. Berglund, "Piglocka," 42.

39. Ulf Kinding, interview by author, January 23, 2002.

40. Ulf Kinding, interview by author, January 23, 2002.
41. Ingvar Strömblad, interview by author, June 24, 2002.
42. Pers Nils Johansson, interview by author, January 3, 2002.
43. Lederhosen aren't Swedish. Cf. the following dialogue from John Landis' 1983 feature film *Trading Places* (USA: Paramount, 1983):
Denholm Elliott: "Let me see now, you would be from Austria, am I right?"
Jamie Lee Curtis: "No, I am Inga, from Sveden."
Denholm Elliott: "Sweden? But you're wearing lederhosen."
Jamie Lee Curtis: "Ja, for sure, from Sveden!"
44. Note that the lameness associated with folk costume in Swedish popular culture is tied primarily to the knee tassel, an element of many male costumes, especially within Dalarna. Part of the anxiety regarding outsiders' views of folk costumes may also be tied to the resulting discrepancy between sexualized female costumes and desexualized or feminized male ones. This concern may be compared with that expressed by many Asians about the colonialist implications of the hypersexualization and exoticization of Asian women and the simultaneous desexualization and feminization of Asian men.
45. Anders and Ulla Bergsten, interview by author, May 28, 2002.
46. This was another performance of the program described in Chapter Seven.
47. Urban Lind, interview by author, June 27, 2002.
48. This is also the case with regard to the Swedish folk music that is sold internationally. The Minneapolis-based Northside label, for instance, which re-issues Scandinavian releases in the United States, sells mixed and/or modernized folk musics almost exclusively. The international polska community has networks through which they can buy and sell "traditional" CDs, which tend to be published exclusively in Scandinavia, where they also reach a more limited audience.
49. A performance of Ale Möller's World Music Orchestra had recently been broadcast on Swedish television.
50. Inger Rydberg, interview by author, April 4, 2002.
51. Annelie Westerlund, interview by author, April 26, 2002.
52. Åsa Grogarn Sol, interview by author, December 25, 2001.
53. E.g., Ling, "Folkmusik—En brygd," 33.
54. The more obvious recent example is the anti-immigrant Sweden Democrat party, who upon entering Swedish parliament in 2010 called for the defunding of federal multicultural programs in favor of a reinvestment in Swedish folklore. For more on this issue, see my own "Keeping Sweden Swedish: Folk Music, Right-Wing Nationalism, and the Immigration Debate," when and if it gets published, or the Postscript to this volume.
55. Pär Moberg, "Re: Digest Number 561," November 7, 2002, http://uk.groups.yahoo.com/group/svenskfolkmusik/message/2523 (accessed August 20, 2011), ellipsis in original. For a discussion of the television program to which he refers, see pages 97–98.
56. Ethel Wieslander, "Re: Digest Number 561," 7 November 2002, http://uk.groups.yahoo.com/group/svenskfolkmusik/message/2524 (accessed August 20, 2011).
57. Vivi Nilsson, interview by author, October 30, 2001.
58. Jan Ling, interview by author, May 23, 2002.
59. Ling, "Folkmusik—En brygd," 20–22; "Upp, bröder," 27–29.
60. Sten Källman, interview by author, January 9, 2002.
61. Ling, "Folkmusik—En brygd," 33.
62. To the extent to which there can be political turmoil in Sweden.
63. The bourgeois bloc had previously held a majority in parliament between 1976 and 1982, under the leadership of Centrist Party prime minister Thorbjörn Fälldin.

64. The primary back-up musicians for Nordman usually mentioned are members of the folk music group Väsen: Roger Tallroth, Mikael Marin, Olov Johansson, and André Ferrari, who joined the trio after meeting them on tour with Nordman. Other Nordman back-up musicians with high profiles within folk music Sweden included Ale Möller, Maria Röjås, and Harald Pettersson.

65. Lars Lilliestam, "Nordman och 'det svenska,'" *Noterat* 4 (1997): 39–40.

66. Camilla Lundberg, *Nyckelfeber*, Sweden: SVT, Television Broadcast, 2002. This is likely the television program to which Pär Moberg refers on page 94.

67. Jan Ling, "Folk Music Revival in Sweden: The Lilla Edet Fiddle Club," *Yearbook of the International Folk Music Council* 43 (1986): 3–4, italics in original.

68. Ling, "Lilla Edet Fiddle Club," 6–7.

69. Jan Ling, "'O tysta ensamhet'—Från känslosam stil till hembygdsnostalgi," *Sumlen*, 1978: 40–58.

70. Ling, "O tysta ensamhet," 55.

71. Ling, "O tysta ensamhet," 56–58.

72. For instance, a documentary film about Jan Johansson's life and music is framed by people listening to *Jazz På Svenska* on headphones, exclaiming about its essential Swedishness; see Anders Østergaard, *Trollkarlen: en film om Jan Johansson* (Denmark: Angel Films, 1999). On the other hand, Erik Kjellberg argues that while this music has been received ideologically, the interest for Jan Johansson himself was always exclusively musical; see Kjellberg's "Jazz på svenska," in *Det stora uppdraget: Perspektiv på Folkmusikkommissionen i Sverige 1908–2008*, ed. Mathias Boström, Dan Lundberg, and Märta Ramsten (Stockholm: Nordiska museets förlag, 2010), 160.

73. This use of folk music as a kind of romanticizing surface ornament in popular rock is of course not unique to Nordman, but has been used enough as an effect to have been satirized in the song "Stonehenge" from Rob Reiner's mock rock documentary *This is Spinal Tap* (USA: MGM, 1984).

74. Nordlek is a tri-annual Scandinavian folk dancers' convention. Scandinavium is Gothenburg's convention center.

75. Rose-Marie Landén Nord, interview by author, May 28, 2002.

CHAPTER 5

—◦◦◦—

A Natural Art

The quality axis finds its point of origin in a folk music conceived as a function of nature and the natural, its secondary pole in artifice. This axis may run parallel to and occasionally overlap with some of the binarisms discussed in previous chapters, tradition/innovation and rural/urban especially. The primary focus of this chapter, however, is on the continuum between natural, raw, and unschooled folk music on the one hand; and the polished formality of art music on the other. A secondary but related focus is the relationship between amateurism and professionalism among folk musicians.

In terms of the global history of the folk music concept, Nature seems to have played an important role since the very beginning.[1] It pervaded Herder's language in his writings on folk song.[2] The natural was also an implicit element due to folk music's initial construction in binary opposition to cultured art music.[3] In Sweden, however, the explicit language of the natural does not seem to saturate writings on folk music until later, the 1840s or so, around the time of the early development of nature as a key symbol for Swedish national identity.[4]

Orvar Löfgren has amply demonstrated that nature has retained its significance as a general marker of Swedishness in the time since as well.[5] Within polska Sweden, meanwhile, the overt symbolic use of material nature (forests, pastures, bears, wolves, etc.) and especially its mythical inhabitants has in recent years come to bear some of the stigma of national romanticism.[6] The idea of folk music being invested natural or supernatural force may be drawn upon by a group like Nordman, for example, but in my experience is today rarely expressed in rhetoric internal to folk music Sweden.[7] This is not to suggest that nature has lost its symbolic value within that sphere. The constant association between Swedish folk music and rural settings via the summer gatherings, for instance, does much to keep that relationship alive.[8] However, when folk music insiders do make explicit some connection between folk music and nature or the

supernatural, more often than not it occurs with some self-ironizing acknowledgment of the cliché.

The same cannot be said for less tangible manifestations of the natural, in
particular those elements of folk music that define it against the artifice of art
music. The notion of folk music as "unschooled and raw" has been a recurring
theme in many of my interviews and conversations. The ideology of amateurism
that was central to the revival has been subject to some critique by professional
folk musicians since that time, but even these musicians will generally accept
the notion that older generations of tradition bearers have by and large been
fairly unschooled. Likewise, I have found raw, rough sound and lack of vibrato
to be generally accepted as stylistic markers of folk music that distinguish it
from the classical.

Amateurs and Professionals

Ironically, while the modern folk music aesthetic tends to be defined in opposition to that of art music, both struggle with an initial inaccessibility that simultaneously marginalizes the music and grants it an intrinsic value. In classical
music the beginning listener's difficulty may stem from a musical complexity
that also demonstrates greater sophistication over modern popular forms (consider, for example, the rhetoric associated with Beethoven's late quartets). Folk
music's inaccessibility, on the other hand, relates to an expectation of refine-
ment associated with the classical: technical mastery, consistency of tone, virtuosity perhaps. The challenge of the folk music enthusiast is to listen through the
spelman's lack of these qualities, to the unpolished diamonds beneath. Greger
Siljebo argues:

> If I listen to an old spelman I have a knowledge-base and familiarity that allows
> me to hear a lot of things that interest me, which for me are invaluable. And
> maybe he isn't that good, purely on a technical level, but he has something very
> strong in his expression that interests me. But an art musician who doesn't
> work with folk music may not understand, because they don't hear what's hap-
> pening underneath. And that has meant that folk music has not been particu-
> larly interesting from an art music perspective.[9]

The raw state of the music grants it a currency of the Natural that mitigates the
loss of Folk accessibility. The old spelman that Siljebo summons further con-
tributes an element of Tradition to the equation.

The term "spelman" can refer not only to the tradition bearer of the past,
however, but also to the amateur player of the present. A similar argument can
be made using this type of spelman, one that also affiliates folk music with the
Natural by distancing it from art music. Inger Rydberg makes the case:

It's kind of fun that there are so many categories, that you can play even though you're not very skilled, even if you're not a professional. I think that's what's so great about this music. That's what I'd like to say. You have a chance to participate and play, because it's so fun, even if you're not that good. I think that art music—it seems this way anyway—that people who play classical music are very restricted, I mean they have to be so good.[10]

Where Siljebo's old spelman grants a sense of Tradition, Rydberg's amateur sphere grants Folk currency by virtue of its participatory nature. Her sort of example is actually more commonly given, perhaps because the inaccessibility associated with folk music's rawness triggers a more acutely felt demand for compensatory Folk value.

Greger Siljebo's choice of example, on the other hand, has everything to do with his status as a professional folk musician. The value granted to amateur communal music-making within folk music Sweden can make it quite difficult for people in his position, as Kajsa Paulsson notes:

The folk music concept is incredibly complicated in many ways. It has the baggage of being a grassroots movement. It has the baggage of being an amateur enterprise as well. And then we have the professional end too, so you have an upper level of musicians also, happily enough. But in between, there's a lot of back and forth around questions of money and so on. The idea that "folk music doesn't need any money. It's only amateurs who play it." But at the same time, within folk music circles, that's what's valuable about it. So that can be both a positive and a negative. It's been a huge battle for professional musicians within folk music. To feel like, "but we can get paid for our work too."[11]

As a professional folk musician, Siljebo must must deal with a certain stigma attached to playing for commercial gain. As such he is less likely to further privilege the modern amateur world over the professional by citing it as a locus for natural rawness.

Amateurism is also in some sense built into the spelman concept, a connotation reinforced by institutions like the spelman gathering and spelman group. The term "spelman" is often contrasted with "musician" (*musiker*), which implies a certain degree of professionalism, and does not necessarily carry a direct association with folk music.[12] Ingvar Strömblad, who actually had a career as a professional accordionist before he tired of being forced to play music in which he had no interest, made the distinction as follows:

Strömblad: Do you know the difference between a spelman and a musician?
Kaminsky: No.
Strömblad: Well, if you say to a musician: "can you play Wednesday at nine o'clock?" "Sure I can, how much does it pay?" And if I say the same thing to a spelman: "Can you play on Wednesday?" "Of course!" [*rubs his hands together*] "When do we start?" A critical difference.[13]

The value of amateur status is thus actually embedded in the standard terminology for Swedish folk music.

To make matters worse for the professional, the term "spelman" can also imply grounded cultural knowledge of the music. Again the word refers not only to the modern amateur player, but also to Siljebo's venerable tradition bearer. When Ale Möller coined the term *folkmusiker* he did so not only to distinguish his circle of folk musicians as professionals, but also to avoid the implication that they were necessarily possessors of deep traditional knowledge:

> I mean from a spelman you can ask very extensive knowledge in tune playing for example, you can ask knowledge about different styles and a certain, a little geography and knowledge of the big personalities, folk music history and so on. Playing for dance for example I think is fairly obvious . . . there is a large skill set that is absolutely necessary if you're going to, I think, be a really good spelman. I'm talking about career roles so to speak right, or musicians' roles. This other thing, to be a folk musician, there you can reduce those demands a little bit, but instead increase other demands, to be able to arrange, to be familiar with a bunch of different interesting parallel rhythmic events for example, to be able to deal with a sound system, to be able to work in a studio and to know, have a fair amount of knowledge about adjacent genres, so that you know how to interact with others and . . . to know harmonic theory and such. Because examples of folk musicians at that time, it's exactly those members of Filarfolket and Groupa for example, that you wouldn't say were independent spelmän, but who know enough to be musicians within the genre.[14]

The creation of this professional folk musician concept further pushes the spelman (its binary opposite) toward the natural end of the spectrum, as a bearer of rooted knowledge, symbol of pre-industrial rural life, and player of unamplified traditional instruments.

During the revival, this spelman/musician divide was reinforced by a new archaic and anti-classical aesthetic for spelmän.[15] With the privileging of amateur status came a hypercorrective erasure of those classical-sounding elements once common among Swedish traditional fiddlers. Here Dan Olsson explains the effect of this phenomenon on revival-era folk music:

> Today we've also filtered out a lot. We've taken certain ideological and aesthetic positions, and as a result there are a lot of *folklig* ways of playing that don't exist today, or aren't highlighted because we don't think they're *folklig*. For example, playing with glissandi and playing with vibrato, a lot of spelmän did that. But today, add vibrato, and it's seen as classical music, and "no, that's not folk." I mean we're still in need of some sort of demarcative border between classical and *folklig* music-making, based on different ideological points of departure. Among other things that people during the twentieth century had classical music as a model, and when the folk music wave in the seventies came along people turned away strongly from that.[16]

Among other things, this reaction manifested in a shift in attitude among spelmän who played for the Zorn badge during the revival years. Märta Ramsten, who was tasked with recording the trials, notes that many young players came in with a new playing technique: heavy, rhythmic, and rough. The previous generations' intricately ornamented Dala, virtuosic Hälsinge, and notation-faithful spelman group styles were all too close to the classical.[17]

The Zorn jury, for its part, supported and reinforced this change. Jan Ling, who was a jury member during a stretch of this period, reports:

> [W]hen someone like Sven Kjellström comes in and sits on the Zorn jury, the criteria for judging get to be a lot about playing clean, and technique. We reacted against that during the seventies, when we tried to encourage alternate intonations, which meant that sometimes we really screwed up. But it could be more complicated than that too. For example, we made a spelman into a riksspelman who many people within spelman circles considered tone deaf. Some spelmän were about to kill us after, that's how mad they were. But now it seems like his playing style has become accepted, so maybe we were right in some sense. . . . [Later in the interview:] At the same time a famous, young fiddler came up for the first time. He was dressed in folk costume, pretty as the day, and played quick and fast and virtuosic. Everyone thought he would get the badge immediately, I mean he just stepped on the gas. But we didn't consider his playing mature and he didn't get anything, which meant people yelled at us and doubted us even more. But we thought the young spelman was on the road to a virtuosity where the substance was lost, and everything was on the technical end. Eventually he became one of Sweden's most celebrated spelmän, who realized that we meant well and wanted him in the "tradition."[18]

This story actually demonstrates two ways in which the Zorn jury used its considerable status-granting powers to control developments within folk music Sweden during the revival. The aesthetic reification of the folk/art boundary was one, of course. The other was to act as a check on the newly developing professional caste of folk musicians, to ensure that they not overshadow "traditional" amateur players.

Even today, the technical advantage that professional folk musicians might have over amateurs in attempting the Zorn trials is still subverted in a number of ways. The adjudicators still explicitly mark technical prowess as secondary to stylistic authenticity. A primary criterion is the ability play in a manner appropriate for dancing, a skill not universally held among professionals. Perhaps most critically, very few musicians are granted the riksspelman title on their first try. Established and respected professionals thus risk a great deal of status in making an attempt at the title. A number have made only one attempt, failed, and chosen not to make a second.[19] The extremely high standards of the adjudicators are thus reinforced, in turn granting more legitimacy to the title. As such, the riksspelman badge has become a mark of status outweighing almost any other, and has remained as open to amateurs as it has to professionals.[20]

These revival and post-revival shifts on the part of the Zorn jury were at least in part a reaction to the rise of a new generation of young professional players. The fact that the changes in criteria have been maintained and reinforced in the decades since may be credited largely to the continued and growing presence of ever-younger and better-trained folk musicians. In the aftermath of the revival, more and more Swedish conservatories have started folk music programs, and folk music has also entered the pre-college curriculum to a considerable degree. Many extra-curricular programs have developed for the grade school set, and at least one Swedish secondary school, Rättviks gymnasium, now has a line for students who wish to specialize in folk music. Semester- and year-long folk music and dance programs at the post-secondary, pre-college *folkhögskola* level have been especially important.

For these younger players today, there can be some question regarding whether to self-identify as spelmän or folk musicians. Within the amateur sphere that both makes up the core Swedish folk music subculture and provides much of the economic support base for professionals, the spelman is in almost every respect privileged over the musician. Furthermore, the folk musician label was a product of a time during which many professional players did not have much of a background in folk music, and thus could not claim the traditional knowledge possessed by older generations. Today most professional players are well embedded in the folk music culture, and would not hesitate to call themselves spelmän out of any doubt of their right to do so.[21]

Yet on the other hand, the tradition-bearer status ascribed to spelmän may seem overly restrictive to professional players with appetites for experimentation, and may also deemphasize the value of the music in favor of the heritage. Karin Eriksson explains:

> I'm a spelman in certain cases, but I can also say that I'm a folk musician, and I can do that because I consider it a genre. . . . I've known people who were involved with folk music or folk dance, or folk art, or *hembygd* conservation, just to preserve something because it's old. . . . [U]nlike them, I think that if the music isn't interesting enough, then its survival is not a priority. Do you understand what I mean? There's a difference between playing music because you like the music—so it survives because there's something to it—and trying to force something to live on because it has value for being old. I think it can be a lot of fun to go to some old spelman, copy him exactly and see what happens. Here's my problem, I go back and forth a little, but I think you can do that, even if you see it as a genre. And even if you experiment. They're just different ways of playing the music.[22]

Eriksson here engages a typical anti-preservationist tactic, implying that excessive interest in heritage serves the music poorly, but not vice versa—the maintenance of traditions can be upheld via the copying of old spelmän, even when it is done as a rewarding musical exercise. She reinforces the connection between amateurism and preservationism by bringing in folk dance and folk art, and by implication the Youth Ring, with its history of cultural and political conservatism. By placing the professional class of folk musicians within which she sees herself in opposition to that culture of preservationism, Eriksson thus re-legitimizes her professional status. The effect is especially powerful as a counter to the anti-commercial argument that stigmatizes playing for pay, given the generally politically progressive tendencies of many who have made that argument during the revival and in the years since.

When I ask Eriksson to elaborate on the difference between spelmän and folk musicians, she shifts easily from one definition of spelman to another, from old tradition bearer to present-day amateur:

> *Kaminsky*: Can you say a little more about the difference between spelman and folk musician?
> *Eriksson*: Yeah, I think I'm a folk musician primarily, but sometimes I'm a spelman.
> *Kaminsky*: What's the difference?
> *Eriksson*: I think that the biggest difference is the attitude I have when I'm playing. I guess it's also different based on whether you think there can be professionals or not. Because if you think, as I do, that there can be a professional stratum—which also means that there can be several different strata—then you can talk about folk musicians. But "spelman" has nothing to do with the quality of playing, or with how it sounds, it has to do with your attitude toward what you're doing. Often when someone says they're a spelman it has more to do with the social aspect, maybe with spelman groups and not so much else; they don't spend a lot of time on stage, and mostly they do it for fun. So I think that there's a pretty big difference. I consider myself to be a folk musician primarily. But that also has to do with the fact that I consider it a genre. Ask me in ten years.[23]

The discursive slip from one binarism to another—preservationist/innovationist to amateur/professional—further reinforces that implied connection between cultural preservationism and amateur folk music enthusiasm.

The New Ensemble Tradition

Perhaps the greatest musical development engendered by the folk music revival was the creation of new instrumentations for folk music groups. The genre thus established has no generally agreed-upon name, though I will call it "ensemble" music, a term I have heard used by a number of insiders.[24] The traditional spelman group and gammeldans settings are typically excluded from this category. Instead, the label generally applies to gigging groups with mixed traditional and non-traditional instrumentation. Iconic examples are Groupa, Filarfolket, Hedningarna, Garmarna, Hoven Droven, and Väsen. Ale Möller's folk musicians, as well as my own "innovationist" category, would both be associated with this genre. Musically, the central characteristics of ensemble folk music are innovations necessitated by the combination of melody instruments with rhythm instruments and/or voice.[25] Champions of the genre laud the creative results, while its detractors complain of a format that homogenizes any potential rhythmic subtleties within the melody line.[26]

Ensemble players made up only a very small portion of the revival, however. The new instrumentation that the revival introduced was largely a result of a few musicians with backgrounds in other genres bringing in the instruments with which they were already familiar. Most beginners, and quite a number of people with other musical training, chose to learn fiddle or nyckelharpa. This was the obvious path given that the music to be played was so very tied to those instruments. Many new fiddlers came to learn their instruments in all-fiddle study circles, which then evolved into spelman groups.[27] The music of Dalarna, where folk traditions were most continuous, came to dominate, and the best-known master fiddle teachers were associated with that province. A few teachers had pre-revival backgrounds in folk music, while others were simply fast enough at mastering the style that they were able to establish themselves as pedagogues.[28]

Where ensemble music could be associated with concepts like "folk musician" and "innovationist," this fiddle-dominated genre can be tied to spelmän, neotraditionalists, and preservationists. Again, there is no generally agreed-upon label; the closest might be "traditional," which I will use here.[29] Musically, this genre has its grounding in the old solo instrumental traditions. Second-fiddle harmonizations, a twentieth-century development associated first with Dalarna but now spread throughout Sweden, are also often included. In some cases, an accordion, harmonium, or bass may undergird the music with chord progressions, but this element may also stretch the boundaries of the genre given its potential for homogenizing melodic rhythm. The spelman group format, which essentially follows this three-part arrangement on a larger scale, is sometimes included here. However, it may also be excluded by proponents of the genre, given the rhythmic homogenization that naturally results from large-scale homophony.[30]

The ensemble format is without a doubt the most commercially viable. Groups with name recognition beyond the folk music subculture almost fall into this category. So do nearly all of the Swedish releases on the Minneapolis-based Northside label, for instance.[31] The traditional category, on the other hand, is host not only to the amateur sphere, but also to the authentic tradition bearer. This marriage of amateurism and authenticity under the same "spelman" label does a great deal to grant priviliged status to obscurity and amateurism within the folk music subculture.

Players of traditional instruments may also attain high status within both of these worlds, as professional musicians as well as tradition bearers. Modern folk music ensembles generally include one or more players of fiddle or nyckelharpa—Olov Johansson in Väsen, Mats Edén in Groupa, Ellika Frisell in Den Fule, Ola Bäckström in Boot, Hans Kennemark in Bäsk, Johan Hedin in Bazar Blå, and so forth. As long as these players maintain a somewhat visible "traditional" career as well, they may have status in both realms. This status may even be cumulative. Very often, these are the musicians who hold the highest-profile teaching positions in the Swedish folk music conservatory system.[32] It does seem, however, to be the traditional side that grants the core of credibility. Nyckelharpa player Ditte Andersson puts the argument in musical terms:

> When Olov [Johansson]—who's played in tradition—plays in an ensemble, it's not a problem. There are two genres. I've done that a lot too. But people who almost only ever play in a group, who just take those Byss-Calle tunes, they become so damn metrical and boring. So that suppleness and flexibility that the soloist or duo has, I hope it doesn't disappear.[33]

The sentiment is common among folk music insiders. Such is the currency of the small-scale tradition that even making this kind of statement can help cement insider status.

Fiddler Hans Kennemark was one person who was fairly entrenched in the traditional side of things before creating the supergroup Bäsk with ensemble players Jonas Simonson (of Groupa) and Sten Källman (of Filarfolket). Here he reflects on the transition:

> It was like there were two different parallel worlds. The part of folk music Sweden exemplified by Groupa and Filarfolket was like another crowd, somehow. What we were doing with Forsmark Tre and Tritonus was more traditional in one way, but we also weren't being as provocative. We were more about affirming what was beautiful in the music, and pure; the fiddle playing was the important thing. It was about finding nice harmonies, not so much the modal approach, the heaviness that Hedningarna had. Only we found our compatriots more in Finland and in the spelmän from Dalarna, from Siljansnäs and Rättvik. That was more the thing. And with the dancers—the Youth Ring.[34]

Kennemark mentions a number of things that I have already established as characterizing the "traditional" world—the fiddle, Dalarna, dancers. He brings other aspects in as well, however. Purity, pleasing harmonies, and beauty are all elements he ascribes to the "traditional" end. One might consider this list curious given the association of those things with the aesthetics of Western art music. These are not normally considered iconic elements of traditional Swedish music (with the possible exception of pleasant harmonies). The probable reason Kennemark cites them here is that they do emerge as audible elements of the music when contrasted with the revival-era ensemble styles, which tended to emphasize harshness and modality.

Ironically, those who were most dedicated to a clear delineation between folk and art musics during the revival were those professional folk musicians who entered the genre with backgrounds in other styles. The members of Groupa and Filarfolket in the early eighties established a distinct preference for older, modal tune types, less obviously influenced by Western art music. Their harmonizations and arrangements likewise tended to emphasize the modal over the tonal, and their playing reflected an aesthetic of rough, dirty sound. Dan Lundberg, Krister Malm, and Owe Ronström, in analyzing Groupa's rendition of the polska "Sparve Lilla," have argued that the group supersaturates their arrangement with such sonic "folk" markers, to the effect that it becomes "more Swedish than Swedish."[35] Thus at the same time Ale Möller coined the term "folk musician" as part of a break from traditionalism and a move towards professionalism, the players to whom he was applying it were actually accentuating, rather than underplaying, the folk/art split in their music.

The emphasis on this split may be read in part as compensation for the relaxation of other genre boundaries among professional folk musicians. Both Groupa and Filarfolket mixed Swedish folk music freely with jazz as well as foreign folk and traditional musics. Most professional folk musicians of the early revival days already had the necessary musical training in other styles, given that they had to hit the ground running the very moment Swedish folk music was rescued from obscurity. The social closeness between the progressive rock and folk music movements was another factor, as was the advantage musical eclecticism meant for individuals seeking performing work.[36]

In Gothenburg, the position of folk music in higher education has also encouraged a certain amount of style mixing for professional musicians in training. It began in 1971 when Jan Ling founded Sämus, an experimental teacher training program dedicated to filling the demands of a 1969 government initiative to begin teaching popular music in grade school music classes.[37] Sten Källman explains:

> It was the radical era. Part of the idea was a move away from the classical and toward popular music for the training of music teachers. The old music director would be swept out, and we would come in as newly minted, somewhat multimusical. . . . You got to play blues, a little jazz and rock, pop music, folk music, and classical music too.[38]

Sämus remained an independent and experimental entity until 1975, when its music education program was incorporated into the School of Music.[39] Since that time folk music has always had a place at Gothenburg University, though never as an independent program—everyone who wanted training in Swedish folk music also had to have it in other styles as well. In the fall of 2002 this principle was reified with the foundation of programs in world music performance and education.

My sense is that this Gothenburg tradition in higher music education has encouraged an exaggeration of the folk/art boundary. Students in these programs are taught to hypercorrect for classical elements in their folk music, so as to create clear delineations between the styles they are learning. The emphasis on dirty sound, on roughness, remains an integral part of the pedagogy. Jonas Simonson, who runs the program, made it a central theme of my private flute lessons with him.[40] Saxophonist Hanna Wiskari reports a similar approach on the part of Sten Källman with regard to their private lessons:[41]

> I think my tunes were kind of pretty and friendly and so on, but he's pretty meaty. I don't know how brutal I am, but I think he's been an influence there. I mean there are a lot of means of expressing yourself, but he says that folk music isn't romantic music, it's dance music to a large extent. . . . [H]e says you should get tough; "think flesh and blood" he said at one point.[42]

Conservatory-trained fiddle players too have engaged in this reification of the boundary between folk and art musics. Ida Norrlöf, who at the time of her interview was a student at the Gothenburg School of Music studying with Hans Kennemark among others, defines folk music in this way: "I think folk music should be unpretentious. It should be joy, primarily. Unlike other genres it doesn't have so much to do with precision. That's when it becomes boring, I think, when it gets to be too perfect. Then folk music loses its strength. It has to live all the time."[43]

If this focus on the folk/art boundary is compensation for fusion with other styles, however, it stands to reason that it would be stronger in a place where such fusion has been emphasized. A school with an autonomous folk music program would not need to maintain itself so carefully against other genres. Dan Lundberg, Owe Ronström, and Krister Malm have noted, for instance, that several groups associated with independent conservatory folk music programs have musical profiles that fit solidly within a subgenre they call "chamber folk music," within which the line between art and folk is blurrier.[44] Many of today's younger professional folk musicians are coming out of a dedicated folk music program at the Royal Music Academy in Stockholm, where the aesthetic of roughness is far less prevalent.

The Folk/Art Connection

The emphasis on the folk/art split is also, of course, a direct result of the construction of those categories in the late eighteenth century. In the time before such a line was imagined it can be debated to what extent it existed at all. In the Swedish seventeenth century, rural musicians served all classes of people.[45] Even when musical class roles became more defined in the eighteenth century, the repertoire of rural peasant players often overlapped with traditions we today would call "art music."[46] The fact that these musicians worked for pay, and that many could read and write music (the only reason we know anything about their repertoire) further challenges the notion that strict lines between art and folk could be drawn during this period.

Even after the introduction of the folk music concept in Sweden, the primary target market of published collections was that of salon singer and pianist. Public performances of "folk music" during the nineteenth century were almost exclusively staged by amateur and professional art musicians. This tradition continued well into the twentieth century with the new technologies of gramophone and radio. Even musicians who dedicated themselves primarily to folk music were strongly affected by classical ideals—virtuosity among the Hälsingland fiddlers who dominated the market in the first half of the twentieth century, and tonally conceived harmonizations among the fiddlers from Dalarna who would later eclipse them.

Seen in this broader context, the aesthetic reification of the art/folk boundary may be understood as an idiosyncrasy of the revival era whose reverberations are still felt today. The consistency of that boundary was necessary to the maintenance of a coherent "folk music," given the disregard with which its other genre boundaries (against jazz, pop, rock, and foreign folk and traditional musics) were being treated during the seventies and eighties. As the genre-bending musical innovations of the revival have since become established folk music subgenres in their own right, the vigilance with which the folk/art boundary must be maintained can be relaxed. As I have already elaborated, however, that boundary remains a fairly powerful aesthetic marker in Gothenburg at least, likely in part to compensate for its lack of significant institutional reification in the local School of Music.

As with other things, the attitude toward the folk/art boundary has been changing in the scholarly world as well as the practical. I have mentioned that Jan Ling, when he served on the Zorn jury, was involved in a conscious and concerted effort to separate the criteria for aesthetic valuations of folk music from those of art music. I have also mentioned, in an earlier chapter, that over the course of the revival he came to see the strict folk/art division as an artificial construct. He has in recent years gone so far as to suggest that folk and world musics, in their modern and developing forms, are in a position to become the new art music, usurping that currently and tenuously held by "new" music. Ling gave a keynote paper at the 2001 European Seminar in Ethnomusicology to that effect, and made similar statements when I later asked him in an interview for his current definition of folk music:

> Folk music today—world music and what's coming out now—is clearly a melting pot, out of which a lot of completely commercial flowers are going bloom. But in part it can also be the dynamic from which the new art music springs; which is to say, a new aesthetic will establish itself. I see it as far more exciting than what's happening with most innovative genres today. Because they're so esoteric. If you listen to what these new people are doing within art music, it's extremely narrow, aesthetically. So it's going to be difficult to get any broader

mooring for that art, which means it will always be marginalized. While what's emerging now out of different fusions involving folk music—which of course builds on Groupa and their music—it's possible that what will happen there will be the same thing that happened with Viennese classicism. They'll become classics.[47]

So far, Lundberg's "chamber folk music" concept and Ling's notion that modern folk music may be the seed of a reincarnated Viennese classicism do not seem to have found purchase outside the realm of Academe. In fact, in most of the cases I have discussed in which the art/folk boundary has been blurred, it has occurred more or less unself-consciously. The musicians themselves have not made explicit reference to, much less problematized the relevant genre labels.

This holds true for the long history of Swedish folk/art music interaction as well. At first the labels did not exist. Then, in the first century and a half of the concept preceding the revival, the categories were defined according to the origin of the tunes—form, perhaps, to a lesser extent—and not how or by whom they were played. Simple arrangements of folk tunes for art musicians would thus qualify unequivocally as folk music. Today that rule for dividing the genres holds consistent from the position of the classical world, yet within the post-revival folk music realm, style has become the primary marker.[48] Thus that history of art musicians playing arrangements of folk tunes now falls within art music (and outside folk music) according to folk music insiders, and within folk music (outside art music) according to art music insiders. The music is neither and both, and no boundary—as defined by either party—is ever actually close enough to be crossed, nor is the surrounding discourse of genre-crossing ever triggered.

From the early days of Swedish radio and throughout the twentieth century, the foremost figure with regard to the tradition of chamber music performances and arrangements of folk tunes was pianist/accordionist Gunnar Hahn. The extensive liner notes to a 1997 compilation CD featuring performances of Hahn arrangements from the sixties, seventies, and eighties demonstrate something of the no-man's-land nature of this sort of project.[49] Terms like "classical" and "art" do not surface at all. In the language of the liner notes, written by former Stockholm concert house director Bengt Olof Engström, this is unequivocally folk music, arranged for chamber ensembles. Yet his romanticized descriptions of folk music as "an important part of our cultural heritage" and of Hahn's ability to capture its "soul," its essential expression of "the people themselves," signal a lack of connection to the late twentieth-century world of folk music Sweden, within which that sort of language would generally be considered anachronistic.

Gunnar Hahn, despite enjoying a popular appeal rivaling that of any other player of Swedish folk tunes at least up until the revival—excepting, perhaps, Jan Johansson—came up only twice in my sixty hours of interviews. The first mention was actually made by me as I listed various players and groups, and asked singer/fiddler Annelie Westerlund to explain which she thought were legitimate folk musicians, and which in her view crossed the line. Gunnar Hahn was one of three (alongside Nordman and Jan Johansson) that seemed to fit into a third category, solidly within another genre, and thus far enough beyond the line to not even to have crossed it:[50]

> *Kaminsky*: Gunnar Hahn?
> *Westerlund*: Is he a folk musician? [*laugh*]
> *Kaminsky*: Yeah, he's made records called "Folk Music My Way" [sic] or something like that.
> *Westerlund*: Right. Of course Jan Johansson has done that too, but I don't think that makes him a folk musician.[51]

The second reference to Hahn in my interviews was made by accordionist Ingvar Strömblad, an individual generally skeptical of genre boundaries and the game of defining the is and is not of folk music. Even here, however, the reference was made in passing, with regard to Gunnar Hahn's involvement in the early years of Concerts Sweden.[52] Perhaps more relevant was Strömblad's suggestion that I familiarize myself with the music of Junekvartetten, a still-active group that plays Swedish folk tunes arranged for string quartet.[53] That group is inheritor of the Hahn tradition in more ways than one—in addition to playing some of his old arrangements, they are similar in that they classify their genre as folk, and not art music. The liner notes to their second album, like those to Hahn's, refer to the "soul of folk music," again signaling the outsider status of the project.[54] And as was the case with Hahn, Ingvar Strömblad was the only one of my consultants to bring them up. Folk musicians would consider them art music, just as the art musicians who produced them consider them folk music.

The inverse of these doubly marginal chamber ensemble projects would be performances of art music repertoire by folk musicians, as if it were folk music. Such performances do occur, and are actually more of a visible presence within folk music Sweden. They tend to fall into two categories. First are those that make use of tunes occupying a liminal space between folk and art musics, sometimes accompanied by explicit reference to the issue of genre crossing. The second involves fiddlers who play canonical art music works in a folk music style.

The most obvious examples in the first category are those involving the so-called "spelman books" of the seventeenth and eighteenth centuries, manuscripts that were kept by musicians as memory aids. Due to their association with "spelmän" these books do possess an obvious affinity with folk music. Yet stylistically the tunes tend to the Baroque and stile galant. The classical-sounding makeup of these manuscripts may be considered due in part to the books being memory aids, and thus unlikely to include local core repertoire. Other contributing factors might be that the books come from a period of history during which Swedish spelmän were not as bound to rural village culture, and that the selection of notated repertoire was not yet mediated by nineteenth-century collectors who might be inclined to exclude music with obvious international influence.

Various folk musicians and groups have revived the tunes in these books in the present day. Hans Kennemark and Bäsk have been responsible for introducing several tunes from Västergötland's Sexdrega collection into the modern collective repertoire. They do not go out of their way to discuss the folk/art boundary in the surrounding discourse, and as such, by associating themselves with these tunes, allow them to land without pomp or circumstance solidly within the folk music tradition as generally understood. On the other hand, scholar/fiddler Magnus Gustafsson, who has conducted archival research on spelman books in Southern Sweden, has been more explicit about their implications with regard to genre boundaries. With various combinations of folk and early musicians, Gustafsson has released three albums grounded in his scholarly work.[55] In more than one of these contexts he has noted explicitly in liner notes the difficulty of determining the status of the spelman book repertoire as art or folk music.[56] In the notes to Höök he writes:

> This music is difficult to label or classify according to genre. Is it folk music or Baroque music? There are in any case very few groups who have taken repertoire or musical inspiration from manuscripts such as these. The main object of this production is not primarily to try to show with an orthodox approach how it might have sounded. Instead we wish to show what a musical treasure is hidden in these manuscripts, and based upon our own musical experiences and subjective perspectives create a pleasing whole, where both present and past can be apprehended.
>
> This is not to say that we are uninterested in performance practice and tradition. On the contrary, we have dedicated much effort to finding out as much as possible about the musical aesthetics of the time, without allowing ourselves to be bound by them. The end result is an interesting example of how it can sound when experienced folk musicians relatively freely approach a genre form that at least in certain respects might be considered Baroque. Here perhaps you get a certain living-tradition aesthetic "free with purchase," which many Baroque musicians instead vainly seek intellectually via books and sources.[57]

Though he ostensibly leaves the question of genre definition unanswered, Gustafsson's discussion of the musicians' choice to play the music based on their own instincts, without excessive deference to historical performance practice, represents a clear favoring of modern practices within the folk over the early music movement. This balancing of musical expression and faithful reproduction is a modern cliché within folk music discourse, pegging these albums as insider projects just as clearly as Bengt Olof Engström's liner notes to Hahn's recordings give away their outsider status.

The second type of performance where I have witnessed art music played in a folk music style has occurred in more informal settings at spelman gatherings, specifically during Musik vid Siljan, by players who have had dual training as folk and classical musicians. Fiddler Lisa Rydberg, for example, in playing for dance at the Östbjörka gathering, has in the past years included one or two Bach melodies in her set, arranged as appropriate dance tunes. In 2003 she ended her set by inviting Pelle Gustafsson on stage to play a Bingsjö polska and two Bach melodies, arranged as a polska and polka. They explained that they had never played Bach for dance before, and that the venture was an experimental one. In 2004 Lisa inserted a Bach melody into the middle of her set, and her marking of the genre-crossing moment was reduced to an easily-missed throw-away line: "next is a Bach polska." The following year she played the same tune again, and said nothing.

At the 2003 Boda spelman gathering I witnessed Pelle Gustafsson, Jeanette Eriksson, and two other fiddlers jokingly insert classical clichés and eventually whole classical pieces into a jam session between the four of them. As in the dance sets played by Pelle Gustafsson and Lisa Rydberg earlier in the week, the players engaged in obvious style fluctuations, moving in and out of classical beauty and folk brutality. Here the verbal language of genre crossing was almost entirely absent, made unnecessary by the lack of a formal audience. In that context, the music itself was the discursive reference—someone would start playing Bach or Vivaldi, and others simply joined. The explicit language of genre crossing may be considered superfluous in these cases, given that the pieces were canonical classics. As such they were also formally and stylistically quite distant from any Swedish folk tradition, unlike the generally anonymous tunes found in old spelman books, which do require explicit heralding to peg as "art music."

In the session with Gustafsson, Eriksson, and the two other fiddlers, the game of mixing folk and classical seemed outwardly lighthearted. My sense was, however, that its self-conscious irony probably also concealed a sincere impulse on the part of at least some of its players to demonstrate virtuosity the regular folk music repertoire does not allow. Furthermore, beyond the capacity of this sort of genre crossing to establish its players as special within the folk music world, it could also do the same within the classical, by demonstrating their ability to move beyond sheet music and the boundaries of art music style. At the same time, while the game set its players apart in these ways, its apparent self-irony did well to camouflage any violation of the Swedish culture of modesty dissuading obvious attempts at demonstrating individual distinction.[58]

On another level the game may be read as a possible strategy for reconciling competing impulses to both draw and erase genre boundaries. How it functions to dissipate such boundaries is obvious enough: The players move easily back and forth between genre-defining styles, like an eraser over an arbitrarily drawn pencil line. By bringing well-known classical pieces into the quintessential folk music context of late-night gathering session, they show the music to be subject to the same laws of free musical innovation to which they might subject any folk tune. Yet the pieces' canonical nature also marks them unambiguously as "art music"; this is in fact the very point of the game, the principle that makes the irony ironic. The boundary is thus also reified because its existence is prerequisite, the net without which the game's back-and-forth volleys would be meaningless. The classical status of the music is also necessarily maintained as a function of its players being classically trained, and thus insiders within a tradition in which genre boundaries are defined by the music's origin, rather than the style in which it is played. The necessity of balancing and maintaining impulses to both meld and separate the art and the folk is thus well-satisfied in this outwardly lighthearted game.

The Axes in Tandem

Of the four axes I have discussed in these chapters, each has its own idiosyncratic patterns of conflict and resolution. This four-player tennis game of art music in folk style reflects such a pattern along the quality axis. Emma Rydberg and Urban Lind, in creating their personal polska dance palettes out of a pan-national set of regional variations, play a similar game along the axis of place. Jan Ling's argument that innovation is an essential element of tradition, and Olle Edström's that schlager is the true Swedish folk music, do the same sort of work along the time and commonality axes, respectively.

The abovementioned examples only reveal part of the picture, however. I have selected them to represent negotiations of individual axes, which to this point I have treated as distinct entities for the purposes of structuring my argument. Taking the broader view, however, one can see the four axes to be in a state of constant interpenetration. For instance, recall that Emma Rydberg and Urban Lind's bringing together of regional and national identities through polska dance also represented a reconciliation along the time axis, by making knowledge of tradition a prerequisite for innovation. The rural/urban continuum, to give another example, represents a nexus along which all four axes intertwine. The phenomenon of urbanization plays out spatially, yet at the same time generates the obscurity central to conflicts along the commonality axis.[59] The occurrence of this drastic change from one century to the next also relates it intimately to the time axis; tradition and innovation are not uncommonly mapped onto the rural and urban. Finally, that rural/urban divide also symbolically represents the dynamic of nature vs. artifice that otherwise defines the axis of quality.

The segregation of the various axes into separate chapters has to this point camouflaged their constant intersection. Now that I have explicated them individually, however, my intention in the following pages is to move into discussions of how people negotiate them in tandem.

124   CHAPTER 5

Notes

1. Matthew Gelbart, *The Invention of "Folk Music" and "Art Music": Emerging Categories from Ossian to Wagner* (New York: Cambridge UP, 2007), 40–79.

2. Philip Bohlman, *The Study of Folk Music in the Modern World* (Bloomington: Indiana University Press, 1988), xviii–xix, 6–7.

3. Gelbart, *Invention*.

4. see, e.g., Richard Dybeck, *Svenska vallvisor och hornlåtar* (Stockholm: Bok och bild, 1974 [1846]), vii-viii; cf. Jan Ling, "'Upp, bröder, kring bildningens fana': Om folkmusikens historia och ideologi," in *Folkmusikboken*, ed. Jan Ling, Gunnar Ternhag, and Märta Ramsten (Stockholm: Prisma, 1980), 21; Orvar Löfgren, "The Nature Lovers," in *Culture Builders: A Historical Anthropology of Middle-Class Life*, ed. Jonas Frykman and Orvar Löfgren (New Brunswick: Rutgers University Press, 1987), 50–57. Recall, for instance, that Carl Envallson's definition of National music in 1802 placed Nature (in the form of the pastoral) in opposition to the National and Traditional; see Carl-Allan Moberg, "Tonalitetsproblem i svensk folkmusik," in *Texter om svensk folkmusik—Från Haeffner till Ling*, ed. Owe Ronström and Gunnar Ternhag (Stockholm: Kungliga Musikaliska Akademien, 1994 [1949]), 173.

5. Orvar Löfgren, "Känslans förvandling: Tiden, naturen och hemmet i den borgerliga kulturen," in *Den kultiverade männsikan*, ed. Jonas Frykman and Orvar Löfgren (Malmö: Gleerups, 1979), 56–73.

6. Jan Ling, "Folkmusik—En brygd," *Fataburen* (1979): 32–33.

7. Such connections were drawn with some frequency at the height of the revival. Jan Ling's vitriolic reaction against supernaturally colored romanticizing elements of Pers Hans and Björn Ståbi's classic *Bockfot!!!* album (Sonet SLP-2514, 1970, 33rpm vinyl LP) and Bo i Ransätt Isaksson's *Folkmusiken i Sverige* (Motala: Borgströms Tryckeri, 1979) may have contributed to the present-day paucity of that sort of language within the Swedish folk music sphere; see Ling, "Folkmusik—En brygd," 29, 33.

8. Orvar Löfgren has argued that, in the twentieth century, the summer vacation and its association with the rural has been a powerful maintainer of nature as a national symbol ("The Nature Lovers," 64–75).

9. Greger Siljebo, interview by author, December 3, 2001.

10. Inger Rydberg, interview by author, April 4, 2002.

11. Kajsa Paulsson, interview by author, December 18, 2001.

12. The term "musiker" can also be contrasted with "musikant," another word for musician which, like "spelman," implies amateurism, playing for the joy of it, and folk music. The suffix -er usually applies to profession-words, things people are (e.g., mekaniker, politiker, akademiker = mechanic, politician, academic), while -ant applies to words associated with callings or things people do (e.g., praktikant, predikant = practitioner, preacher). Thus "musiker" implies professionalism to a much greater extent than the English "musician," given its opposition to secondary terms lacking in English.

13. Ingvar Strömblad, interview by author, June 24, 2002.

14. Ale Möller, interview with Mats Johansson, October 29, 2000, qtd. in Mats Johansson, "Stil som retorik och praxis: En musikantropologisk studie av nutida svensk folkmusik" (MA Thesis, Universitetet i Bergen, Bergen, 2001), 51, ellipses in original.

15. Märta Ramsten, "De nya spelmännen: Trender och ideal i 70-talets spelmansmusik," in *Folkmusikvågen*, ed. Lena Roth (Stockholm: Rikskonserter, 1985), 67–73; also, this volume, pages 31–32.

16. Dan Olsson, interview by author, May 20, 2002.

17. Ramsten, "De nya spelmännen," 65–67.

18. Jan Ling, interview by author, May 23, 2002.

19. The "famous young fiddler" to whom Jan Ling refers did eventually gain the title of riksspelman, however.

20. Ironically, one of the only ways to gain status above that granted by the
riksspelman title is to become an A-lister without ever making an attempt at the Zorn
trials. The cachet gained in this manner is a direct result of demonstrating a lack of need
for the adjudicators' approval. Also ironic is that, since only players of traditional instruments can make the choice not to participate in the Zorn trials, only they may enjoy this
special super-riksspelman status. Because the title of riksspelman is so valued and useful,
however, very few A-list spelmän actually fall into this category. Fiddlers Mats Berglund, Ola Bäckström, and Ellika Frisell are the only three I know of.

21. cf. Johansson, "Stil som retorik och praxis," 52–53.

22. Karin Eriksson, interview by author, January 5, 2002.

23. Karin Eriksson, interview by author, January 5, 2002.

24. See, for example, "Sax" Mats Nilsson's second quote on page 29, or Ditte
Andersson's quote on page 115.

25. Swedish folk song before the revival would typically have been accompanied by
chordal instruments like guitar or zither (cittra or hummel) or not at all; see, e.g., Margareta Jersild, "Om förhållandet mellan vokalt och instrumentalt i svensk folkmusik,"
Svensk Tidskrift för Musikforskning 58, no. 2 (1976): 53–54.

26. This stigmatizing of the rhythm section also dovetails with Adornian criticisms
of popular music, according to which overtly expressed meter "pre-digests" the music for
the listener. See, for example, Theodore Adorno, "On Popular Music," *Studies in Philosophy and Social Science* 9 (1941): 17–48.

27. Hôl i Vägga and Kristians Kapell are two spelman groups in Gothenburg that
began as revival-era study circles.

28. Jonny Soling, famously, taught fiddle lessons to his fellow students at Sämus
(see below) while he was still very much in the process of learning himself.

29. Another name sometimes applied to this genre is "fiddle playing" (fiolspel). I
have chosen to use "traditional" because, while fiddle playing is certainly iconic for this
genre, few would argue that instruments like clarinet and nyckelharpa fall outside its
boundaries.

30. Generally, the inclusion or exclusion of spelman groups from this genre depends
on the position of the speaker. Those who wish to compare "traditional" style favorably
to ensemble music will generally exclude the spelman group format, given the need to
emphasize the rhythmic subtleties that ensemble music lacks. Those who wish to extol
the creativity associated with ensemble music, on the other hand, may include the homogenized spelman group in the "traditional" category (see, e.g., "Sax" Mats Nilsson's
second quote on page 29).

31. The exceptions are traditional albums by members of ensemble bands also represented on the Northside label. Väsen's Olov Johansson also has a traditional solo album
on Northside, as does Hedningarna's Anders Norudde.

32. Players of other instruments do teach at conservatory, but they are typically restricted to teaching players of their own instruments. Roger Tallroth teaches guitar, Björn
Tollin teaches percussion, and so forth. (Roger Tallroth has taught fiddle groups as well,
but on these occasions he typically plays fiddle.) Fiddler Ellika Frisell, on the other hand,

has been called upon to teach percussionist Petter Berndalen how to "fiddle on percussion."

33. Ditte Andersson, interview by author, May 10, 2007. This interview is from a later phase of fieldwork, not centered around Gothenburg.

34. Hans Kennemark, interview by author, January 8, 2002. Kennemark's first group, Forsmark Tre, played for public workshops held by Skjortor och Särkar in the 1980s (Ulla Bergsten, interview by author, May 22, 2002).

35. Dan Lundberg, Krister Malm, and Owe Ronström, *Musik—Medier—Mångkultur: Förändringar i svenska musiklandskap* (Hedemora: Gidlunds, 2000), 148–149.

36. The connection between professionalism and musical eclecticism was further reflected with the 1981 foundation of the Swedish Folk Music and Dance Association (RFoD). This institution provided an alternative to SSR and its narrow focus on Swedish traditions and amateur folk music life, with an expanded purview that included both native Swedish and immigrant musics, and advocacy for professional as well as amateur musicians.

37. Philip Tagg, "The Göteborg Connection: Lessons in the History and Politics of Popular Music Education and Research," *Popular Music* 17, no. 2 (1998): 221–222, 226–227; see also Stig-Magnus Thorsén, "SÄMUS – musiklärarutbildning på försök," *Svensk Tidskrift för Musikforskning* 1974, no. 2 (1974): 5–10. Sämus is short for *Särskild Ämnesutbildning i Musik* (Special Subject Training in Music).

38. Sten Källman, interview by author, January 9, 2002.

39. Tagg, "The Göteborg Connection," 235n.

40. I took my lessons with Jonas Simonson privately, outside the auspices of the University. Nevertheless, I consider his pedagogical approach relevant, given that he was charged with developing the Gothenburg University world music program.

41. Jonas Simonson and Sten Källman played together in Bäsk, and have played separately in Groupa and Filarfolket, respectively. Both teach at the Gothenburg School of Music.

42. Hanna Wiskari, interview by author, December 28, 2001.

43. Ida Norrlöf, interview by author, May 10, 2002.

44. Lundberg, Malm, and Ronström, *Musik—Medier—Mångkultur*, 151.

45. Greger Andersson, "Stad och landsbygd," in *Musiken i Sverige I: Från forntid till stormaktstidens slut*, ed. Bengt R. Jonsson, Ann-Marie Nilsson, and Greger Andersson (Stockholm: Fischer & Co, 1994), 385.

46. Greger Andersson, "Städerna som musikmiljöer," in *Musiken i Sverige II: Frihetstid och Gustaviansk tid 1720–1810*, ed. Bengt R. Jonsson and Anna Ivarsdotter-Johnson (Stockholm: Fischer & Co, 1993), 167–168.

47. Jan Ling, interview by author, May 23, 2002. See also, Jan Ling, "Svensk folkmusik blir världsmusik: En intervju med Johan Hedin om hans väg från spelman till tonsättare," in *Allt under linden den gröna: Studier i folkmusik och folklore tillägnade Ann-Mari Häggman*, ed. Anders G. Lindqvist, Christoffer Grönholm, Kurt Sohlström, and Nina Stendahl (Vasa: Finlands svenska folkmusikinistitut, 2001), 335–356.

48. In a thought experiment to which I subjected almost all of my consultants, I made a series of statements and asked them to classify them as descriptions of folk music or not. Overall, my consultants tended to deem the style in which a tune was played more of a defining factor than the origin of the tune, its player, or the context in which it was performed.

49. Bengt Olof Engström, "Gunnar Hahn och hans musik," liner notes from *Svenska låtar på mitt sätt*, Gunnar Hahn, LadyBird Productions LBCD 0023, 1997, One Compact Disc.

50. Early on in the list Westerlund mentions Groupa as a band that consistently maintains a position across that line. When I mention Nordman and Gunnar Hahn, however, she clearly places them in another category, nowhere near the line. About Nordman she says, for instance, "I don't call that folk music at all, actually. They're a rock band that makes use of folk music instruments, but it's not folk music. No one will ever get me to say that, they're not a folk music group. They're a rock band. But the fact that they have a nyckelharpa, it doesn't matter so much. They might as well have a synthesizer" (Annelie Westerlund, interview by author, April 26, 2002).

51. Annelie Westerlund, interview by author, April 26, 2002.

52. Ingvar Strömblad, interview by author, June 24, 2002.

53. The group has now added a bass and calls itself Junekvintetten (The June Quintet).

54. Mart Hallek, et al., "Folkmusik i Frack II," liner notes from Junekvintetten med vänner, *Folkmusik i Frack II*, 2004, Intim Musik IMCD 095, compact disc.

55. Sågskära, *Krook! Musik bland trumslagare, bröllopsspelmän och bergtagna kvinnor*, 1997, Drone DROCD010, compact disc; Höökensemblen, *Höök! Musik bland stadsmusikanter, krigsfångar och mästertjuvar*, 1995, Drone DROCD007, compact disc; *Polski dantz: 1600-talsmelodier på vandring*, 2002, Drone DROCD026, compact disc.

56. Magnus Gustafsson, "17th and 18th Century Swedish Music," liner notes from Höökensemblen, *Höök! Musik bland stadsmusikanter, krigsfångar och mästertjuvar*, 1995, Drone DROCD007, compact disc; "Polski Dantz: 17th century melodies in migration...," liner notes from Höökensemblen, *Polski dantz: 1600-talsmelodier på vandring*, 2002, Drone DROCD026, compact disc.

57. Gustafsson, "17th and 18th century."

58. This doubleness may also be related to a common feature of session playing in general, a veneer of egalitarianism that can act to mask subtle internal hierarchies. The session as an institution tends to be explicitly open, yet its supposed openness provides any subset of its members opportunities to elevate the difficulty beyond the playing capacity of the others, especially if members of that subset share a pre-existing repertoire. In the specific context of the Swedish spelman gathering, such strategies may be especially prevalent, given that the common rule of etiquette is that anyone can join any session. Karl Malbert describes the phenomenon as follows:
"During these spontaneous sessions as they're called, the feeling is that it's really free, and anyone can join in. But sometimes someone wants to play with particular people, and maybe they don't want to play with others. They want to play tunes only they know, difficult tunes. So you get the sense when you're playing that if you take up the wrong tune it'll be ignored or interrupted, almost in the way described in feminist theories about techniques of domination. It can happen that when you start playing, someone will run right over you, playing harder and stronger and starting in on another tune that's more fun. But at the same time anyone can be involved, because if you ask if you can play they'll usually say yes. Unless they're rehearsing for a specific occasion or something. But if it's one of these sessions, and you know some of the people, you can play, even though usually some of the people only want to play with a few of the people there. It's just that you can't do that, because it's not a culture where you can leave with your

clique and say 'but you can stay here, because we don't want to play with you any more'" (Karl Marlbert, interview by author, December 11, 2001).

59. This is why I place my discussion of that continuum at a point of transition between chapters on axes of place and commonality.

CHAPTER 6

—‹vv›—

Three Definitions of Folk Music

The evolution of the modern Swedish folk music concept out of its initial, relatively stable position in the early nineteenth century may be read as a result of the slow dissociation of its original four ways of being understood—national romanticism's once tightly interwoven strands of Tradition, Nation, the Folk, and the Natural. The present chapter concerns itself with the ways in which interview subjects negotiate this dilemma in response to my asking them to define the term. My analyses of their answers are rooted in the theoretical frame I established in my introduction, and draw upon that discussion of the inner workings of individual axes explicated in the intervening chapters. I owe a special debt here to the principles of phenomenography, a school of thought based upon the theory that the learning of any concept involves the integration of multiple and finite "ways of understanding" it.[1] My particular use of phenomenography is to theorize the four axes along which discussions of folk music tend to move as distinct ways of understanding that concept.[2]

I have asked almost all of my interview subjects to define folk music, and elicited quite a variety of responses. Nearly everyone notes how difficult the question is to answer, and some argue that definition should not even be attempted. Most acknowledge conflicts along one axis or another—usually time, place, or commonality. They might make a statement about older traditions and then immediately qualify it with one about the possibilities of innovation; or mention dance band music as a truly popular form, and then leaven that with a statement about older peasant traditions. Those who answer with more confidence usually do so because they can quote Jan Ling, or at least utilize one of his strategies for mitigating intra-axial conflicts: defining folk music as a modern(izable) genre based on older peasant traditions, or arguing constant innovation to be a traditional aspect of the music. Also fairly common is a discussion of some ineffable quality to the music itself, a visceral element that resonates with the (individual or folk-) soul, setting it apart from other musics.

The vast majority of my consultants did their best to move on to the next question as quickly as possible. The only real exceptions were Joar Skorpen, "Sax" Mats Nilsson, and Magnus Ek, the three musicians I introduced in chapter 2 as archetypal examples of neotraditionalist, innovationist, and neomedievalist perspectives, respectively. Each of these men spent a considerable amount of time attempting their own definition, refusing to give up until they seemed to find some measure of satisfaction in their own answers.

In doing so, each navigated serially through the axes of time, place, commonality, and quality. This tactic, whereby an interview subject moves from one way of understanding a concept to another in response to a single interview question, has been called "intra-contextual conceptual shift" by phenomenographers.[3] My sense is that the tactic is especially suited to an essentially contested concept like "folk music," as a function of the following principles: First, because folk music is conceived along axes and not according to fixed categories, answers are necessarily dynamic and unstable to begin with. This provides a certain momentum for conceptual shifts, which can then easily be triggered by logical difficulties or inconsistencies along a single axis. Second, the impossibility of defining an essentially contested concept by drawing external boundaries around it means that its inner terrain must be covered extensively in order to identify its broader landscape. The traversal of multiple axes thus becomes a definitional necessity. Third, logical conflicts between axes force an impetus toward their resolution, favoring discourse that covers multiple axes simultaneously. Shifts between axes may thus occur easily, in the form of subtle and layered modulation.

Joar Skorpen

At the fairly late point in the interview when I asked Joar Skorpen to define folk music for me, much of our discussion had already been focused upon that concept and his understanding of it. A prominent theme had been a recurring acknowledgment that others might disagree with his perspective, and he with theirs. Statements to that effect are fairly prominent in that selection of Skorpen's quotes in chapter 2, in which I argue that he self-consciously deploys his own understanding of the concept as a counterbalance to Norwegian conservatism and Swedish permissiveness. He uses the techniques of heteroglossic refraction and reported speech to map the logically inconsistent terrain of the concept, tracing the arguments of multiple disagreeing subjects.

This technique is also consistent with Skorpen's approach to definition, in which he allows himself to draw dividing lines that reflect his own ideas about the meaning of the term, boundaries he acknowledges might not enjoy general acceptance. Throughout his interview Skorpen positions himself with some consistency on specific points along the various axes, staking his claim and defending it from counterarguments offered not by me, but rather by generic past or hypothetical others. The consistency of his positions seem in part to be made possible by the narrowness of the conceptual terrain he claims, in leaving out not only dance band, but also genre-bending groups like Väsen, Hedningarna, and Garmarna. Along the commonality axis he thus cuts folk music off from both fusion and popular music. Along the quality axis, he argues that folk and classical music are two entirely different areas, and sees no need to mix the two. When I ask him directly for a definition of folk music, his primary concern is with the remaining two axes of time and place:

> *Kaminsky:* I'm asking about, well, how you define folk music. You've said that you—I can ask that question again. Or more directly. How do you define folk music?
> *Skorpen:* It's what I was talking about before. I mean, for me what's really important is the dialects in relation to the geography. I think that's very, very important. And that's something new, because of course they didn't think that way before. Today you'll hear that as a counterargument: "but they didn't think that way before." No, they didn't, because they didn't have to, because they didn't have the communications we have now.

The existence of musical dialects and their specific regional variations is central to Skorpen's concept of folk music, as I have already shown in chapter 2. Together with his acknowledgment that his definition may be narrower than that of others, this affords him a very defensible position. Skorpen focuses on regional dialects rooted in natural boundaries and communication routes, mountains and waters. He insists that national borders are culturally and musically insignificant before the turn of the twentieth century, allowing for a folk music that goes back to ancient times, while simultaneously avoiding the politically charged nationalism that might otherwise go hand in hand with that kind of traditionalism. Skorpen then summons a potential threat to his position, the ghost of past counterarguments, a protest that the conceptual focus on regional specificity is actually a modern phenomenon. He summarily banishes it with the argument that today's self-conscious focus on regionalism compensates for a natural regional isolation now lost in the face of modern communications.

Skorpen's implication that the tradition should necessarily be maintained, however, summons yet another specter, that of stale preservationism. Skorpen answers this problem in the following way:

> And you have to be very careful there, since it's easy to wind up in that museum curators' camp. But I actually don't feel like that's me at all. For me there's huge difference between focusing rigorously on tradition, and not allowing the music to live and breathe. Because I prefer to play for dance. I think it's a lot more fun to play for dance than for concerts. And those dancers who follow the music and get a lot of joy out of the dance are the ones who are fun. Of course, if they also do it in the tradition, that's a plus. But I react against

people who are so hung up on tradition that it paralyzes them, so they can't even play.

Skorpen ingeniously wards off that threat of inertness by invoking another critical marker of folk music, functionality. Folk music is dance music, still practiced today and in living tradition. No better proof could be presented of dedication to life, the present moment, and the dynamic than a commitment to dance. Skorpen further protects himself from this preservationist specter by distancing himself from straw-man conservatives whose tradition-mania forces them to lose contact with the music.

Having defined himself against innovationists earlier in the interview (by removing genre-bending groups from the folk music category) and now preservationists, Skorpen reiterates his neotraditionalist thesis:

> I also think that it has to do with uncertainty, actually. For people who are secure in the tradition—it goes back to that idea that if you're secure within a tradition area you can permit yourself a lot of leeway as well. Because you'll never lose that core, since it's so ingrained.

Skorpen shores up his defense against preservationism by asserting that excessive conservatism marks a lack of traditional knowledge. In so doing he usurps for his neotraditionalist camp the authority associated with respect for tradition claimed by preservationists. Thus fortified against that more conservative element, he turns once again to face the innovationists, and one of the arguments they levy against his traditionalism:

> And when I discuss this with people, I often get the argument that "but it's supposed to be fun." As if that has to be the most important thing. And I'm surprised, and sometimes a little provoked by that, because I don't understand why that needs to be mentioned. That's a given. If it wasn't fun you wouldn't be doing it. But it's very foreign if you come from the classical world, where that's never been an issue. I've strayed a little from the question. But I've never understood the idea that wanting to be rigorous and thorough in delving into an area should stand in opposition to it being fun.

At this point in the discussion Skorpen observes that he has moved away from the question at hand, and returns to his neotraditionalist method for learning a tradition, which I have previously quoted in chapter 2:

> How did I get into this, again? What was the question? It was what I put into "folk music." Well, I'm interested in going as far as I can, as far as I'm able to find sources. And when I can't get any further, that's when I try to somehow find a reasonable solution for myself. I'll happily discuss it with others also, to see if they also think that "yeah, that sounds probable; that's the way it might have been." And then you think, well, I'll keep going with that for another few years.

Here Skorpen begins to work the quality axis into his argument, with a discussion of how certain ineffable qualities of the music can identify it as traditional:

> I have a friend named Unni Løvlid, who studies *folklig sång*. She's done six years at the School of Music in Oslo, and she's doing her *hovedfag* now.
> *Kaminsky: Hov—*?
> *Skorpen: Hovedfag* is a post-graduate program, following ordinary undergraduate programs. She was born and raised in Horningdal, and has visited a lot of older people. She talks about this gut feeling, it sounds flaky as hell, but I've come to realize it's really important. Sometimes you can just tell—this guy Sigmund Eikås does the same thing, for example—it doesn't have to be supported, because it's just apparent, there's something there that isn't right, that isn't working. And in most areas you can't always explain why, but there are certain things that just feel like they stick out in some strange way.

Here I would suggest that Skorpen is drawing upon a tradition of understanding folk music as the product of a slow evolutionary process, identifiable to the initiated by its satisfying wholeness and lack of awkward edges, as a product of natural selection.[4] In this view of folk music, Nature and Tradition are implicitly intertwined in their mutual adherence to Darwinian principles. In this way Skorpen can easily integrate the quality axis into his otherwise time-and-place-heavy discussion of how to responsibly play music in a weak tradition area:

> And that's the thing with the music from Bohuslän also. I try to be strict with myself, especially because it's so thin. If it were a really big area I wouldn't be. But it feels like it's important to be rigorous, since you run the risk that since there are so few practitioners, what you do can be accepted as truth. So you should at least have taken a real position with regard to what you're doing in advance. And then you can revise it after five years, when you've figured out, "oh that was wrong." But you still really have to try to find a credible concept.

At this point in the interview Skorpen implies he might be done answering the question, to which I respond by implying that he is not. I quickly follow, however, by offering him a way out, suggesting that a complete answer is unnecessary, perhaps even impossible:

> *Skorpen:* Does that answer your question?
> *Kaminsky:* The question was how you define folk music.
> *Skorpen:* Yeah, that's hardly an answer to that question, of course—[*laugh*]
> *Kaminsky:* [*laugh*] But nobody has answered that question yet, so that, everyone answers differently.
> *Skorpen:* Yes, exactly. Because of course if you're going to answer it directly, then you get into these categories, and then there isn't that much more to it.

Skorpen then ties up his definition by returning to the point at which he started, along the axes of time and place:

But back to what I mentioned in the beginning, the dialect thing. I guess that's what I define as folk music. I mean those old dialect roots, that also go together with communications, where you can see clear delineations between areas. Which areas didn't have contact with each other, which areas did have contact with each other, all that is mirrored very often in both folk music and to a certain extent dance. And in linguistic dialects. Ah, at last, I've cracked the code. Linguistic dialects, because that's the whole point of departure. That folk music follows the same patterns as the linguistic dialects. And that's almost entirely consistent, as I see it.[5]

Effectively, the narrowness of Skorpen's definition is what allows him to stake out a consistent position and gain some satisfaction in his own answer in the end. He can reject modern developments and simultaneously maintain his position as an insider because he is so careful to reproduce the effects of pre-industrial lifestyle on his own music-making, taking care to counteract the homogenization threatened by the modern ease of communication.

"Sax" Mats Nilsson

The project of definition becomes quite a bit more complicated, however, when innovationist developments are to be integrated under the "folk music" rubric. Exemplifying this problem is "Sax" Mats Nilsson's response to my definition question, marked as it is by a struggle to reconcile modern and historical practice. He begins by immediately splitting his definition in two:

> *Kaminsky:* My second, second big question then is if you have some definition of folk music.
> *Nilsson:* Yeah, that's a difficult question. As I see it there are two ways to define things. On the one hand you can try to put together a technical definition of folk music, and on the other you can create an emotional, personal one. For example, when I use concepts like "rock and roll" and "jazz," that's really emotional. When I say "wow, rock and roll!," then it's like what we talked about earlier. And I can also say "there's a lot of folk music in this." And what I mean by that on an emotional level is fairly self-evident, both to me and to a number of people in my surroundings.

Nilsson's definition as he begins it bears certain striking resemblances to elements of Skorpen's: that ineffable quality, recognizable to insiders, yet impossible to put into words. My sense is that he opens with this we-know-it-when-we-see-it qualification because he knows in advance that his technical definition, constrained by the inner pitfalls of the concept, will not convey what is most important about the music.

Indeed, Nilsson does struggle with this problem as he moves on:

But if you're going to look at the technical aspect, it's not so self-evident. A few years ago someone defined it as music that came from a specific place and wasn't born of the Western tradition. But that's not quite right either, because if you take Ireland for example, they really have a folk music, in the true meaning of the word. Ireland is a fairly young nation, and for that reason their folk music is very much born of the Western musical tradition. Not to mention the United States, of course, which is also a very young nation, and has a lot of folk music that's also based on the building blocks of Western music. But Swedish folk music, in the form we're talking about now, isn't based on those building blocks. And neither is Balkan music for example, and absolutely not the Arabic and Turkish and so on. So it's a little hard to define it, I think.

In an approach again bearing some affinities with Skorpen's, Nilsson begins his technical discussion of the music by drawing a boundary. Unlike Skorpen, however, Nilsson places that initial defining line across the quality axis, separating folk music from Western tonally conceived forms. This boundary he draws between folk and non-folk is not entirely unproblematic, of course. Nilsson must restrict this aspect of his definition to Swedish music, and even here qualify it as "music in the form we're talking about now." Recall that he faced a similar snag in chapter 2, having to acknowledge that tonally conceived Swedish accordion tunes were also folk music.

The necessary restriction of his initial sound-based definition to the Swedish further forces a shift to the place axis:

> I don't want to define it in terms of Swedishness, or anything like that. I mean, folk music is stuff that's come from outside, and has been treated in a local context. That's folk music.

The notion of a folk music that has come from outside and been locally developed has been espoused in many of my interviews and conversations. It effectively mitigates the paranoid xenophobia of the original ideology of preservationism and the strict patrolling of boundaries tied up with nationalism, while still acknowledging the significance of local variation and identity. In this case it also allows Nilsson to draw a second boundary, against popular music:

> I mean the opposite is today's pop industry, which is always working with a global objective. When folk music was created the objective wasn't global. Global didn't exist. The objective was local.

Nilsson's discussion of locally specific folk musics, like Skorpen's, represents a nexus along axes of time and place, situating regional traditions in the past tense. Diverging from Skorpen's path, however, Nilsson observes some depersonalization in the regionalist model, a criticism perhaps fueled by his innovationist predilection to focus on individual creativity and talent:

It's the same thing with the musical dialects, what I was talking about earlier. I don't think it has anything to do with pure geography. I think there have been spelmän who were dominant in certain areas, who may have been very good. Pekkos Per, for instance. What we call "Bingsjö" today is the Pekkos family. There have been a number of fantastic spelmän, who together with their environment—which is to say, the people who have danced locally—have developed a typical music, a typical phrasing. We've wanted to pin that on a bush, but that's what I think has happened.

Nilsson's statement about people misguidedly wanting to pin local signature styles "on a bush" also suggests another element to his discomfort at assigning musical traditions to localities rather than individuals. The bush represents not only place by its stasis, but also—and perhaps more obviously—the natural. The metaphor thus reflects the connection between nature and place implied by the traditional regions model, also exemplified in Skorpen's description of regions bounded by mountains and waters.

Having explicitly rejected that aspect of regionalism by focusing on individual musicians and their agency, Nilsson returns to a description of folk music's historical development otherwise quite akin to Skorpen's:

And that's how I think it is with folk music. That's what has happened, and the outside influences have been fairly minimal, because that's how the world was structured at that time. So it's often developed in some degree of isolation. And you can hear that. But at the same time it's also the case that you have traditions that span whole countries. Or entire regions. And in those cases it's just word of mouth that's done its thing. But I think that's what folk music is, purely on a technical level.

At this point, having established a view of what folk music was historically, Nilsson faces the challenge of integrating his own contemporary practices into the concept. He makes his first attempt by returning to an earlier point, opening modern folk music to the possibility of a global target audience:

While today you can even sit down and write a tune with a global objective. There's a really huge difference there, because that demands everything that doesn't have to do with music. The whole marketing thing, all of that.

This strategy is flawed, however, in that it erases his previously established boundary between folk and popular musics. Perhaps sensing that to pursue this line of reasoning is to risk unraveling his definition as it stands, Nilsson immediately changes course. He backtracks and reiterates points along the time and place axes, again crediting individual spelmän with the development of regional dialects:

If you look at it, often there have been religious motives. A lot of folk music out there in the world has spread as religious music. A lot of our Swedish folk music is religious music, especially the vocal tradition. And it's wandered in that way. But even so, it's developed locally, or regionally. That's why the chorales sound different at what's really a pretty close distance. But it comes from outside. The polska came over the sea, down to the folk, and so on. It came to Pekkos Per in Bingsjö, and he took and worked out something special, and it came to someone else here and someone else there. Niklas Larsson [in Svarteborg] and so on. Who are extremely different. But you hear the basic structure in it. So for me, I guess folk music on a purely technical level is music that's been created in that way. And folk music today continues to be influenced all the time. It does.

Here Nilsson has finally found a passable link between folk musics past and present, a variation on Ling's notion of innovation as tradition. Having thus connected his own practices to his broader technical definition, he returns to the emotional:

Emotionally, folk music for me is very much about distinctiveness from ordinary music. That's very much my own emotional interpretation. "Whoa, it sounds different." You notice that we weren't around when this was going on, or when it was made. That's folk music.[6]

Nilsson's emotional definition, in turn, is connected to his initial technical one—both lie upon the quality axis, involving a distinction between folk music and more mundane-sounding fare.

Also notable at the very end of Nilsson's definition is a return to the focus on the past that has marked much of his discussion. His statement that "we weren't around when this was going on" quite clearly excludes modern practice. Recall that this oscillation between images of folk music as static past and malleable present is a common mark of the innovationist perspective, which alternately includes itself within and excludes itself from the tradition.

Magnus Ek

This darting back and forth across the time axis is even more prevalent in drummer Magnus Ek's response to the definition question. Ek opens by immediately dismissing the significance of the commonality axis:

Kaminsky: I think there's a big question that I, or a big area that I have left. And that's the question of definition—do you have a definition of folk music?
Ek: What it is?
Kaminsky: Yeah.
Ek: Yes. I do. I think it's a shortcut, or it's to make yourself popular to say that dance band music—a la Vikingar—is folk music.[7] Because that's not what people mean by that anyway, so that's more to attract attention.

After this opening, Ek, like Skorpen, plays his definition primarily along axes of time and place. He begins with a fairly conservative position, associating folk music directly with Tradition and National identity:

> Folk music is the traditional music in different countries. I think it's often performed under fairly simple conditions. That's not a value judgment; it's just what I think it is. I mean, when you're out traveling, you say to yourself "damn, I'd like to hear some folk music, how does it sound here in this place?" Then most often you try to find your way away from the big stages and the hotels, to some sort of bushes, where you think you're going to find these little villages and the like. And I think that's where folk music flourishes.

Also reminiscent of Skorpen's definition is the intertwining of the Natural with the Traditional, which Ek does here by raising images of bush and village, familiar rural chronotopes.[8] In placing large stages and hotels in opposition to these villages and bushes, Ek also casually flips the commonality axis to align its obscure end with Nature and Tradition, further segregating folk from modern popular musics. In his description of the international traveler he suggests a connection between large-stage popular music and superficial tourism, to be contrasted with the cultural discoveries offered by folk musics found off the beaten path. One subtle implication might be that Swedes unfamiliar with Swedish folk music are in some sense tourists in their own country—an insinuation camouflaged by Ek's casting of himself as the tourist, and in a foreign land.

Like Nilsson, Ek also grants the rural folk music a personification:

> It's often old men—there it is again, right, tradition bearers—so you think it's old men and women who do it best. Okay, they've been doing it, they have the tradition in their blood, and often they make fantastic music. And that's what I consider folk music.

The tradition bearer is central to Ek's conception of folk music, yet as one might glean from the above quote, he has earlier in the interview acknowledged that icon to be somewhat problematic. He thus quickly leavens this image, and its previously-acknowledged ties to a conservative view of folk music, with an innovationist qualification:

> But then I also consider, in connection to this, that folk music would be dead if young people didn't come and take hold of it and do whatever pleased them. Because out of that, it can look unkempt and motley, like in Sweden right now, there are a bunch of groups like us who completely rootlessly do whatever strikes our fancy. Without respect we create bad and good music.

Ek here creates a clear division of labor between the tradition bearers who function as a source of the music, and innovators like himself who keep it alive. Further securing his rightful presence in the folk music realm, he suggests that traditional legitimacy is simply a matter of timing:

And if you look a hundred years in the future, those who interview people then, they're going to see that that's probably a part of folk music, much more than we think it is now.

Having thus argued for the legitimacy of the innovationist approach, Ek returns again to his traditional rural source, over which he remains conflicted:

But the actual core, that's what you get it from, and that still usually has to do with those small-scale contexts. What's been inherited from generation to generation, it—I can't really get away from that. Maybe because it's most unchanged there. So it's easy to find the central components there.

Ek concludes by appending a secondary definition regarding that ineffable quality that sets folk music apart from other genres:

Folk music. There is another definition, that it has an inherent powerful force, and a healing capacity. It's like a story about the people's way of life, of looking at their life. You hear it in those notes, in how they play, and so on, so that to me is folk music.[9]

Ek's addendum here suggests that he feels his primary definition to be somehow incomplete, not entirely successful in conveying what is truly powerful about the music. The consistent inclusion of this element of the visceral in each interview—Skorpen's "gut feeling," Nilsson's "emotional definition," Ek's "healing capacity"—I think reflects an impulse to express what is truly special about the music on all three accounts. Its segregation from the rest of the discussion in each of the three cases can be read as a discursive strategy for separating the soul of the music itself from the heady debates that inevitably surround it.[10] Each of these three men have taken on the task of defining a term beset by a complex of moving parts and an entrenched history of political and ideological debates, yet which for each of them is also connected to a personal deep history of visceral musical experience. That they should experience an impulse to separate the personal from the political should come as little surprise.

Staging the Concept

Ek's little story-of-a-people tag at the end of his definition centers a folk music that is otherwise constantly on the move, first a tradition of the old and rural, then an innovative practice of the young and rootless, and back again. The instability counteracted by Ek's final words is born of his clear desire to steer away from a definition tied to the aged tradition bearer, and his ultimate acknowledgment of an inability to do so. This inner conflict gives energy and forward momentum to his definition, which flitters back and forth along the time axis between pure unchanging source material and the innovative practices of a newer age.

This frenetic back and forth is also a product of the limitations of the interview context, which demands unambiguous meaning, and therefore makes difficult the logical explication of an essentially contested concept. The next chapter regards ways in which the folk music and folk dance concepts can be dealt with on stage, where multiplicity of meaning may be a more acceptable part of the discourse. Chapter 7 begins with a discussion of staged "folk dance" and the issues associated with that concept, and ends with an analysis of concerts put on by Raun, a folk rock group led by Magnus Ek. In that performance context, Ek will be able to grapple far more successfully with the problems inherent to the folk music concept, with a presentational style full of humor and ambiguous irony.

Notes

1. Ference Marton and Shirley Booth, *Learning and Awareness* (Mahwah: Erlbaum, 1997), 114.

2. Phenomenographers have also developed their own system for interview analysis, which for practical reasons I have not followed. One minor departure, for example, is that the prescribed approach assumes interviews to be conducted specifically for the purpose of being analyzed phenomenographically, whereas I have applied my theoretical frame after the fact. In actuality, though, in practical terms I have not strayed too far from the phenomenographers' path here. Their approach to interview technique essentially mirrors that of the ethnographer, "non-directive except with respect to 'leading' the interviewee to focus on pre-determined content in particular contexts" (Eleanor Walsh, "Phenomenographic analysis of interview transcripts," in *Phenomenographic Research: Variations in Method: The Warburton Symposium*, ed. John A. Bowden and Eleanor Walsh (Melbourne: Royal Melbourne Institute of Technology, 1994), 17). Where I truly diverge from traditional phenomenographic methodology is in the process by which I have elicited the four ways of understanding folk music from my materials and experience. My primary theoretical departure involves my having had to adapt to certain complications that arise from applying the phenomenographic model to an essentially contested concept, postulating the existence of dynamic axes in place of fixed categories. My main methodological departure has been that I have not elicited these ways of understanding the concept via the careful group process used by phenomenographers for the purpose of mitigating subjective bias. The process by which I have educed these axes has been individual, a cyclical ethnographic progression of observing, asking, and thinking. That procedure has been thorough, to be sure, and based upon a far wider fieldwork experience than simple interview analysis, yet has been subject to none of the rigorous external controls prescribed by phenomenographers (Walsh, "Phenomenographic Analysis," 26–29). I have compensated for this absence in part with feedback analysis. A number of Swedish folk music insiders, including several of my consultants, have consented to review a late draft of this work. Some have argued in their critiques that I may have given short shrift to certain important events, people, and phenomena; but none have taken issue with—and several have commented positively upon—my theoretical frame.

3. Ference Marton and Wing-yan Pong, "Conceptions as Ways of Being Aware of Something—Accounting for Inter- and Intra-Contextual Shifts in the Meaning of Two Economic Phenomena" (paper read at the symposium: New Challenges to Research and Learning, Helsinki, March 22, 2001), 14. The intra-contextual conceptual shift may be distinguished from the inter-contextual conceptual shift in that the latter refers to a change effected by a new interview question on the same concept (12, 14).

4. See, e.g., Maud Karpeles, "Some Reflections on Authenticity in Folk Music," *Journal of the International Folk Music Council* 3 (1951): 11, 14–15.

5. Joar Skorpen, interview by author, November 18, 2001.

6. "Sax" Mats Nilsson, interview by author, January 9, 2002.

7. Ek may be responding specifically to views espoused by fellow band mate Harald Pettersson, among others. In his response to my definition question, Pettersson argued that modern popular forms are in fact today's folk music (Harald Pettersson, interview by author, July 3, 2004).

8. "Chronotope" is a term coined by Mikhail Bakhtin for a place that signifies a particular time or kind of time; in his words: "the primary means for materializing time in space" (Mikhail Bakhtin, "Forms of Time and the Chronotope in the Novel: Notes toward a Historical Poetics (X. Concluding Remarks)," in *The Dialogic Imagination* (Austin: University of Texas Press, 1981 [1973]), 250).

9. Magnus Ek, interview by author, April 2, 2002.

10. This partitioning may also be an attempt to shield that essential element from the politicization of its description, given the reliance of that description upon romanticizing imagery.

CHAPTER 7

—⁓—

Two Public Performances

Ethnographers have an established tradition of acknowledging the self-conscious awareness of our subjects that they are participating in something called "culture," a set of practices that help define them as a group, and which they are aware we are there to study. As early as 1972, Milton Singer coined the term "cultural performance" to describe any performative event that might function as a unit of observation for purposes of ethnographic analysis; so recognized not only by himself, but also by his consultants:

> As I observed the range of cultural performances (and was allowed, sometimes asked, to photograph and record them) it seemed to me that my Indian friends—and perhaps all peoples—thought of their culture as encapsulated in these discrete performances, which they could exhibit to visitors and to themselves.[1]

My experiences in Sweden were certainly consistent with Singer's in this regard. Staged folk music and folk dance performances are almost by definition self-conscious presentations of culture. In Sweden, where general knowledge about these traditional arts is fairly minimal among the wider populace, the imparting of self-knowledge to Swedes is often an implicit and not rarely an explicit goal of such performances.

Yet the presentational performance of Swedish folk music is a double-edged sword. Many of its enthusiasts would argue that the act of staging itself subverts its true form.[2] Folk music is meant to be functional dance, or wedding, or funeral music. To put it on stage is to remove it from that Natural context and weaken the boundary between folk and art. Further, it challenges one of the most powerful markers of authenticity for tradition bearers, namely their lack of self-consciousness regarding the fact that what they do is called "folk music." In claiming to represent the tradition, the staged cultural performance thus reveals itself as representation, as facsimile.

This problem is compounded by the long history of staged folkloric performances in Sweden now generally acknowledged by folk music and dance insiders to have seriously distorted the objects they purported to represent. In the nineteenth century, folk songs were arranged to be performed in four-part choral harmonizations, or for soprano solo voice and piano. Folk dances were shaped according to the needs of the public stage and the narrative trajectory of the folklife play; most famously by Anders Selinder for the Stockholm Opera, but also for folkloric performances staged by college student groups.[3] In other words, faithful reproduction was not a central concern in the nineteenth century, as much as was satisfying an interest in rural folk culture among the bourgeoisie.

The earliest issues of the Youth Ring's journal in the early 1920s reveal that by that point, strict reproduction for the purposes of heritage preservation had become a central value in the folk dance movement. By this time, however, the material to be preserved was primarily made up of those choreographed dances of the nineteenth-century folklife stage. As I have mentioned, during the folk music revival this traditional folk dance group repertoire was challenged as inauthentic by the new school of polska dancers. Yet the old-school folk dance group has weathered this attack, having remained a significant folk movement in Sweden throughout the twentieth and early twenty-first centuries, to a much greater extent than their challengers. A comparison between the two dance movements reveals a manifestation of the dilemma inherent in staging (and thereby popularizing) folkloric events—for the dance to enjoy popular success, the original material must be altered to generate visual and dramatic interest.

The spelman competitions of the early twentieth century also represented that ideological shift toward cultural preservationism in the performance realm, and one that offered a less distorted view of village culture than in the world of folk dance. Yet these never enjoyed the longevity of the folk dance movement. Further, the most successful acts that came out of these competitions were those Hälsingland players whose repertoire was of a fairly recent virtuosic tradition, again developed primarily for the stage. These were later eclipsed by spelman groups, who enjoyed brief popular successes, but which again never had the consistent pan-national visibility accorded the folk dance group via midsummer celebrations.[4] Neither did the spelman group represent past peasant traditions with any real accuracy, as fiddle groups larger than two would have been rare before the twentieth century.

If folk music fusion is to be considered a unitary subgenre, one might argue that it has been the one to enjoy the most consistent visibility in the past fifty years, in one form or another. From Jan Johansson in the sixties, Kebnekajse and Merit Hemmingsson in the seventies, Groupa and Filarfolket in the eighties, to Hedningarna and Garmarna in the nineties and early aughts, the mixing of folk music with other genres has proven an effective recipe for popular appeal.[5]

Yet as in the realm of folk dance, some voice concern at the distortion entailed by this sort of adaptation. Here territorial losses along the time and place axes may not be considered worth gains along that of commonality.

In short, of the various types of staging that Swedish folkloric culture has seen over the past century, the two that have been the most visible and long-lasting are the folk dance group performance on the one hand, and the folk music fusion concert on the other. Both are marked by their respective histories at the crossroads of insider subculture and outsider superculture.[6] These crossroads become focal points for the tensions within and between all four axes of the folk music concept, tensions that occasionally manifest by becoming part of the performances themselves. This phenomenon may be seen as further evidence as to the essential contestedness of these concepts. Given that performances are planned for public display, simply to present the conflicts embedded in "folk music" or "folk dance" at the end of a process of rehearsal and preparation functions practically as an admission of the inability to resolve those conflicts. In making them public, the cultural performace acknowledges that they are central to the cultures they represent.

This chapter is dedicated to the analysis of performances by two different ensembles, one a folk dance group, the other a folk fusion band. The youth section of National, Gothenburg's largest folk dance group, was a group of mostly teenage dancers under the direction of Emma Rydberg, Urban Lind, and Magnus Ewaldz. Raun was a folk rock band led by Magnus Ek, comprising musicians from both Gothenburg and Stockholm.

The Youth Section of Folk Dance Group National

These days many folk dance groups have been affected by the rebirth of polska dance in the aftermath of the folk music revival. Even Philochoros has expanded their repertoire beyond the traditional elaborately choreographed folk dances for which it was a conduit into the twentieth century, to include both polskor and gammeldans. While many folk dance groups today concentrate exclusively on stage dances, and some smaller number dance polskor exclusively, this phenomenon of doing both is not unusual.

Folk Dance Group National's youth section is one example of a group that engages in both polska and stage dancing. They are actually somewhat unusual in that they occasionally include "modern" dance in their repertoire as well—lindy hop, tango, foxtrot, jive, one-step, samba, rumba, and so forth. When most of these dances were first popular in Sweden, the Youth Ring erected strict boundaries against them; a legacy that may have lost some of its ideological charge today, yet has had a lasting effect in terms of their typically remaining excluded from the regular repertoire. Some folk dance groups will dance these dances at their informal social gatherings, but National's youth section is unusual in actually learning them during official rehearsal times, and on rare occasions, even performing them.[7]

Emma Rydberg proposed the reintroduction of these modern dances to the group's repertoire after a long hiatus at the last rehearsal of the 2004 spring semester, to the dancers' popular approval. Her interest in including these dances may be read in part as a challenge to the Youth Ring's history of cultural and political conservatism, a problem about which Rydberg has verbalized a certain degree of frustration. She is not the first to deal with this sort of issue in this way—during the seventies, the Gothenburg folk dance group Näverluren was created both as an element of and a reaction against the Youth Ring. Rydberg's position is made somewhat more difficult, however, by the fact of her youth group's affiliation with a larger adult folk dance group, and the absence today of the revolutionary leftist sail winds of the seventies.

Where Näverluren explored polskor and other forms to balance out the established dance group repertoire, for instance, the repertoire of National's youth section today remains weighted toward those choreographed stage dances. In part this may be due to the fact that polska dance is no longer in any danger of extinction, and thus less likely to draw fervent advocates. Practical issues related to the specific structure of the group are perhaps of greater significance here, however. The adult section favors the stage dances, and shares a good deal of its repertoire with the youth section; the youth dancers often fill out the adult group in their public performances. Also, the younger dancers especially enjoy the social cohesion entailed by group forms, and are often less interested in the gender politics of the couple dances. When the leaders ask the dancers for a request, their first choice is often a complex stage form called "hörnstolpadans," made chaotic fun by the quick tempo at which the musicians tend to play it.

The older and more experienced members of the youth section, fewer in number, tend to favor the polska dances. Where high tempos challenge the group in the stage forms, here the steps are more demanding of the individual and the couple, and subtler in their variations. Gender relations and sexual dynamics are more pronounced in the couple dances as well, of course. Polska dance abilities also open the door to spelman gatherings and the Folk Music Café, which tend to be more interesting places to the older teenagers, few of whom choose the path to National's adult section. Interest in these couple dances is also stoked by the leaders of the group, all three of whom are accomplished polska dancers.

In a group that commands both stage and polska dances, the tendency in actual performances will be to favor the stage dances, for the obvious reason that they are more interesting visually, being designed for public viewing. This may pose a problem, however, for the choreographers of such performances, if they do not wish to perpetuate the notion that stage dance is "true" folk dance. The question becomes: how does one create an entertaining program that also accurately represents traditional folk culture?

In 2002, folk dance group National's youth section had a dance program that addressed this problem quite effectively. I first saw it performed publicly in Gothenburg's Bältespännar park, as part of a potpourri put on by several of the Youth Ring's local member dance groups for Sweden's national day, June sixth. Their opening contrasted markedly with those of other folk dance groups on the program. Where the traditional opening has dancers promenade or dance in from one or two sides of the floor to the strains of the first tune, here the young dancers walked in haphazardly, from all corners of the floor, greeting each other, play-acting casual conversation, absent any music. The girls were dressed in full folk costume, but the boys wore no vests. Urban Lind stood with another fiddler on the stage above, observing, until he spoke through his microphone: "The members of National's youth section are going to dance a set representing their views on how *folklig dans* became stage dance."

The dancers went through a number of Western Swedish village dances: an engelska, several polskor, a schottische.[8] The dancing was improvisatory. Couples did not coordinate their moves with those of other couples. Into this scene walked Magnus Ewaldz, observing, taking notes in a green book, interrupting the dancers to ask questions. Eventually he took the upper stage with the musicians, and while the dancers vacated the floor, made an announcement: "I am ballet master Selinder from Stockholm. I have traveled around Sweden observing village dances, and I have created some simple compositions that my dance troupe will now perform."

The dancers took to the floor once more, this time looking much more the folk dance group part. The boys were now fully dressed in their vests.[9] The dancers moved in sync to the music as a group. The four choreographed stage dances that followed looked much like the dance presentation of any other folk dance group.[10]

Following this program, Lind invited the audience up to join the dancers, and he and the other fiddler went back to playing village dances, a schottische and three polskor.[11] Few audience members joined the dance, however. More stepped to the floor when Lind and his partner were replaced by another set of folk dance musicians, Heimdal's spelmän, who shifted into the gammeldans repertoire, alternating pairs of schottisches, waltzes, polkas, and hambos.

The leaders of National's youth section who created this program did an effective job of negotiating the visual monotony of social village dancing and the problematic nature of its mediation in being adapted for the stage. The explicit narrative showing the historical relationship between the two types of dances allowed stage dances to be used to demonstrate their own background. At the same time, village dances could be integrated into a folk dance performance as part of a narrative, without needing to dominate the event.

The performance also revealed negotiations along axes of time, place, commonality, and quality, all of which the Swedish folk dance concept shares with that of folk music. Because the axes were stretched along a narrative timeline, their logical knots could be loosened and unraveled. Village dance traditions became Selinder's innovative choreographies, while improvisation turned to fixed form. Ideas were culled from the rural countryside for an urban stage, transformed from the regionally specific to the nationally representative. Popular dances were reinvented as elitist ballet for trained dancers, unschooled rawness exchanged for professional artifice.[12]

Yet the satisfyingly tidy picture this performance draws relies upon its self-restriction to events preceding the amateur folk dance group movement. The more recent history that actually led to the existence of a folk dance group that can perform both stage and village dances has done a great deal to re-tangle the axes so neatly stretched out over the nineteenth-century timeline of the above-described performance. As we move into the first half of the twentieth century, Selinder's innovations become new Traditions, guarded by institutions like the Youth Ring. Later Henry Sjöberg's village dance revival completes this reversal by reclaiming its improvisatory essence against the conservative stage dance tradition. At the same time, however, Sjöberg's revival reaffirmed the original nineteenth-century orientation of the time axis by claiming age and authenticity for the polska.

The twenty-first century also holds reversals along the commonality axis, exemplified at the point in the June sixth event when Lind opened the floor to the audience. The behavior of the crowd once asked to take the floor belies—even flips—the popular/elitist dichotomy suggested by National's performance. Unfamiliar with the polska, most only step up when given the opportunity to dance gammeldans or easy-to-learn choreographed group dances, perhaps familiar from midsummer and similar events.

Along the quality axis, while Selinder's nineteenth-century troupe was indeed made up of professional stage dancers, in the twentieth century the folk dance group movement has become Sweden's amateur dance movement *par excellence*, with essentially no professional aspect. *Folklig dans*, on the other hand, like folk music, has in recent years entered into the higher education school system, with a special program at the Stockholm University of Dance and Circus as well as at a number of other institutions.

In sum, while in the nineteenth century Selinder's folk dances represented a move away from the original ways of understanding folk music and dance, the twentieth century has overlaced this motion with reversals and re-reversals. The disjointed classification system regarding what is and is not considered *folklig dans*, described in chapter 4, is one product of this complex relationship between stage and village dances today.[13] Just as some have argued schlager and dance band to be modern folk musics, so others have allowed for a generous list of modern *folklig dans* forms, including, in some cases, house and hip hop.[14] Significantly, however, they have generally not included stage-oriented folk dances on that list.[15] This despite the qualifications of staged folk dance as a clear development out of village traditions, as well as its current amateur status and national ubiquity, far beyond that of the polska subculture. The lacuna is especially noteworthy considering that the liberal claim of including house and hip hop under *folklig dans* simultaneously violates both the National and Traditional as ways of understanding that concept, demonstrating an otherwise exceptional openness with regard to the rubric.[16]

One explanation for this exclusion may be that, when Ernst Klein originally coined the term *folklig dans*, he did so explicitly to distinguish it from staged *folkdans*. The reason why the force of this distinction has been maintained in common usage, where *folklig dans* has otherwise expanded generously, may be that the false claim staked by the name "folk dance" remains a threat against the perceived cultural legitimacy of polska. To acknowledge folk dance as a *folklig* form would be to reinforce that claim, and to risk even greater marginalization to modern polska culture as a result.

On the other hand, placing old village dances in the same category as today's club music allows each to benefit from the currency of the other. The polska's authenticity rubs off on club music, and club music's cultural relevance rubs off on the polska. Both can enjoy a reunified conception of the *folklig* as simultaneously folk and popular. Staged folk dance groups have little to offer either in terms of currency, meanwhile, and are kept out of the picture. The folk dance movement of the twentieth and twenty-first centuries is inconvenient here in its being both more popular and more amateur than today's polska subculture. This is why National's narrative dance performance must stop short of the twentieth century in the story it tells.

Raun

I move now to a different sort of cultural performance, by the folk rock group Raun. My primary analysis will be of a live concert they put on as part of a world music series at Bommens Salonger, an upscale Gothenburg bar, on March 17, 2002. I also bring in some discussion of a show they did just over a month later, on April 26, at the Folk Music Café, as well as their two albums and individual interviews with all four band members.

Before the Bommens Salongen performance I had called Magnus Ek, the band's front man, in order to secure permission to record the event. He had been friendly on the phone, and warned me that there would be theatrics before the concert proper. When I arrived at the bar, I found Ek and introduced myself to him. I then staked out a spot where I thought the stability of my microphone stand would not be compromised, and waited for the show to begin.

Eventually an odd assemblage of characters began to wander the audience. Ek was among them, sporting a curly blond wig and makeshift glasses from what looked to be the remains of a metal tea strainer, waving a vacuum hose. A second man meandered the room singing ballads. A woman also wandered the crowd, behaving in a manner she would later describe to me in an interview as "generally fascistic."[17] The fourth member of the strange troupe approached me, standing as I was somewhat conspicuously under a microphone stand with a digital camera hanging around my neck. He held an alto recorder in each fist. I began to feel the uneasy feeling I associate with the knowledge of immanent harassment by avant-garde theater folk with no regard for the fourth wall. The exchange went as follows, in English:

> *Recorder player*: Folk music? You like folk music?
> *Ethnomusicologist*: Yes. I like folk music.
> *Recorder player*: I would like to show you an old Swedish tradition, from the north, east and west of Sweden.[18]

He lifted the recorders, each to a nostril, and began to play a simple accompaniment figure, to which he sang a song I did not know. I learned later it was "Hello You Old Red Indian," a dance band classic that had topped the charts in 1973.[19]

Raun was of primary interest to me because they, more than any other group I knew of, actively negotiated the conflicts inherent to the folk music concept in performance. The theatrics of their live shows were a virtual parade of paradoxes they bent back and forth to entertain their audience. Where National's youth section created in its Selinder story a narrative that allowed a crooked concept to stretch out and straighten itself over a timeline, Raun compressed conflicts and presented them side by side and on top of one another, juxtaposing them to comedic and musical effect. In the case of the recorder player's dance band performance, Tradition and the Folk were both conjoined and mutually alienated via a grotesque "traditional" arrangement of an already-grotesque popular song.

The band was founded by singer Helena Ek, and led by her brother Magnus Ek on percussion. Both lived in Gothenburg. Recorder player Göran Månsson and hurdy-gurdy player Harald Pettersson, who both lived in the Stockholm area, rounded out the group.[20] Each of the four band members had considerable experience in other musical genres. Magnus Ek played music from a wide range of percussion traditions, and his experience as a theater musician informed much of the group's live performance aesthetic. Helena Ek was a classically trained singer whose contacts with Pettersson and Månsson came first through the Swedish early music scene.

Musically the group fit rather well within the subgenre Dan Lundberg calls "drone rock," among bands like Hedningarna, Garmarna, and Hoven Droven.[21] One striking connection between Raun and Garmarna, for instance, was their common use of stark contrasts between a harsh and rough-sounding instrumental palette and a pure, polished vocal sound on the part of the female lead singer.[22] Göran Månsson describes Raun's use of this technique:

> It's a lot about what *klang* we want in the group, what "sound" as they say. It's centered around the percussive aspect. There's a lot of pulse, a lot of rhythm in it. And I have a part in that as well, with my instruments. Harald too, who has joined the group now. The hurdy-gurdy is also very rhythmic in that way, and I

use a lot of percussive sounds in my recorders when I play. And then Helena's voice goes on top.[23]

As I understand it, the simultaneous performance of rough playing and pure, steady voice effectively functions to resolve any potential tensions along the quality axis.

While the vocal/instrumental interplay best recalled Garmarna among other established drone rock groups, the instrumentation itself had more in common with Hedningarna's neomedievalist palette. Like Hedningarna, the group played a panoply of instruments between them, only a few of which I mention here. Tellingly, no one played the modern fiddle. Månsson's recorders suggested an early music connection, and the vague archaism of Nordman. Pettersson's hurdy-gurdy and bagpipe were the classic resurrected folk music instruments. The bow harp occasionally played by Helena Ek also fell into that category, as Sweden's oldest known string instrument. Magnus Ek's percussion may have fulfilled a similar function. Drumming in Swedish folk music was almost unheard of before the revival, yet in Sweden as anywhere drums can signify the primeval. They may be connected to Saami sacred drumming (a tradition long ago broken by Christian missionaries) or an otherwise unknowable past.

Percussion also offered serendipitous flexibility for Magnus Ek's aesthetic of improbable mixing. His esoteric kit carried associations with music both modern and ancient, primal and popular, rural and urban:

Now I've landed in more of a kind of city-influenced story, where my arsenal is a mixture of three components. We're talking about skin, standard drums: I have a custom-made drum that's something like a mixture between *bombo* and bass drum. It's very similar to another drum from Småland whose name I've forgotten, but which comes from the military and was used in folk music there.[24] Then there's metal, to blend into youth music [*laugh*]. No, but to give a little tougher sound. I like metal when it doesn't cool it down, but it makes it fresh and crisp. And then sampled sounds.[25]

Ek's skin drums suggested nature, the primitive and prehistoric. His scrap metals connected to the modern, human-made, urban. Yet often these were also found objects, and as such formed a link to older traditions, simple instruments of bark or bone. Ek's third category, sampled sounds, fulfilled a similar bridging function. Highly technologized, yet also in some sense unmediated, sampling presents the truest possible record of sonic past; the more modern the technology the more faithful the reproduction.

Sociologist Tricia Rose has noted the use of sampling in rap music as an act of homage, of making connections to musical roots.[26] Ek's dubbing of old field recordings into his own music represented a use of that technology to similar effect. In the title track to Raun's second album, *Dance Jon*, he used two cuts from old Bohuslän field recordings, one of vocable singing by Martin Martinsson, the other a collector's announcement of an upcoming fiddle tune.[27] The track opens with a repetitive hurdy-gurdy lick, joined by a regular drum kick and sub-contrabass recorder bass line figure, over which the collector's announcement is then heard: "Old polska from Bohuslän recorded by the spelman Niklas Larsson from Bohuslän." This sample is then sampled in turn: "Niklas Larsson. Niklas Larsson. Nikla- Nikla- Nik- Niklas Larsson, Nikla- Nikla- Nik-Niklas Larsson," and followed by the Martin Martinsson vocable lick. The remainder of the six-minute track is marked by permutations of these and a few other fragments, with the eventual addition of Helena Ek singing over and above.

The sort of folk techno effect created here was not unique to Raun. Hedningarna had made extensive use of it on their 1997 album *Hippjokk*, for example.[28] The use of sampled field recordings, however, seems to have been a new innovation in this context, and one typical of Magnus Ek's aesthetic of improbable mixing. Ek stamped the music "traditional folk" in a way traditional folk music does not allow, weaving the collector's announcement, a literal marker of authenticity, into the musical fabric itself. With the same gesture he connected the music to old and new, marking it folk according to the musical rules of the electronic dance club.[29]

Here and in Raun's live performances, Magnus Ek's primary theme was the rural/urban dichotomy, powerful in its capacity to allow multiple axes of the folk music concept to manifest within itself simultaneously. His "city-influenced" percussive palette offered a blend of the natural and artificial, old and new, the skin drums of ancient folk cultures and the fresh metallic sounds of today's popular youth culture. *Dance Jon* in its urban club dance aesthetic offered its appreciation of old rural traditions in an innovative way, popping up the folk, re-musicking Martin Martinsson's natural singing voice through digital sampling artifice. Even Ek's Salvation-Army-bin costuming at the opening of the Bommen's Salonger concert navigated multiple axes by way of the urban/rural dichotomy. The tea-strainer glasses were actually special folklife research spectacles, he revealed later in the performance. Innovation to study tradition, and a loaded commentary: alienating citified technology whose metal weaving completely hid his observing eyes from his rural subjects, and in the process partially obscured his own vision. The vacuum hose, Helena Ek informed me in her interview, was meant to clear the urban air for folk music. The original plan, she says, had been to use a pine tree air freshener, but they were unable to find one of sufficient size. These objects again formed comical links between axial poles—the vacuum hose a most modern device to clear the city air for ancient sounds; the pine tree air freshener the same and furthermore a pointed commentary on the artificial representation of nature.

Of Magnus Ek's arsenal of pastorality-producing urban objects, however, none was more effective than his megaphone. He made some use of it in the prelude to the Bommens Salonger concert, but allowed it to figure more prominently in the opening of the later performance at the Folk Music Café. Foregoing the audience-participation prelude, the group opened that show by parading toward the stage from the back of the crowd. As a processional Ek sang the well-known traditional lullaby "Byssan lull" through the megaphone, in a dead-on gender-ambiguous impression of a faltering old tradition-bearer. His wavering voice distorted through the bullhorn created a sound uncannily like an old field recording. While perhaps the most obviously urban of all his devices, the megaphone could thus also conjure an established sound of rural authenticity. The bullhorn's physical form reversed the relationship between singer and mediating object established with phonograph recordings, a cone sung out of, rather than into. This thoroughly modern, technological device was able to generate a live field recording, as if to eliminate the mediator of time in bringing the tradition bearer's song to our ears. A marriage of urban and rural, a body of city, voice of the country, it removed the distance between. Like the vacuum hose and the tea-strainer glasses, however, the object pointed to its own absurdity and by extension the absurdity of the entire field recording aesthetic; that machine-induced distortion and petrification should be sonic markers of the genuine. Nor did Ek allow his authentic-sounding performance of the lullaby to stand. He broke off in the middle to announce: "folk music!" before he completed the song, a self-conscious internal labeling that, paradoxically, marked its inauthenticity.

Ek went even further in mocking the currency ascribed to the rural tradition bearer, and the futility of insisting on a folk music free from urban influence, in a song he sang only at live shows. Here is the introduction and performance of this number at the Bommens Salonger concert:

Magnus Ek: As promising young musicians such as ourselves, who work in the folk music business, it's very important to keep contact with our roots, that is, backwards, and we work a lot with older people.
Man in audience: Thanks.
Magnus Ek: And, right. You're welcome up on stage, we can—Thomas also works with folk. And I'm talking even older than Thomas. They're 80, 85 preferably. That's when they're at their prime. Then they're real role models, because that's when they're TRADITION BEARERS! Yes. LET'S COUNT TO THREE FOR OUR SWEDISH TRADITION BEARERS! ONE TWO THREE! One more time [*as members of the audience join in*]: ONE TWO THREE! A new custom. And it goes in the plus column if these people are little odd, original. That is, not to say detached, but also not quite, they're not so keen on internalizing current societal norms. Only they live some place far out in the forest, there's a path, no warm water, no soaps at night, no TV. At the most there are some newspapers on the floor; instead of vacuuming they just turn the pages. The hygienic ones, they do it every day. We heard about two sisters, Carmencita and Berit Persson are their names, who live in a red cottage someplace in Sweden, and we're not going to tell you where they live—then you'll also sneak off there and dig around in this folk music treasure they're hiding. We were fortunate enough to hitch a ride on a welfare helicopter that flies there once a week with food and drops it on the lawn outside, because they're very shy, these sisters. They dart out like little mice, then right back in again. We caught a ride on one of these food packages and after various episodes we were

able to win the sisters' trust, and they revealed to us the following song, which is for those who long for the genuine in folk music. We will attempt to reproduce it as accurately as possible:

[*Ek sings in his faltering old tradition bearer voice:*]
Oh, the boy, he went to the rosy grove
    There he met a girl, so good and round
They went to the place of love
    There he was shocked, and she went mute
[*insecure humming*] and then took himself out—
We www, we will not say what happened there
    But 9 months later she's screaming "dear god"
A boy he was—[*Pauses, then says:*] Um, wait, this is it:
He ate and he grew senselessly
    But suddenly a bushy tail became visible
A changeling he was, is, and shall be
    Where he then went, we swear we do not know
We think he became a politician or an executive
    Now the song is over, and we say thanks and good bye.[30]

In the last refrain, the punch line, Ek once again made use of humorous juxtaposition to join rural to urban, old to new. Yet on the whole the humor of this segment operated on a subtler level. Recall that Ek's answer to the definition question in his interview revealed a certain ambivalence about tradition bearers, as icons both necessary and problematic. In this performance context, he was able to conjure these icons and at the same time deflect their implicit claim of exclusive rights to his music, forming a hermetic circle of irony around them. This strategy is similar to that used by those spelman gathering players who humorously inject virtuosic classical pieces into their sessions, the overt irony leavening any sincere desire to demonstrate instrumental prowess; or by those who make self-mocking use of national romantic clichés to describe what about folk music speaks to them.

While satire was central to Raun's performance, there was also a sincere joy in linking the past to the present, rural to urban. Consider the song "Frej," which the group had originally developed for a street procession program. At the end of the Bommens Salonger concert, Pettersson and the Eks returned to the stage, and Magnus gave the following introduction:

Magnus Ek: You've shown a musical maturity that I haven't seen in any audience before in my entire life. [*Audience laughter.*] And we want to give you a tribute for tonight by playing a kind of music that has its roots far far far back in time. Far far far. Far far far. Ancient Nordic mythology. We have a figure there, a god named Frej. Yes! Somebody knows him there. He's a male sex god. A little narrow, maybe. He's a kind of global erotic symbol, an archaic man. No doubt a Gothenburger. [*audience laughter*] Frej! Okay, are you ready?
Harald Pettersson: Yes.

Magnus Ek: We work in three. [*More audience laughter as the band begins to play. Ek and Pettersson scream the lyrics in a manner more rock than folk, repeating them ad nauseam:*]

> He's a sex machine! Go on! Keep it going!
> He's a sex machine! Go on! Keep it going!
> He's a sex machine! Go on! Keep it going!
> He's a sex machine! Go on! Keep it going!
> Pretty is he, stylish is he, pretty is he as he dances!
> Pretty is he, stylish is he, especially when he chances!

Soon a transformed Göran Månsson reentered, wearing a plastic horned helmet (a single rhinoceros-style horn projected out the front) and a flasher's trench coat, dancing his way to the stage to audience applause and hoots. Once on stage he pulled a flute out of his pants, attached to a rubber hose that led behind his shirt and up to his mouth. He held his instrument erect and played a countermelody, dancing along suggestively.

> He's a sex machine! Go on! Keep it going!
> He's a sex machine! Go on! Keep it going!
> He's a sex machine! Go on! Keep it going!
> He's a sex machine! Go on! Keep it going!
> Pretty is he, stylish is he, pretty is he as he dances!
> Pretty is he, stylish is he, especially when he chances![31]

Here Månsson's props again bridged old and new, his helmet ostensibly representing the pre-historic, his trench coat the contemporary. His penis flute parodied ancient fertility symbols; the rubber hose that allowed him to play it a modern innovation. The sex god/sex machine Månsson played was also binary in this sense; ancient god, modern machine, the time between bridged by a timeless institution.[32]

To my mind Raun exemplified negotiations along the various axes of folk music so well precisely because the conflicts inherent to them supplied the kinetic force behind their performance aesthetic, as both music and theater, satire and sincerity. They did not apologize for playing a music that did not belong to the modern city, but rather claimed it as their own. Or as Magnus Ek put it in the liner notes to their first album:

> Raun is like an age-old Nordic folk musician who has always believed he could only live in the country. Suddenly, he finds himself in the city and to his great surprise he is enchanted by the urban pulse . . . and there is a swing about him wherever he goes.[33]

Here was where Ek could offer his best definition of Swedish folk music. The discursive arena of "stage show" allowed him far greater flexibility in engaging with the concept than he was afforded in that of "ethnographic interview." Not expected in the performance context to answer questions clearly and unambiguously, here he had no need to chase the folk music concept back and forth along its various axes. The group's props and jokes, even their instruments superimposed the urban on the rural, the new over the old. This simultaneity was not only made possible by, it was a guiding principle behind their humor and their music.

Conclusion

In organizing this book my intention was to construct a narrative flow from a set of neatly organized theoretical ideas into a far messier reality. I began by outlining and then artificially isolating the four constituent strands I identified within the Swedish folk music concept, and followed by allowing them to merge, intertwine, and finally jumble in the final pages. Raun's chaotic performance of the concept at Bommens Salonger was for me, as soon as I saw it, the validation of my theories and the obvious conclusion to the work.

Yet Raun's concert was exceptional in the extent to which it went to expose folk music's conceptual innards. Like the performance by National's youth section and my interviews with Joar Skorpen, "Sax" Mats Nilsson, and Magnus Ek, I selected it for analysis not on the basis of its being average or representative, but because it told what I thought was the relevant story. The "average" performance or interview would have kept these issues below the surface. Most would allow the music and dance, the meetings they create, and the spaces they inhabit to form the core essence of the concept.

This leads me to what I found to be the most surprising result of my feedback analysis, though in retrospect it was highly predictable. I sent a late draft of this work to a number of mostly Swedish readers, with the instructions that "[i]f you find spelling errors or factual mistakes, I am very happy to get corrections. But mostly I am interested in your ideas about my ideas, whether you agree or not." My supposition was that my topic and theoretical frame, drawn and expanded as they were from some of the most common conversations among Swedish scholars and practitioners of folk music, would generate a continuation of those discussions. As it turned out, the few comments I received on my broader theoretical ideas were simple nods of approval. Those comments that did not address factual or spelling errors were instead generally dedicated to some phenomenon or event that a reader felt I had missed; the second great Ransäter debate for example, or the Polska Dancer sphere, or Skeppsholms-gården, the Folk Music Café's analogue in Stockholm.[34]

The general lack of comment on my overall frame, save for the odd head-nod, is in one sense a sign that my analysis has been valid. But it may also mean that it seems less relevant than my discussions of the actual contexts in which negotiations over the folk music concept take place. Reader suggestions that I include discussions of elements like Skeppsholmsgården have been made not with the goal of benefiting my argument, but rather that they might complete the image I have drawn of the subculture. What some of my readers find lacking here, I think, is a confirmation of all the essential contexts in which folk music happens. The reason I miss some of these is that, naturally, those contexts are not consistent across the entire pathway of Swedish folk music. People in Stockholm will prioritize them differently from people in Gothenburg, as will players as opposed to singers as opposed to folk dancers as opposed to Polska Dancers, and so forth. .

Because of this inevitable variation, and because my stated purpose was never a complete picture of folk music Sweden, I can justify leaving out or de-prioritizing some of the phenomena my readers may deem important. Or at least, I can do so as long as I believe I have been trying to answer the right question. Here is the more troubling issue brought up by my readers' comments (or absence thereof): Have I been too eager to allow my consultants to shape my discussion with their utterances, and missed what was not being said? Have I, after all this, asked the wrong question?

I ask this not as a rhetorical exercise, but sincerely as a result of an unexpected set of reader responses, and I believe the answer to be not uncomplicated. In my favor, I do believe that I have answered a question that was clearly being posed by Swedish scholars of folk music. Not only that, but I believe my contribution to the ethnographic tradition to be significant, in that my mapping of disagreement over a unified conceptual field represents a model for ethnographic analysis that does much to solve the old dilemma of how to describe broad cultural concepts without camouflaging the persistence of individual ideas and differences.

Yet for the people I have studied, all this may matter less than the acknowledgment this work can offer to the sociomusical contexts that make them who they are. Where the materials I collected in the field became, for me, evidence to prove a point, from the perspective of my Swedish readers, the point had never been anything other than the "evidence" itself. The frame is all well and good, but more significant is the content that holds it up. And though the presentation of this content was never my primary goal, my sense is that I have inadvertently succeeded in it nevertheless. The "missing" elements of which some of my readers complain are, after all, relatively few, and I have gone back and addressed them all in one way or another.

So, I stand by the question I have asked, and the answer I have given. My final admission that my theoretical framework may be secondary to its content might, I admit, provide a somewhat unsatisfying conclusion. Yet it is an honest one, and perhaps befitting a book regarding a question whose very defining characteristic is its unresolvability.

Notes

1. Milton Singer, *When a Great Tradition Modernizes: An Anthropological Approach to Indian Civilization* (Chicago: University of Chicago Press, 1972), 71.

2. See, for instance, the quotation by Greger Siljebo on pages 81–82.

3. For a discussion of the process by which Selinder's choreographies entered the folk dance movement, see page 76; or, for more detail, Göran Andersson's "Anders Selinder: Nationalromantikens företrädare inom svensk dans," in *Norden i dans: Folk—Fag—Forskning*, ed. Egil Bakka and Gunnel Biskop (Oslo: Novus, 2007), 206–214; "Philochoros—Grunden till den svenska folkdansörelsen," in *Norden i dans: Folk—Fag—Forskning*, ed. Egil Bakka and Gunnel Biskop (Oslo: Novus, 2007), 309–318.

4. The walking tune Gärdebylåten, as recorded by Rättvik's spelman group, became a nationwide hit in the late 1940s; see Jan Ling and Märta Ramsten, "The Gärdeby Folk Melody—A Musical Migrant," in *Analytica: Studies in the Description and Analysis of Music*, ed. Anders Lönn and Erik Kjellberg (Stockholm: Almqvist & Wiksell, 1985), 301–321.

5. Jan Johansson was only the best-known of several Swedish jazz artists who experimented with folk fusion in the 1960s. For more on the other artists involved, see Toivo Burlin's "Skyskrapornas och de röda stugornas musik: Ett försök till förståelse av fusionen av jazz och svensk folkmusik," *STM Online* 3 (2000).

6. cf. Mark Slobin, *Subcultural Sounds: Micromusics of the West* (Hanover: Wesleyan University Press, 1993), 11.

7. I have not seen National's youth section rehearse or perform modern dance. According to Emma Rydberg they have been doing it less and less over the years (personal correspondence with the author, July 19, 2005). I have, however, seen a performance including elements of swing, line dancing, cancan, hip hop, halling, and engelska by the Sveg youth dancers from Härjedalen, performed to the music of Hoven Droven at Urkult in 2004. One example of a folk dance group that dances "modern" dances socially is Göteborgs Folkdansvänner, at their annual midsummer retreat.

8. Specifically: engelska från Ytterby, slängpolska från Valle, polska från övre Klarälvsdalen, polska från Skepplanda, and mixed schottisches.

9. Magnus Ewaldz later gave me a typewritten program of the dance used as a memory aid by the group. At the point in the program marked "Selinder" a handwritten note adds: "klädbyte" (costume change), and by it the letters "K" and "D," for *Kavaljerer* (Gentlemen) and *Damer* (Ladies). By the K the note says "väst på" (vest on), while D is left blank. The inclusion of the D suggests to me an initial idea of having both boys and girls dress up to symbolize their transformation into Selinder's dance troupe, the blank space reflecting the impracticality of losing any piece of the female costume for the first half of the program.

10. The dances were: daldans (shortened), väva vadmal, övals på linje, and långdans från Närke. Only the first was actually choreographed by Selinder himself; Magnus Ewaldz noted to me after the performance that they had taken that liberty self-consciously. In fact, when the group was short on men, they actually changed the character of Selinder to Lotten Åström, one of Selinder's female dancers who also became a dedicated collector, choreographer and teacher, and who had some affiliation with National.

11. Bingsjö, Boda, and Klarälvsdalen.

12. Magnus Ewaldz also made some of these distinctions verbally explicit in the group's May 31 rehearsal preceding the national day performance. He directed the open-

ing greeting scene as the beginning of a typical social dance at a village crossroads. For the daldans he coached the dancers to look more "professional" than in the village dances.

13. See this volume, pages 76-77.

14. e.g., Mats Nilsson, *Dans—Kontinuitet i förändring* (Gothenburg: Etnologiska Föreningen, 1998).

15. The closest I have seen to a challenge to the exclusion of "folk dance group" from *folklig dans* is the question asked by the title to Gunnel Biskop's book: *Folkdans inom folkdansrörelsen—Folklig dans?* [Folk Dance within the Folk Dance Movement— *Folklig Dans?*] (Åbo: Folkloristiska institutionen vid Åbo akademi, 1990). When the book is opened, however, her answer is revealed to be "no" (31).

16. "Dans" Mats Nilsson has commented, upon reading this: "Your reasoning about why I don't include staged forms of folk dance within '*folklig dans*' is nothing to argue with. And you can also extend the reasoning and the thought further. An extreme viewpoint I take is that it's not really *folklig dans* at all when the dances are formalized within the educational system, as they are for example in Tobo. And when the students at the School of Dance in Stockholm express themselves, they talk about '*folklig dans* on stage,' that's just the same as *folkdans* to me" ("Dans" Mats Nilsson, personal communication with the author, July 7, 2005).

17. Helena Ek, interview by author, April 2, 2002.

18. Göran Månsson, fieldnotes by author, March 17, 2002.

19. Harald Pettersson told me several years later that he and Göran Månsson were planning to expand on this idea, to put on dance band outfits and play dance band classics arranged for recorder and hurdy-gurdy. The projected project title was "Popular Tunes for Unpopular Instruments" (personal conversation, July 3, 2004). The song "Hallå du gamle indian" (also sung in English as "Hello You Old Red Indian") is best known today as a dance band classic from the seventies, though in fact it had first been a big band hit in 1941.

20. Harald Pettersson joined the group after the release of their first album.

21. Dan Lundberg, Krister Malm, and Owe Ronström. *Musik—Medier—Mångkultur: Förändringar i svenska musiklandskap* (Hedemora: Gidlunds, 2000), 150–153. Lundberg, Ronström, and Malm divide what they call "Swedish world music" into two categories: "drone rock" and "chamber folk music" (150–153).

22. This gendered sonic distinction between male instrumentalists and female vocalists tends to be preserved in drone rock even when the men start singing. When Harald Pettersson performs a solo song his voice is raw and gravelly; so too with the men of Hedningarna, Den Fule, and Nordman.

23. Göran Månsson, interview by author, July 25, 2003.

24. See Magnus Gustafsson, "'Därnest spelmännarne med violer, säckpipa, hautbois och trumma...' Något om en folklig trumtradition i Värend," *Noterat* 8 (2000): 5–20.

25. Magnus Ek, interview by author, April 2, 2002.

26. Tricia Rose, *Black Noise: Rap Music and Black Culture in Contemporary America* (Hanover: University Press of New England, 1994), 79.

27. Raun, *Dance Jon*, 2003, Drone DROCD036, compact disc.

28. Hedningarna, *Hippjokk*, 1997, Northside NSD6003, compact disc.

29. Ek did, however, leave a significant disjuncture between the signifier and signified. Niklas Larsson is announced but his music is absent; instead the only other sample we hear is Martin Martinsson's vocable lick. Both samples were taken from the same

collection, *Music Sveciae: Folk Music in Sweden 20: Visor & låtar från Bohuslän*, 1997, Caprice CAP 21543, compact disc (tracks 17 and 40).

30. Magnus Ek, field recording by author, March 17, 2002.

31. Magnus Ek and Harald Pettersson, field recording by author, March 17, 2002.

32. Sex.

33. Magnus Ek, "Raun," liner notes from Raun, *Raun*, 2000, Prophone PCD 056, compact disc, ellipsis in original.

34. Another common comment regarded my interview quotations, which several readers felt I had not cleaned up enough. I have since re-edited them.

POSTSCRIPT

—*∿*—

Return of the Nationalist Right

An issue that informs this book throughout, sometimes overtly and at other times covertly, is that of the relationship of folk music to nationalist politics. I am sure that for many of my consultants, the troubles they have had defining the term have stemmed at least in part from the difficulty of reconciling their own leftist or center-left political beliefs with their love of a genre that was originally formed to serve the agenda of conservative nationalism. At the very least I can say that I find myself in that position.

My revisions were nearly complete when this issue came to a head with the 2010 election of the Sweden Democrats to parliament with 5.7 percent of the national vote. An extreme-right anti-immigrant party with roots in the neo-Nazi movement, the Sweden Democrats have called for an end to all federal funding for multicultural programming in favor of a reinvestment in Swedish folklore and music.[1] As a result, several folk music organizations have written position statements condemning the Sweden Democrats, public debates have been held between prominent folk musicians and members of that party, and demonstrations have been held around the country by a new group calling itself "Folk Musicians against Xenophobia."[2] Battle lines have been drawn.

In the final words to his chapter on folk music and ideology in *Folkmusikboken*, Jan Ling wrote: "*Folk music will be colored by differing ideologies as long as it is a living reality and not a museum object. It will serve progressive or reactionary movements. All you have to do is help yourself to it!*"[3] I am not sure, however, that folk music is quite so politically plastic as Ling suggests here. While it is certainly the case that both the left and the right have made use of it at various points in history, my sense is that in a moment like this, when both lay claim to the concept, its essential ingredients combine to favor the conservative over the progressive. The trifecta of Folk, Nation, and Tradition defines a group of people whose identity stems from their common heritage and historical association with a specific body of land. The folk are further rooted to the earth by the fourth, Natural element; their value predicated on their constancy and identity with that place. Emigration, immigration, urbanization, industrialization, modernization, mass-communication, and globalization are all threats to that identity. As long as those four elements remain fundamental to the concept—which I believe they do, even today—folk music will be best suited to the ideological needs of the xenophobic and reactionary.

On the other hand, there seems to be fairly little correlation of interest in traditional folk music to anti-immigrant sentiment in Sweden. The Swedish folk music community has multiple constituencies, most of which in my view either either to skew to the left or conform to the general political demographic. In my years of fieldwork in Sweden, I can think of very few openly xenophobic statements made by folk music insiders, compared to a great many more in Swedish society at large.

Nor, for that matter, is there evidence that a nation with a more forward-looking view of folk music would be more open to immigration. In her book *Ilmatar's Inspirations*, Tina Ramnarine describes a Finnish "new folk" revival that seems unconcerned with limiting itself according to the conventions of a distant past, and welcomes international influence far more unequivocally than (what I have experienced of) its Swedish counterpart.[4] Yet at the same time, Finland has limited immigration to a much greater extent than Sweden. The Sweden Democrats' 5.7 percent in 2010 pales in comparison to the anti-immigrant True Finns' 19.1 percent in the 2011 Finnish national election. This at a time when Finland's foreign-born population stands at under three percent, the lowest in the EU, compared to Sweden's fifteen percent.[5] In other words, folk music's ideological baggage may simply not weigh significantly on the scale of national politics, on either side of the equation.

The folk community's public denouncement of the Sweden Democrats may thus be enough to distance folk music from anti-immigrant rhetoric in the public imagination, despite the conformity of that rhetoric to the logic of the concept. The Sweden Democrats do not seem to have a lot of folk musicians, or even people who actually like folk music, in their camp.[6] And the same factors that have kept the Swedish populace from folk music in the first place—its presumed association with the politically reactionary, combined with its musical inaccessibility—may also operate to alienate that populace further from the Sweden Democrats.

Nevertheless, for those who dedicate their lives to folk music, and who experience within it a great emotional affect, and yet who oppose xenophobic public policy, the Sweden Democrats' talking points must raise uncomfortable questions. What exactly is it that people find so compelling about folk music? Is there nothing to the natural beauty of its unmediated face-to-faceness, the immortality of its connection to the past, the comfort of its connection to a like-minded community unalienated by modern technologies? Can it really be said that this nineteenth-century romance does not resonate at all in the twenty-first century? And if it does resonate, doesn't that mean that what people in the folk music community value, on some level, is an underpopulated, conservative, insular society? Is that what I value in this?

The implicit ideals of the Swedish folk music concept as I have described them here stand very much at odds with my own political leanings. I see tensions in human life between rootedness and migration, communities and individuals, cultural specifics and human universals, but would not privilege one side over the other arbitrarily. Moreover, I believe that the Herderian view that grants intrinsic value to the rooted traditional community is fundamental not only to the narrative of extreme nationalism, but also to its logical conclusion in genocide and ethnic cleansing. I understand no ethical justification for forcibly preventing someone from crossing an imaginary line simply because of where or to whom they were born, or to deny them equal rights for crossing it. This puts me so far on the other side of the fence from political nationalism as to place me in opposition to the immigration laws of every country in the world.

But I would be lying if I were to claim that the Herderian narrative does not resonate with me on a visceral level. The localized communal event of music-making and dance that lies at the center of folk music Sweden appeals to me like nothing else. It is a place where I am valued, as a musician, dancer, and friend. That world binds me to my childhood years in Umeå, oversaturated memories of the forest near our house and Jan Johansson on my father's tape player. This is my fantasy of Sweden, and not altogether different from the one upon which the Sweden Democrats have based their nostalgic political campaign.

So when a journalist or reporter at a folk music gathering starts asking me the same questions to which I have subjected my consultants, I suffer from the same conflicts. What does folk music mean to me? I have learned to warn them that my answer will be useless, confused and clinical. Even after asking scores of people that same question, writing this book, then revising it, I am still sorting it out for myself. It comes down to the question of how we can reconcile the beauty of Herder's vision with its consequences. All I can say is that this dilemma will be at the center of my work for years to come, as an ethnomusicologist, as a scholar, and as a teacher.

Notes

1. Sverigedemokraterna, *En återupprättad välfärd: Sverigedemokraternas skuggbudget våren 2010* (Sverigedemokraterna, 2010), 58, http://sdu.nu/Skuggbudget_2010.pdf (accessed August 20, 2011). For information on the party's neo-Nazi roots, see, e.g., Stieg Larsson and Mikael Ekman, *Sverigedemokraterna: Den nationella rörelsen* (Stockholm: Ordfront, 2001).

2. For a detailed analysis of these protests, proclamations, and debates, see my own "Keeping Sweden Swedish: Folk Music, Right-Wing Nationalism, and the Immigration Debate," as yet unpublished.

3. "'Upp, bröder, kring bildningens fana': Om folkmusikens historia och ideologi," in *Folkmusikboken*, ed. Jan Ling, Gunnar Ternhag, and Märta Ramsten (Stockholm: Prisma, 1980), 42, italics in original.

4. Tina Ramnarine, *Ilmatar's Inspirations: Nationalism, Globalization, and the Changing Soundscapes of Finnish Folk Music* (Chicago: University of Chicago Press, 2003), 50–51, 173–220.

5. For information on the Finnish foreign-born population, see "Background note: Finland" (US Department of State, 2010), http://www.state.gov/r/pa/ei/bgn/3238.htm (accessed August 20, 2011). For the Swedish foreign-born population, see "Befolkning efter bakgrund" (Statistiska centralbyrån, 2010), http://www.scb.se/Statistik/BE/BE0101/2010-A01b/Utrikes_fodda_och_utlandsk_bakgrund.pdf (accessed August 20, 2011).

6. See, e.g., Pontus Mattsson, *Sverigedemokraterna in på bara skinnet: Reportage* (Stockholm: Natur & kultur, 2009), 146–147.

APPENDIX A

—〜〜—

List of Interviews

NAME	DATE
Ditte Andersson	May 10, 2007
Håkan Bengtsson	June 25, 2002
Göran Berg	July 18, 2003
Ulla & Anders Bergsten	May 22, 2002
Alf Bergstrand	May 21, 2002
Anders Dahlgren	February 21, 2002
Ida Heinö Djunovic	February 7, 2002
Olle Edström	March 27, 2002
Helena Ek	April 2, 2002
Magnus Ek	April 2, 2002
Karin Eriksson	January 5, 2002
Martin Hillbratt	December 4, 2001
Johan Hogenäs	February 4, 2002
Lilian Håkansson	October 26, 2001
Gunnel Johansson	July 24, 2002
Pers Nils Johansson	January 3, 2002
Hans Kennemark	January 8, 2002
Ulf Kinding	January 23, 2002
Joanna Kober	April 29, 2002
Sten Källman	January 9, 2002
Kjell Leidhammar	January 12, 2002
Urban Lind	June 27, 2002
Jan Ling	May 23, 2002
Karl Malbert	December 11, 2001

Svante Mannervik	June 25, 2003
Lennart Mellgren	August 4, 2002
Göran Månsson	July 25, 2003
"Dans" Mats Nilsson	December 7, 2001
"Sax" Mats Nilsson	January 9, 2002
	July 15, 2003
Vivi Nilsson	October 30, 2001
Rose-Marie Landén Nord	
(with Ulf Henningson & Rolf Persson)	May 28, 2002
Annika Nordström	July 1, 2002
Ida Norrlöf	May 10, 2002
Gunilla Ohlsson	February 27, 2002
Dan Olsson	April 12, 2002
	May 20, 2002
Kajsa Paulsson	December 18, 2001
Harald Pettersson	July 3, 2004
Göran Premberg	May 16, 2002
Emma Rydberg	March 13, 2002
Inger Rydberg	April 4, 2002
Per Sandberg	December 28, 2001
Greger Siljebo	December 3, 2001
Jonas Simonson	June 13, 2002
Joar Skorpen	November 18, 2001
Åsa Grogarn Sol	September 28, 2001
	October 5, 2001
	December 25, 2001
Ingvar Strömblad	June 24, 2002
Sara Uneback	April 5, 2002
Anders Waernelius	January 18, 2002
Bernt Wennberg	April 11, 2002
Annelie Westerlund	April 26, 2002
Lotta Vesterlund	January 3, 2002
Margareta Lundquister Wignall	November 23, 2001
Hanna Wiskari	December 28, 2001

APPENDIX B

—*~~*—

Glossary of Terms

Allégården. Senior citizen's social center in Gothenburg. Current venue for the Together Group on Friday evenings, the Folk Music Café on Friday nights, and the folk dance group Näverluren on Thursday evenings.

Bingolotto. Popular Swedish Saturday night television program, combining features of a variety show, game show, and lottery drawing. Often cited by Swedes within and outside of folk music circles as an example of modern *folklighet*.

Bingsjö. Small hamlet in Rättvik parish, eastern Dalarna, near the Hälsingland border. Home to iconic fiddler Hjort Anders Olsson (1865–1952), and location of Dalarna's largest annual spelman gathering. The hamlet is also associated with a specific polska music and dance style, even in meter (beat two is equidistant between beats one and three, and receives similar emphasis) and movement (couples rotate at a constant rate, with no up-and-down motion).

Concerts Sweden (*Rikskonserter*). State foundation for the promotion of musical life in Sweden, founded in 1963, dismantled as of 2011.

engelska (pl. engelskor). Lit. "English." Group dance and music form identified with Swedish coastal areas of the west and south, descended from music and dance of Britain and Ireland.

Falun Folk Festival. Folk and world music festival founded in 1986, once Sweden's largest, defunct as of 2004.

folk dance group (*folkdanslag*). The first of these in Sweden was Philochoros, founded in 1880 in Uppsala. Traditional repertoire is made up of group dances, mostly compositions designed specifically for the stage. Some social couple dances (village dances, gammeldanser, and choreographed forms called gillesdanser) have also entered the repertoire in the past thirty years or so.

folklig dans. A term invented by Ernst Klein to distinguish old village dances (*folklig dans*) from staged folk dances (*folkdans*).

gammeldans. "Old Time Dance." Name given to popular dances of the nineteenth century (waltz, polka, schottische, snoa, hambo, mazurka) in the wake of their general displacement by newly-imported African-American dance forms in the 1920s and 30s.

hambo. Gammeldans form. The dance most closely resembles the polska from the Dala village of Boda, combined with a regularly recurring promenade and kick step.

hembygd. *Hem* means "home." *Bygd* means, approximately, "rural settled area." *Hembygd* is not generally used to describe a literal home area, however, but rather as a near-synonym for *bygd*. My sense is that the addition of the *hem*-prefix functions to imply a historical cultural connection of modern Swedes to a distant rural past. The term *hembygd* thus operates as a powerful chronotope for pre-industrial peasant folklife.

kappleik (pl. *kappleikar*). Norwegian folk music performance contest. The subject of Chris Goertzen's *Fiddling for Norway*.

Korrö. Historically preserved hamlet in Småland, southern Sweden. Location of Sweden's largest folk music festival, founded in 1985.

Lekarlaget. Approx. "the spelman group" ("lekare" being an older word for "spelman"). Student-run Swedish folk music ensemble at the Gothenburg School of Music, 1994–2000. Founded by Joar Skorpen and Henrik Silverhjelm.

Mellgrens blandning. "Mellgren's Mixture." Gothenburg Polska Dance group specializing in polskor from multiple provinces, led by fiddler Lennart Mellgren.

National. "National." Gothenburg's largest folk dance group, founded in 1916.

nyckelharpa (pl. nyckelharpor). Lit. "key harp." Keyed fiddle, sometimes also translated as "bowed hurdy-gurdy." Sweden's unofficial national instrument.

Näverluren. "The Birch Bark Horn." Gothenburg folk dance group founded by Vivi Nilsson in 1965.

Philochoros. "Love of the Dance." Sweden's first folk dance group, founded in 1880 in Uppsala.

polska. "Polish" (i.e., from Poland). Swedish folk music and dance form, almost always in triple meter, with multiple regional variations.

Ransäter. Hamlet in Värmland, home to Sweden's largest spelman gathering.

riksspelman (pl. riksspelmän). "National spelman." (See entry under "Riksspelman gathering" for curious etymology.) A musician who has been awarded the silver or gold badge by the Zorn jury, established in 1933 by the Youth Ring. The Zorn jury holds trials each year in a different location, usually hosted by a local spelman organization. The silver badge is the highest mark attainable for those who play before the jury. The gold badge is a merit award decided by the jury in advance, usually awarded to a musician who has already attained the silver badge.

riksspelman gathering. 1. "National gathering of spelmän" (*riks/spelmansstämma*). Event at Skansen in 1910 to which a number of spelmän from all around Sweden were invited to perform. Anders Zorn created a silver medal for the occasion, which was distributed to all participating spelmän. 2. "Riksspelman gathering" (*riksspelmans/stämma*). Annual event initiated by the Youth Ring in 1933, marking the culmination of the week's Zorn trials, for which musicians audition to become "riksspelmän."

Skansen. Large outdoor museum of Swedish folklife in Stockholm, founded by Arthur Hazelius in 1891.

Skeppis. Skeppsholmsgården, the location of Stockholm's regular Sunday-evening folk music and dance nights.

snoa. Gammeldans in duple meter, in which couples spin together 360° every two beats. Often danced to marches and walking tunes.

spelman (pl. spelmän). Lit. "play man." A term applied primarily to folk musicians, regardless of gender. Generally implies strong connection to a musical tradition as well as amateur status, someone who plays for the joy of playing. Sometimes contrasted with the term "folk musician" (*folkmusiker*), coined by Ale Möller in the early 1980s to refer to professional musicians who played in folk music bands, often with backgrounds in other musical genres. Due to the predominance of fiddle in Swedish folk music, the term "spelman" is often translated as "fiddler."

spelman gathering (*spelmansstämma*). An annual event at which spelmän gather and play. Often at these events spelmän enter free, while others pay a minimal entrance fee. Smaller spelman gatherings might be attended only by members of a single spelman group and their friends, while the larger gatherings regularly boast attendance in the thousands. The first Swedish spelman gathering was held in 1910 in Stockholm (see entry under riksspelman gathering).

spelman group (*spelmanslag*). An organization of spelmän, usually dominated by fiddlers, who play folk music together. The first of these was The Dala Association's spelman group (*Dalaföreningens spelmanslag*), formed in Stockholm in 1940. Music played by these groups is usually characterized by simple arrangements, with most members playing the melody, and some smaller subset playing a pre-determined harmony part. Common instruments beyond the fiddle include chromatic nyckelharpa, clarinet, flute, recorder, guitar, bass, and accordion. Spelman groups usually center their repertoire around the music of their home area. These are by and large amateur organizations; money from performances generally goes to fund the group and its activities.

spelman organization (*spelmansförbund*). A broad umbrella folk musicians' association, usually associated with one of Sweden's twenty-five provinces.

The first of these, Södermanland's spelman organization, was established in 1925. Sweden's fifteen spelman organizations are today organized as chapters of SSR. The various spelman organizations are often involved in hosting spelman gatherings and organizing youth programming for young musicians.

Spelmannen. Quarterly journal of SSR, the National Organization of Swedish Spelmän.

SSR (*Sveriges Spelmäns Riksförbund*). "The National Organization of Swedish Spelmän." Founded in 1947 under the name *Sveriges Spelmäns Riksstyrelse* ("The National Council for Swedish Spelmän"), present name adopted 1951. Publishes the journal *Spelmannen.*

Svenska låtar. "Swedish Tunes." Twenty-four-volume collection including 7,910 tunes from all but five of Sweden's provinces (Lappland, Norrbotten, Västerbotten, Ångermanland, and Gotland are excepted). Published 1922–1940, reprinted by Svenskt Visarkiv in 1978 and 2001. Standard reference for Swedish folk melodies.

Swedish Folk Music and Dance Association (Riksförbundet för Folkmusik och Dans, RFoD). Organization founded in 1981 as a broader alternative to SSR, serving dancers as well as musicians, professionals as well as amateurs, and international as well as Swedish genres. Publishes the journal *Folkmusik och dans.*

Sämus. *Särskild Ämnesutbildning i Musik* (Special Subject Training in Music), abbrev. Experimental teacher training program formed in 1971 under the direction of Jan Ling at Gothenburg University. Ceased to exist as independent entity in 1975, when integrated into School of Music.

Urkult. "Ur-Cult." World music festival in Näsåker, Ångermanland, founded in 1994.

The Youth Ring (*Ungdomsringen*). The Swedish Youth Ring for Village Culture (*Svenska Ungdomsringen för Bygdekultur*). National Swedish folk dancers' umbrella organization, within which most Swedish folk dance groups are member organizations. Generally dedicated to preservation and presentation of traditional folk arts, including dance, music, costumes, and crafts. Founded in 1920 under the name "The Swedish Folk Dance Ring" (*Svenska Folkdansringen*), the organization changed its name to "The Youth Ring" in 1922, then back to "The Folk Dance Ring" in 2005. They publish the journal *Hembygden*.

Bibliography

Adorno, Theodore. "On Popular Music." *Studies in Philosophy and Social Science* 9 (1941): 17–48.

Allmo, Per-Ulf. *Säckpipan i Norden* [The Bagpipe in the Nordic Countries]. Stockholm: Allwin, 1990.

Allmo, Per-Ulf, and Jan Winter. *Lirans hemligheter: En studie i nordisk instrumenthistoria* [The Hurdy-Gurdy in the Nordic Countries]. Stockholm: Ordfront, 1985.

Alsmark, Gunnar. "Folktraditionens roll vid utformandet av nationell och regional identitet" [The Role of Folk Tradition in the Creation of National and Regional Identity]. In *Folktradition och regional identitet i Norden*, edited by Aili Nenola-Kallio, 25–39. Åbo: Nordiska institutet för folkdiktning, 1982.

Andersson, Greger. "Stad och Landsbygd" [City and Country]. In *Musiken i Sverige I: Från Forntid till Stormaktstidens Slut*, edited by Bengt R. Jonsson, Ann-Marie Nilsson, and Greger Andersson, 359–395. Stockholm: Fischer & Co, 1994.

———. "Städerna som musikmiljöer" [The Cities as Musical Milieus]. In *Musiken i Sverige II: Frihetstid och Gustaviansk tid 1720–1810*, edited by Bengt R. Jonsson and Anna Ivarsdotter-Johnson, 143–168. Stockholm: Fischer & Co, 1993.

Andersson, Göran. "Anders Selinder: Nationalromantikens företrädare inom svensk dans" [Anders Selinder: The Agent of National Romanticism within Swedish Dance]. In *Norden i dans: Folk—Fag—Forskning*, edited by Egil Bakka and Gunnel Biskop, 206–214. Oslo: Novus, 2007.

———. "Philochoros—Grunden till den svenska folkdansörelsen" [Philochoros—Foundation of the Swedish Folk Dance Movement]. In *Norden i dans: Folk—Fag—Forskning*, edited by Egil Bakka and Gunnel Biskop, 309–318. Oslo: Novus, 2007.

Arcadius, Kerstin. *Museum på svenska: Länsmuseerna och kulturhistorien* [Museum in Swedish: The County Museums and Cultural History]. Stockholm: Nordiska museets förlag, 1997.

Baehrendtz, Nils Erik. "Artur Hazelius och Skansen" [Arthur Hazelius and Skansen]. In *Boken om Skansen*, edited by Nils Erik Baehrendtz, 12–13. Höganäs: Bra Böcker, 1980.

Bakhtin, Mikhail Mikhailovich. "Discourse in the Novel." In *The Dialogic Imagination*, 259–422. Translated by Caryl Emerson and Michael Holquist. Austin: University of Texas Press, 1981. Original publication, 1934–1935.

———. "Forms of Time and the Chronotope in the Novel: Notes toward a Historical Poetics (X. Concluding Remarks)." In *The Dialogic Imagination*, 243–258. Translated by Caryl Emerson and Michael Holquist. Austin: University of Texas Press, 1981. Original publication, 1973.

Beaudry, Nicole. "The Challenges of Human Relations in Ethnographic Enquiry." In *Shadows in the Field: New Perspectives for Fieldwork in Ethnomusicology*, edited by Timothy Cooley and Gregory Barz, 63–83. New York: Oxford University Press, 1997.

Berg, Jonas. "Folkmusikens första början på Skansen och Skansens ordinarie spelmän 1891–1930" [The Beginnings of Folk Music at Skansen and Skansen's Regular Spelmän 1891–1930]. *Noterat* 6 (1998): 5–18.

Berglund, Håkan. "Piglocka: Dragspelets införande och anpassning" [Squeezebox: The Introduction and Adaptation of the Accordion]. *Sumlen*, 1987: 39–70.

Biörnstad, Arne. "Flytta hus" [Moving Houses]. In *Boken om Skansen*, edited by Nils Erik Baehrendtz, 118–119. Höganäs: Bra Böcker, 1980.

———. "Svenska flaggans dag" [Swedish Flag Day]. In *Boken om Skansen*, edited by Nils Erik Baehrendtz, 96–97. Höganäs: Bra Böcker, 1980.

Biskop, Gunnel. *Folkdans inom folkdansrörelsen—Folklig dans?* [Folk Dance Within the Folk Dance Movement—Folklig Dance?] Åbo: Folkloristiska institutionen vid Åbo akademi, 1990.

Blom, Jan-Petter, and Tellef Kvifte. "On the Problem of Inferential Ambivalence in Musical Meter." *Ethnomusicology* 30, no. 3 (1986): 491–517.

Bohlman, Philip. *The Study of Folk Music in the Modern World*. Bloomington: Indiana University Press, 1988.

Bohman, Stefan. "Folkmusiken" [Folk Music]. In *Boken om Skansen*, edited by Nils Erik Baehrendtz, 148–149. Höganäs: Bra Böcker, 1980.

———. "Folkmusiken på Skansen" [Folk-Music at Skansen]. *Fataburen*, 1979: 35–68.

Bohman, Stefan, and Lars Faragó. "Nationalinstrument—Splittrar mer än förenar" [National Instruments—Divide More than Unite]. *Svenska Dagbladet*, March 17, 2002.

Boström, Mathias, Dan Lundberg, and Märta Ramsten. "Förord" [Preface]. In *Det stora uppdraget: Perspektiv på Folkmusikkommissionen i Sverige 1908–2008*, edited by Mathias Boström, Dan Lundberg, and Märta Ramsten, 7–8. Stockholm: Nordiska museets förlag, 2010.

Bringéus, Nils-Arvid. *Människan som kulturvarelse* [The Human as Cultural Being]. Lund: LiberLäromedel, 1981.

Burke, Peter. "Popular Culture between History and Ethnology." *Ethnologia Europaea* 14 (1984): 5–13.

Burlin, Toivo. "Skyskrapornas och de röda stugornas musik: Ett försök till förståelse av fusionen av jazz och svensk folkmusik" [Music of the Skyscrapers and Red Cottages: An Attempt at Understanding the Fusion of Jazz and Swedish Folk Music]. *STM Online* 3 (2000). http://musikforskning.se/stmonline/vol_3/burlin.

Carter, Angela. *Wise Children*. London: Chatto & Windus, 1991.

Clarke, Simon, and Steve Garner, *White Identities: A Critical Sociological Approach*. New York: PlutoPress, 2010.

Dybeck, Richard. *Svenska vallvisor och hornlåtar* [*Swedish pastoral songs and horn tunes*]. Stockholm: Bok och bild, 1974. Original edition, 1846.

Edström, Olle. *Schlager i Sverige 1910–1940* [Schlager in Sweden 1910–1940]. Gothenburg: Novum Grafiska, 1989.

Ehn, Billy, Jonas Frykman, and Orvar Löfgren. *Försvenskningen av Sverige: Det nationellas förvandlingar* [Making Sweden Swedish: Transformations of the National]. Stockholm: Natur och Kultur, 1993.

Ek, Magnus. "Raun." Liner notes from Raun, *Raun*, Prophone PCD 056, 2000, compact disc.

Elbourne, Roger. "The Question of Definition." *Yearbook of the International Folk Music Council* 7 (1976): 9–29.

Emsheimer, Ernst. "Tollabössa och videpipa: Två traditionella folkliga ljudverktyg hos barn" [Popgun and Willow Whistle: Two Children's Sound Producing Implements in the Swedish Folk Tradition]. *Sumlen*, 1984: 9–23.

Engström, Bengt Olof. "Gunnar Hahn och hans musik" [Gunnar Hahn and His Music]. Liner notes from Gunnar Hahn, *Svenska låtar på mitt sätt*, Lady-Bird Productions LBCD 0023, 1997 [1959, 1960, 1962–1965, 1967, 1974, 1983], compact disc.

Enqvist, Bengt. "Vart spel har sin plats" [Every Instrument Has Its Place]. *Spelmannen*, 2001, no. 2: 12.

Eriksson, Karin. *Bland polskor, gånglåtar och valser: Hallands spelmansförbund och den halländska folkmusiken* [Among Polskor, Walking Tunes, and Waltzes: Halland's Spelman Organization and the Folk Music of Halland]. Gothenburg: Gothenburg University Press, 2004.

Fahlander, Thomas, and Daniel Höglund. "a," "SV: a," "SV: a," "SV: a" [a, RE: a, RE: a, RE: a], October 28, 1999. http://uk.groups.yahoo.com/group/svenskfolkmusik/message/556 through 559 (accessed August 20, 2011).

Finnegan, Ruth. *The Hidden Musicians: Music-Making in an English Town*. Cambridge: Cambridge University Press, 1989.

Folkdansringen, Svenska. "Svenska Ungdomsringen byter namn till Svenska Folkdansringen" [The Swedish Youth Ring Changes Its Name to the Swedish Folk Dance Ring]. Press Release, January 14, 2005.

Franzén, Lars-Gunnar. "Märklig stadga på Ransätersstämman" [Strange Statute at the Ransäter Gathering]. *Spelmannen*, 1999, no. 3: 12.

Frykman, Jonas, and Orvar Löfgren. *Culture Builders: A Historical Anthropology of Middle-Class Life* [Den kultiverade människan]; translated by Alan

Crozier. New Brunswick: Rutgers University Press, 1987. Original edition, 1979.

Gallie, W.B. "Essentially Contested Concepts." *Meeting of the Aristotelian Society* 56 (1956): 167–198.

Geijer, Erik Gustaf. "Anmälan" [Introduction]. *Iduna* 1 (1811): 3–10.

Gelbart, Matthew. *The Invention of "Folk Music" and "Art Music": Emerging Categories from Ossian to Wagner.* New York: Cambridge UP, 2007.

Gellner, Ernest. *Language and Solitude: Wittgenstein, Malinowski, and the Habsburg Dilemma.* Cambridge: Cambridge UP, 1998.

Glassie, Henry. "Tradition." *Journal of American Folklore* 108 (1995): 395–412.

Goehr, Lydia. *The Imaginary Museum of Musical Works: An Essay in the Philosophy of Music.* Oxford: Clarendon Press, 1992.

Goertzen, Chris. *Fiddling for Norway: Revival and Identity.* Chicago: University of Chicago Press, 1997.

———. "The Norwegian Folk Revival and the Gammeldans Controversy." *Ethnomusicology* 24, no. 1 (1998): 99–127.

Guilbault, Jocelyne. *Zouk: World Music in the West Indies.* Chicago: University of Chicago Press, 1993.

Gudmundson, Per. "Djäwul'ns blåsbeöl'e: Om säckpipans uppgång, fall, och återuppståelse" [The Devil's Bellows: On the Bagpipe's Rise, Fall, and Revival]. In *Musik och Kultur,* edited by Owe Ronström, 247–290. Lund: Studentlitteratur, 1990.

Gustafsson, Magnus. "17th and 18th century Swedish music." Liner notes from Höökensemblen, *Höök! Musik bland stadsmusikanter, krigsfångar och mästertjuvar,* Drone DROCD007, 1995, compact disc.

———. "'Därnest spelmännarne med violer, säckpipa, hautbois och trumma . . .' Något om en folklig trumtradition i Värend" ["Immediately Thereafter the Spelmän with Viols, Bagpipe, Hautbois and Drum . . .": Something on a Folk Drum Tradition in Värend]. *Noterat* 8 (2000): 5–20.

———. "Polski Dantz: 17th century melodies in migration . . . " Liner notes from Höökensemblen, *Polski Dantz: 1600-talsmelodier på vandring,* Drone DROCD026, 2002, compact disc.

Hale, Amy, and Philip Payton. "Introduction." In *New Directions in Celtic Studies,* 1–14. Exeter: University of Exeter Press, 2000.

Hallek, Mart, et al. "Folkmusik i frack II" [Folk Music in Formal Wear II]. Liner notes from Junekvintetten med vänner, *Folkmusik i frack II,* Intim Musik IMCD 095, 2004, compact disc.

Hamilton, Carolyn. *Terrific Majesty: The Powers of Shaka Zulu and the Limits of Historical Invention.* Cambridge: Harvard University Press, 1998.

Harrison, Frank. "Tradition and Acculturation: A View of Some Musical Processes." In *Essays on Music for Charles Warren Fox,* edited by Jerald C. Graue, 114–125. Rochester: Eastman School of Music Press, 1979.

Haugen, Bjørn Sverre Hol. "Polsdans frå finnskogen" [Pols Dance from the Finnish Woods]. Liner notes from Various Artists, *24 Polsdanser frå Finnskogen*, Finnskogen Kulturverksted FiKCD 1960, 2002, compact disc.

Hobsbawm, Eric, and Terence Ranger. *The Invention of Tradition*. Cambridge: Cambridge University Press, 1983.

Hoerburger, Felix. "Once Again: On the Concept of 'Folk Dance.'" *Journal of the International Folk Music Council* 20 (1968): 30–32.

Holmberg, Rune. "Vad menas med begreppet folkmusik?" [What is Meant by the Term Folk Music?] *Hembygden* 51, no. 5 (1972): 13.

Honeyman, William Crawford. *Strathspey, Reel and Hornpipe Tutor*. Blyth: Dragonfly Music, 1988. Original edition, 1898.

Hopkins, Pandora. *Aural Thinking in Norway: Performance and Communication with the Hardingfele*. New York: Human Sciences Press, 1986.

Isaksson, Bo i Ransätt. *Folkmusiken i Sverige* [Folk Music in Sweden]. Motala: Borgströms Tryckeri, 1979.

Ivarsdotter-Johnson, Anna. "Upptäckten av folkmusiken" [The Discovery of Folk Music]. In *Musiken i Sverige III: Den nationella identiteten 1810–1920*, edited by Leif Jonsson and Martin Tegen, 53–70. Stockholm: Fischer & Co, 1992.

Ivarsdotter-Johnson, Anna, and Märta Ramsten. "Folkmusiken som nationell och provinsiell symbol" [Folkmusik as a National and Provincial Symbol]. In *Musiken i Sverige III: Den nationella identiteten 1810–1920*, edited by Leif Jonsson and Martin Tegen, 237–250. Stockholm: Fischer & Co, 1992.

Ivy, Marilyn. *Discourses of the Vanishing: Modernity, Phantasm, and Japan*. Chicago: University of Chicago Press, 1995.

Jersild, Margareta. "Om förhållandet mellan vokalt och instrumentalt i svensk folkmusik" [On the Relationship Between the Vocal and the Instrumental in Swedish Folk Music]. *Svensk Tidskrift för Musikforskning* 58, no. 2 (1976): 53–66.

Jersild, Margareta, and Märta Ramsten. "Grundpuls och lågt röstläge—Två parametrar i folkligt sångsätt" [Basic Pulse and Low Vocal Tessitura—Two Parameters in Folk Song Style]. *Sumlen*, 1987: 132–146.

Johansson, Mats. "The Concept of Rhythmic Tolerance: Examining Flexible Grooves in Scandinavian Folk Fiddling." In *Musical Rhythm in the Age of Digital Reproduction*, edited by Anne Danielsen, 69–83. Burlington: Ashgate, 2010.

———. "Stil som retorik och praxis: En musikantropologisk studie av nutida svensk folkmusik" [Style as Rhetoric and Practice: A Musical-Anthropological Study of Present-Day Swedish Folk Music]. MA Thesis, Universitetet i Bergen, Bergen, 2001.

Johansson, Ulf, et al. " . . . och det blev . . . Musikens genrer" [. . . and it's . . . The Genres of Music]. *Göteborgs-Posten*, November 16, 2001, 1–7.

Kaminsky, David. "Gender and Sexuality in the Polska: Swedish Couple Dancing and the Challenge of Egalitarian Flirtation." *Ethnomusicology Forum* 20, no. 2 (2011): 123–152.

———. "Hidden Traditions: Conceptualizing Swedish Folk Music in the Twenty-First Century." Ph.D. diss., Harvard University, 2005.

———. "Keeping Sweden Swedish: Folk Music, Right-Wing Nationalism, and the Immigration Debate." Unpublished manuscript.

———. "The Zorn Trials and the Jante Law: On Shining Musically in the Land of Moderation." *Yearbook for Traditional Music* 39 (2007): 27–49.

Karpeles, Maud. "Definition of Folk Music." *Journal of the International Folk Music Council* 7 (1955): 6–7.

———. "The Distinction between Folk Music and Popular Music." *Journal of the International Folk Music Council* 20 (1968): 9–12.

———. "Some Reflections on Authenticity in Folk Music." *Journal of the International Folk Music Council* 3 (1951): 10–16.

Kelley, Robin D.G. "Notes on Deconstructing 'The Folk.'" *The American Historical Review* 97, no. 5 (1992): 1400–1408.

Kimberlin, Cynthia Tse. "Traditions and Transitions in Ethiopian Music: Event as a Catalyst for Change." *Intercultural Music* I (1995): 131–142.

Kjellberg, Erik. "Jazz på svenska" [Jazz in Swedish]. In *Det stora uppdraget: Perspektiv på Folkmusikkommissionen i Sverige 1908–2008*, edited by Mathias Boström, Dan Lundberg, and Märta Ramsten, 148–67. Stockholm: Nordiska museets förlag, 2010.

Klein, Ernst. "Folkdans och folklig dans" [Folk Dance and Folklig Dance]. In *Om Folkdans*, edited by Mats Rehnberg, 64–84. Stockholm: LTs förlag, 1978. Original publication, 1927.

Kvideland, Reimund. "Den folkelege songtradisjonens funksjonelle aspekt" [The Functional Aspect of the Folk Song Tradition]. In *Visa och visforskning*, edited by Ann-Mari Häggman, 137–165. Helsingfors: Svenska litteratursällskapet i Finland, 1974.

Larsson, Stieg, and Mikael Ekman. *Sverigedemokraterna: Den nationella rörelsen* [The Sweden Democrats: The National Movement]. Stockholm: Ordfront, 2001.

Lilliestam, Lars. "Nordman och 'det svenska'" [Nordman and "the Swedish"]. *Noterat* 4 (1997): 39–47.

Liman, Ingemar. "Folkdans" [Folk Dance]. In *Boken om Skansen*, edited by Nils Erik Baehrendtz, 134–135. Höganäs: Bra Böcker, 1980.

———. "Vårt Sverige i miniatyr" [Our Sweden in Miniature]. In *Boken om Skansen*, edited by Nils Erik Baehrendtz, 76–77. Höganäs: Bra Böcker, 1980.

Lindroth, Bengt. "Svensk spelmansmusik—Finns den?" [Swedish Spelman Music—Does it Exist?] *Spelmannen*, 2002, no. 4: 11.

Ling, Jan. "Folk Music and Popular Music in Sweden." In *Tradition and Modern Society*, 103–110. Stockholm: Almqvist & Wiksell, 1989.

————. "Folk Music Revival: A Case Study of Swedish Folk Music Today Focused on the Keyed Fiddle Club of Lilla Edet (Historical background)." In *Tradition in den Musikkulturen, heute und morgen*, edited by Günter Mayer, 51–55. Leipzig: VEB Deutscher Verlag für Musik, 1985.

————. "Folk Music Revival in Sweden: The Lilla Edet Fiddle Club." *Yearbook of the International Folk Music Council* 43 (1986): 1–8.

————. "Folk Song from Gärdeby: A Case of Musical Emigration and Immigration." In *Trends and Perspectives in Musicology: Proceedings of the 1983 World Music Conference of the International Music Council*, edited by Sven Wilson, 154–159. Stockholm: Kungliga Musikaliska Akademien, 1985.

————. "Folkmusik—En brygd" [Folk Music—A Brew]. *Fataburen*, 1979: 9–34.

————. "Groupa and Ransäterspôjker'a, Folk Music Ensembles in Transition." *Studia Instrumentorum Musicae Popularis* 10 (1992): 30–40.

————. "Nyckelharpan: Dialog mellan nutid och dåtid" [The Nyckelharpa—A Dialogue Between Present and Past]. In *Nyckelharpan nu och då*, edited by Birgit Kjellström, 7–21. Stockholm: Musikmuseet, 1991.

————. *Nyckelharpan: Studier i ett folkligt instrument* [The Keyed Fiddle: Studies on a Folk Instrument]. Stockholm: Norstedts & Söner, 1967.

————. "'O tysta ensamhet'—Från känslosam stil till hembygdsnostalgi" [From "Empfindsamer Stil" to Village Nostalgia]. *Sumlen*, 1978: 40–58.

————. *Svensk Folkmusik* [Swedish Folk Music]. Stockholm: Prisma, 1964.

————. "Svensk folkmusik blir världsmusik: En intervju med Johan Hedin om hans väg från spelman till tonsättare" [Swedish Folk Music becomes World Music: An Interview with Johan Hedin about his Path from Spelman to Composer]. In *Allt under linden den gröna: Studier i folkmusik och folklore tillägnade Ann-Mari Häggman*, edited by Anders G Lindqvist, Christoffer Grönholm, Kurt Sohlström, and Nina Stendahl, 335–356. Vasa: Finlands svenska folkmusikinistitut, 2001.

————. "'Upp, Bröder, Kring Bildningens Fana': Om Folkmusikens Historia och Ideologi" ["Up, Brothers, Around the Banner of Knowledge": On the History and Ideology of Folk Music]. In *Folkmusikboken*, edited by Jan Ling, Gunnar Ternhag, and Märta Ramsten, 11–43. Stockholm: Prisma, 1980.

Ling, Jan, Erik Kjellberg, and Owe Ronström. "Sweden." In *The Garland Encyclopedia of World Music*, vol. 8, *Europe*, edited by Timothy Rice, James Porter, and Chris Goertzen, 434–450. New York: Garland, 2000.

Ling, Jan, and Märta Ramsten. "The Gärdeby Folk Melody—A Musical Migrant." In *Analytica: Studies in the Description and Analysis of Music*, edited by Anders Lönn and Erik Kjellberg, 301–321. Stockholm: Almqvist & Wiksell, 1985.

————. "Gärdebylåten: En musikalisk ut- och invandrare" [Gärdebylåten: A Musical Migrant]. *Sumlen* 1984: 37–65.

————. "Tradition och förnyelse i svensk folkmusik: Leksandsspelet förr och nu" [Tradition and Renewal in Swedish Music of Traditional Performers: Playing in Leksand, Then and Now]. In *Musik och Kultur*, edited by Owe Ronström, 211–246. Lund: Studentlitteratur, 1990.

Ling, Jan, Gunnar Ternhag, and Märta Ramsten, eds. *Folkmusikboken* [The Folk Music Book]. Stockholm: Prisma, 1980.

Löfgren, Orvar. "Kring nationalkänslans kulturella organisation" [On the Cultural Organization of National Sentiment]. *Nord-Nytt* 25 (1985): 73–85.

————. "Känslans förvandling: Tiden, naturen och hemmet i den borgerliga kulturen" [The Change of Emotion: Time, Nature, and the Home in Bourgeois Culture]. In *Den kultiverade männsikan*, edited by Jonas Frykman and Orvar Löfgren, 21–130. Malmö: Gleerups, 1979.

————. "Nationaliseringen av Sverige" [The Nationalization of Sweden]. Paper read at the seminar "Den svenska modellens kulturella ansikte," Umeå University, January 14–16, 1987.

————. "Nationella arenor" [National Arenas]. In *Försvenskningen av Sverige: Det nationellas förvandlingar*, edited by Billy Ehn, Jonas Frykman, and Orvar Löfgren, 21–117. Stockholm: Natur och Kultur, 1993.

————. "The Nature Lovers" [Människan i naturen]. In *Culture Builders: A Historical Anthropology of Middle-Class Life*, edited by Jonas Frykman and Orvar Löfgren, 42–87. Translated by Alan Crozier. New Brunswick: Rutgers University Press, 1987.

Lord, Albert. *The Singer of Tales*. Cambridge: Harvard University Press, 1960.

Lucy, John A. "General Introduction." In *Reflexive Language: Reported Speech and Metapragmatics*, edited by John A. Lucy, 1–4. Cambridge: Cambridge University Press, 1993.

Lundberg, Dan. "Folkmusik—en definitionsfråga" [Folk Music: A Question of Definition]. In *Det stora uppdraget: Perspektiv på Folkmusikkommissionen i Sverige 1908–2008*, edited by Mathias Boström, Dan Lundberg, and Märta Ramsten, 225–38. Stockholm: Nordiska museets förlag, 2010.

Lundberg, Dan, Krister Malm, and Owe Ronström. *Musik—Medier—Mångkultur: Förändringar i svenska musiklandskap* [Music—Media—Multiculture: Changes in Swedish Musical Landscapes]. Hedemora: Gidlunds, 2000.

Lundberg, Dan, and Gunnar Ternhag. *Folkmusik i Sverige* [Folk Music in Sweden]. Smedjebacken: Gidlunds, 1996.

Marton, Ference, and Shirley Booth. *Learning and Awareness*. Mahwah: Erlbaum, 1997.

Marton, Ference, and Wing-yan Pong. "Conceptions as Ways of Being Aware of Something: Accounting for Inter- and Intra-Contextual Shifts in the Meaning of Two Economic Phenomena." Paper read at the symposium: New Challenges to Research and Learning, Helsinki, March 22, 2001.

Mattsson, Pontus. *Sverigedemokraterna in på bara skinnet: Reportage* [The Sweden Democrats Up Close and Personal: A Report]. Stockholm: Natur & kultur, 2009.

Middleton, Richard. "Editor's Introduction to Volume 1." *Popular Music* 1 (1981): 3–7.

Moberg, Carl-Allan. "Tonalitetsproblem i svensk folkmusik" [Tonality Problems in Swedish Folk Music]. In *Texter om svensk folkmusik—Från Haeffner till Ling*, edited by Owe Ronström and Gunnar Ternhag, 173–193. Stockholm: Kungliga Musikaliska Akademien, 1994. Original publication, 1949.

Moberg, Pär. "Re: Digest Number 561" [svenskfolkmusik Yahoo! Discussion Group], November 7, 2002. http://uk.groups.yahoo.com/group/svenskfolkmusik/message/2523 (accessed August 20, 2011).

Myers, Helen. "Ethnomusicology." In *Ethnomusicology: An Introduction*, edited by Helen Myers, 3–18. New York: W.W. Norton & Co, 1992.

Narváez, Peter, and Martin Laba, eds. *Media Sense: The Folklore-Popular Cultural Continuum*. Bowling Green: Bowling Green State University Press, 1987.

Needham, Rodney. "Polythetic Classification: Convergence and Consequences." *Man* 10, no. 3 (1975): 349–369.

Nettl, Bruno. *Folk Music in the United States: An Introduction*. 3rd ed. Detroit: Wayne State University Press, 1976. Original edition, 1960.

Nilsson, Katarina, and Elisabet Classon. "Folkmusiken och dess utövare!" [Folk Music and Its Practitioners!] *Hembygden* 51, no. 4 (1972): 12.

Nilsson, Mats. *Dans—Kontinuitet i förändring* [Dance—Continuity in Change]. Gothenburg: Etnologiska Föreningen, 1998.

Nketia, J.H. Kwabena. "African Traditions of Folklore." In *Jahrbuch: Internationale Gesellschaft fur Urheberrecht E.V.*, vol. 4, 221–230. Vienna: Manzsche Verlags- und Universitatsbuchhandlung, 1979.

Nordström, Annika. *Syskonen Svensson: Sångerna och livet. En folklig repertoar i 1900-talets Göteborg* [The Svensson Family, Songs and Life—A Popular Repertoire in Gothenburg during the Twentieth Century]. Gothenburg: Göteborgs Stadsmuseum, 2002.

Norlind, Tobias. *Svensk folkmusik och folkdans* [Swedish Folk Music and Folk Dance]. Stockholm: Natur och Kultur, 1930.

Nylin, Lars. "Kaksi!" Liner notes from Hedningarna, *Kaksi!*, Silence SRSCD 4717, 1992, compact disc.

Nyqvist, Niklas. *Från bondson till folkmusikikon: Otto Andersson och formandet av "finlandssvensk folkmusik"* [From Farmer's Son to Folk Music Icon: Otto Andersson and the Formation of Finland Swedish Folk Music]. Åbo: Åbo Akademis förlag, 2007.

Ohlmarks, Åke, and Nils Erik Bæhrendtz. *Svensk kulturhistoria: Svenska krönikan* [Swedish Cultural History: The Swedish Chronicle]. Borås: Forum, 1993. Original edition, 1981.

Ohlsson, Gert. "Lysande stadga!" [Brilliant Statute!] *Spelmannen*, 1999, no. 3: 12–13.

Olsson, Dan. "Officiella och verkliga orsaker" [Official and Actual Reasons], October 15, 1999. http://uk.groups.yahoo.com/group/svenskfolkmusik/message/497 (accessed August 20, 2011).

Olsson, Dan. "Osanningar och konspirationsteorier" [Untruths and Conspiracy Theories]. *Spelmannen*, 2003, no. 1: 11.

Racy, Ali Jihad. *Making Music in the Arab World: The Culture and Artistry of Tarab*. Cambridge: Cambridge University Press, 2003.

Ramnarine, Tina K. *Ilmatar's Inspirations: Nationalism, Globalization, and the Changing Soundscapes of Finnish Folk Music*. Chicago: University of Chicago Press, 2003.

Ramsten, Märta. "De nya spelmännen: Trender och ideal i 70-talets spelmansmusik" [The New Spelmän: Trends and Ideals in the Spelman Music of the Seventies]. In *Folkmusikvågen*, edited by Lena Roth, 43–74. Stockholm: Rikskonserter, 1985.

———. "Folkmusiken" [Folk Music]. In *Musiken i Sverige IV: Konstmusik, folkmusik, populärmusik 1920–1990*, edited by Leif Jonsson and Hans Åstrand, 279–310. Stockholm: Fischer & Co, 1994.

———. "'Genuint svenskt' med folkmusikaliska förtecken" ["Authentically Swedish" with Folk Music Overtones]. In *Folkmusik och etnicitet*, edited by Johanna Björkholm, 22–29. Vasa: Finlands svenska folkmusikinstitut, 2005.

———. "Med rötter i medeltiden—Mönster och ideal hos 1960- och 1970-talets balladsångare" [With Roots in the Middle Ages—Patterns and Ideals Among The Balladeers of the 1960s and 1970s]. In *Återklang: Svensk folkmusik i förändring 1950–1980*, 140–146. Stockholm: Svenskt Visarkiv, 1992.

———. *Återklang: Svensk folkmusik i förändring 1950—1980* [Reverberations: Swedish Folk Music in a State of Change, 1950—1980]. Stockholm: Svenskt Visarkiv, 1992.

Ramsten, Märta, ed. *The Polish Dance in Scandinavia and Poland: Ethnomusicological Studies*. Stockholm: Svenskt Visarkiv, 2003.

Rehnberg, Mats. *Folk: Kaleidoskopiska anteckningar kring ett ord, dess innebörd och användning under skilda tider* [Folk: Kaleidoscopic Notes on a Word, its Meaning and Use at Various Times]. Stockholm: Akademilitteratur, 1976.

Roempke, Ville. "'Ett nyår för svensk folkmusik: Om spelmansrörelsen" ["A New Year for Swedish Folk Music": On the Spelman Movement]. In *Folkmusikboken*, edited by Jan Ling, Gunnar Ternhag and Märta Ramsten, 263–296. Stockholm: Prisma, 1980.

Ronström, Owe. "Inledning" [Introduction]. In *Texter om Svensk Folkmusik—från Haeffner till Ling*, edited by Owe Ronström and Gunnar Ternhag, 9–27. Stockholm: Kungliga Musikaliska Akademien, 1994.

————. "Making Use of History—Revival of the Bagpipe in Sweden in the 1980s." *Yearbook for Traditional Music* 21 (1989): 95–108.

————. "Nationell musik? Bondemusik? Om folkmusik begreppet" [National Music? Peasant Music? On the Concept of Folk Music]. In *Gimaint u bänskt*, edited by Bengt Arwidsson, 9–19. Visby: Länsmuséet Gotlands Fornsal, 1989.

Rosander, Göran. "Den regionala identiteten: Exemplet Dalarna" [Regional Identity: The Dalarna Example]. *Nord-Nytt* 25 (1985): 27–42.

————. "Turismen och den folkliga kulturen" [Tourism and Folk Culture]. In *Turisternas Dalarna*, edited by Göran Rosander, 213–225. Falun: Dalarnas museum, 1976.

Rose, Tricia. *Black Noise: Rap Music and Black Culture in Contemporary America*. Hanover: University Press of New England, 1994.

Rosenberg, Neil V. "Introduction." In *Transforming Tradition: Folk Music Revivals Examined*, edited by Neil Rosenberg, 1–25. Urbana: University of Illinois Press, 1993.

Roy, William G. *Reds, Whites, and Blues: Social Movements, Folk Music, and Race in the United States*. Princeton: Princeton University Press, 2010.

Sandberg, Björn. "Börja visa lite hänsyn, alla dragspelare!" [Start Showing Some Respect, All You Accordionists!] *Spelmannen*, 2001, no. 1: 13.

Sharp, Cecil J. *English Folk-Song: Some Conclusions*. 2nd ed. London: Novello & Co., Ltd., 1936. Original edition, 1907.

Shelemay, Kay Kaufman. *Let Jasmine Rain Down: Song and Remembrance among Syrian Jews*. Chicago: University of Chicago Press, 1998.

————. "Toward an Ethnomusicology of the Early Music Movement: Thoughts on Bridging Disciplines and Musical Worlds." *Ethnomusicology* 45, no. 1 (2001): 1–29.

Shils, Edward. *Tradition*. Chicago: University of Chicago Press, 1981.

Singer, Milton. *When a Great Tradition Modernizes: An Anthropological Approach to Indian Civilization*. Chicago: University of Chicago Press, 1972.

Sjöberg, Henry. "Vad betyder polska för dig?" [What Does Polska Mean to You?] In *Polska: En bok till folkmusik och dansåret 1990*, edited by Per-Ulf Allmo et al., 19. Stockholm: Organisationskommittén för Folkmusik och dansåret 1990, 1990.

Slobin, Mark. *Subcultural Sounds: Micromusics of the West*. Hanover: Wesleyan University Press, 1993.

Sporr, Karl. "Om vår folkmusik och arbetet för dess bevarande" [On Our Folk Music and the Work for its Preservation]. *Nordisk Folkdans*, 1921, Julnummer [Christmas Edition]: 20–23.

Stahl, Sandra K. D. "The Personal Narrative as Folklore." *Journal of the Folklore Institute* 14 (1977): 9–30.

Statistiska centralbyrån. "Befolkning efter bakgrund" [Population by Background]. Statistiska centralbyrån, 2010. http://www.scb.se/Statistik/BE/BE-0101/2010A01L/Utrikes_fodda.pdf (accessed August 20, 2011).

Strömblad, Ingvar. "Det är skillnad på dragspelare och spelmän med dragspel" [There's a Difference between Accordionists and Spelmän Who Play Accordion]. *Spelmannen*, 2001, no. 3: 11.

Sverigedemokraterna. *En återupprättad välfärd: Sverigedemokraternas skuggbudget våren 2010* [A Welfare Reinstated: The Sweden Democrats' Spring 2010 Shadow Budget]. Sverigedemokraterna, 2010. http://sdu.nu/Skuggbudget_2010.pdf (accessed August 20, 2011).

Tagg, Philip. "The Göteborg Connection: Lessons in the History and Politics of Popular Music Education and Research." *Popular Music* 17, no. 2 (1998): 219–242.

Tedlock, Dennis, and Bruce Mannheim, eds. *The Dialogic Emergence of Culture*. Urbana: University of Illinois Press, 1995.

Ternhag, Gunnar. "'Att rädda några dyrbara lemningar af fordna tiders musik': Om folkmusikens källor" ["To Save Some Valuable Remnants of the Music of Olden Times": On the Sources of Folk Music]. In *Folkmusikboken*, edited by Jan Ling, Gunnar Ternhag and Märta Ramsten, 44–65. Stockholm: Prisma, 1980.

———. "Folkmusik och etnicitet" [Folk Music and Ethnicity]. In *Folkmusik och etnicitet*, edited by Johanna Björkholm, 15–21. Vasa: Finlands svenska folkmusikinstitut, 2005.

———. *Hjort Anders Olsson: Spelman, artist* [Hjort Anders Olsson: Spelman, Artist]. Hedemora: Gidlunds, 1992.

———. "Playing and Handling Bagpipes: Two Swedish Cases." *STM Online* 7 (2004). http://musikforskning.se/stmonline/vol_7/ternhag.

———. "Spelmanstävlingarna: Tävlandets och musikens sammanhang" [The Spelman Contests: The Context of the Competition and the Music]. In *Det stora uppdraget: Perspektiv på Folkmusikkommissionen i Sverige 1908–2008*, edited by Mathias Boström, Dan Lundberg, and Märta Ramsten, 69–83. Stockholm: Nordiska museets förlag, 2010.

———. "The Story of the Mora-Harp: Museumization and De-museumization." *STM Online* 9 (2006). http://musikforskning.se/stmonline/vol_9/ternhag.

Thornton, Shannon. "Reading the Record Bins: The Commercial Construction of Celtic Music." In *New Directions in Celtic Studies*, edited by Amy Hale and Philip Payton, 19–29. Exeter: University of Exeter Press, 2000.

Thorsén, Stig-Magnus. "SÄMUS – Musiklärarutbildning på försök [SÄMUS – Experimental Music Education Program]." *Svensk Tidskrift för Musikforskning* 1974, no. 2 (1974): 5–10.

Titon, Jeff Todd. "Knowing Fieldwork." In *Shadows in the Field: New Perspectives for Fieldwork in Ethnomusicology*, edited by Gregory F. Barz and Timothy J. Cooley, 87–100. New York: Oxford University Press, 1997.

Upmark, Gustaf. "Skansen 25 år" [Skansen 25 Years]. *Fataburen*, 1916: 97–194.

US Department of State. "Background note: Finland." http://www.state.gov/r/p-a/ei/bgn/3238.htm (accessed August 20, 2011).

Walsh, Eleanor. "Phenomenographic analysis of interview transcripts." In *Phenomenographic Research: Variations in Method: The Warburton Symposium*, edited by John A. Bowden and Eleanor Walsh, 17–30. Melbourne: Royal Melbourne Institute of Technology, 1994.

Whisnant, David. *All That Is Native and Fine: The Politics of Culture in an American Region*. Twenty-Fifth Anniversary Edition. Chapel Hill: The University of North Carolina Press, 2009. Original edition, 1983.

Wieslander, Ethel. "Re: Digest Number 561" [svenskfolkmusik Yahoo! Discussion Group], 7 November 2002. http://uk.groups.yahoo.com/group/svensk-folkmusik/message/2524 (accessed August 20, 2011).

Wiora, Walter. "Concerning the Conception of Authentic Folk Music." *Journal of the International Folk Music Council* 1 (1949): 14–19.

Wittgenstein, Ludwig. *Philosophical Investigations* [Philosophische Untersuchungen]; translated by G. E. M. Anscombe. 3rd ed. Malen: Blackwell, 2001. Original edition, 1953.

Žižek, Slavoj. *The Plague of Fantasies*. New York: Verso, 1997.

Åkesson, Ingrid. *Med rösten som instrument: Perspektiv på nutida svensk vokal folkmusik* [With the Voice as an Instrument: Perspectives on Current Swedish Vocal Folk Music]. Stockholm: Svenskt visarkiv, 2007.

———. "Recreation, Reshaping, and Renewal among Contemporary Swedish Folk Singers: Attitudes toward Tradition in Vocal Folk Music Revitalization." *STM Online* 9 (2006). http://musikforskning.se/stmonline/vol_9/akesson.

Discography and Videography

Berglund, Mats, Göran Håkansson, Atle Lien Jenssen, and Olav Sæta. *24 polsdanser frå finnskogen*. Finnskogen Kulturverksted FiKCD 1960, 2002, compact disc.

Dervish. *Live in Palma*. Kells KM-9516, 1997, 2 compact discs.

Ellika & Solo. *Tretakt takissaba*. Xource XOUCD 133, 2002, compact disc.

Gilliam, Terry. *Time Bandits*. Feature Film. UK: Handmade Films, 1981.

Hedningarna. *Hippjokk*. Northside NSD6003, 1997, compact disc.

Hedningarna. *Kaksi!* Silence SRSCD 4717, 1992, compact disc.

Hedningarna. *Trä*. Silence SRSCD 4721, 1994, compact disc.

Höökensemblen. *Höök! Musik bland stadsmusikanter, krigsfångar och mästertjuvar*. Drone DROCD007, 1995, compact disc.

Höökensemblen. *Polski dantz: 1600-talsmelodier på vandring*. Drone DROCD026, 2002, compact disc.

Johansson, Jan. *Jazz på svenska*. Megafon MFLP S4, 1964, 33rpm vinyl LP.

Landis, John. *Trading Places*. Feature Film. USA: Paramount, 1983.

Lundberg, Camilla. *Nyckelfeber* [Key Fever]. Documentary Film. Sweden: Sveriges Television, 2002.

Moodyson, Lukas. *Fucking Åmål*. Feature Film. Sweden: Memfis Film, 1998.

Music Sveciae: Folk Music in Sweden 20: Visor & låtar från Bohuslän. Caprice CAP 21543, 1997, compact disc.

Raun. *Dance Jon*. Drone DROCD036, 2003, compact disc.

Raun. *Raun*. Prophone PCD 056, 2000, compact disc.

Reiner, Rob. *This is Spinal Tap*. Feature Film. USA: MGM, 1984.

Ståbi, Björn, and Pers Hans. *Bockfot!!!* Sonet SLP-2514, 1970, 33rpm vinyl LP.

Sågskära. *Krook! Musik bland trumslagare, bröllopsspelmän och bergtagna kvinnor*. Drone DROCD010, 1997, compact disc.

Various Artists. *Trance 2001, The 3rd Edition*. EMG Records Sweden AB 5002, 2001, 2 compact discs.

Willemark, Lena, Kirsten Bråten-Berg, Per Gudmundson, Gunnar Stubseid, and Ale Möller. *Suède • Norvège: Musiques des vallées scandinaves*. Ocora C 560008, 1993, compact disc.

185

Østergaard, Anders. *Trollkarlen: En film om Jan Johansson* [The Wizard: A Film about Jan Johansson]. Documentary Film. Denmark: Angel Films, 1999.

Index

24 polsdanser frå finnskogen, 56, 71n49

Abrahamsson, Axel, 58
Abrahamsson, Ernst, 58
accordion, 20, 35; chromatic, 12, 28–29, 30, 36, 38n4, 83–88, 93, 101, 114; diatonic, 19, 86–88
Adorno, Theodor, 125n26
African music, ix–xi, xiiin4, 62–63
Alingsås, 89
Allégården, xii, 1, 13n1, 28, 50, 52, 77, 82, 96, 98, 103n23, 146, 167; specific events at, 62, 92, 149, 152–53
Allmo, Per-Ulf, xii
allspel, 39n9
amateur vs. professional, 108–13, 126n36, 148
American folk music, ix, 73–74n79, 135
Americanization, 95–96
American Scandinavian Foundation, xiii
Andersson, David, 58, 71n52
Andersson, Ditte, 115, 165
Andersson, Nils, 46
Andersson, Otto, 39n9
animal horn, 20, 32, 86
anthropology, 3, 5, 15–16n19, 16n29, 143; linguistic, 7–8, 16n29
anti-immigrant sentiment. *See* xenophobia
Arab music, xiiin4, 135
Arcadius, Kerstin, 46, 59
archaic fiddle style, 12–13, 31, 110, 117
art vs. folk. *See* axis of quality; folk vs. art
Atlantic Orchestra, 59–60
aural tradition, ix–x, 78; vs. written, 117–18
authenticity, 3, 21–22, 23, 143–44, 148–49, 152–53
axis of commonality, xi, 4, 10–11, 17n43, 17n45, 30, 67, 75–101, 123, 128n59, 129–31, 137–38, 145, 147–48

axis of place, 10–11, 45–66, 123, 128n59, 129–30, 135, 147–48; nation vs. international culture sphere, 55–63; nation vs. region, 45–54
axis of quality, 10–11, 17n43, 101, 107–23, 130, 133, 135, 137, 147–48; amateur vs. professional, 108–13, 126n36, 148; folk vs. art, 10, 19, 25, 38n2–3, 102n14, 108–11, 115–23, 131, 143; raw vs. polished, 108–12, 117, 148, 150–51
axis of time, 10–11, 19–38, 42n39, 51–52, 123, 129–30, 137–40, 147–48; innovation as tradition, 21–25, 39n11, 123, 129, 137

Bach, Johann Sebastian, 43n62, 122
Bagaregården's spelman group, xii
bagpipe, Swedish, 24, 32, 33, 35–36, 100, 151
Bain, Aly, 60, 71n60
Bakhtin, Mikhail, 7, 16n28–29, 16n33. *See also* chronotopes, heteroglossia
bakmes, 49, 69n18
Balkan music, 135
ballad, 33, 42–43n56, 149
Baroque music, 120–21
basic polska, 49–51
bass, 29, 169; acoustic, x, 72n64, 88, 114, 127n53; electric, 28, 33
Baywatch, 80
Bazar Blå, 115
Beaudry, Nicole, xi
Beethoven, Ludwig van, 108
Bengtsson, Håkan, xii, 165
Berchtold, Andreas, 76
Berg, Göran, xii, 165
Berglund, Mats, 56, 59, 125n20
Bergsten, Anders, xii, 50–51, 90, 165
Bergsten, Ulla, xii, 50–51, 90, 165

Bergstrand, Alf, xii, 165
Berndalen, Petter, 125–26n32
Bildt, Carl, 97
Billquist, Ulla, 67
Bingolotto, 79–80, 103n18, 167
Bingsjö, 41n27, 62–63, 72n67, 93, 167;
    polska from, 49–51, 122, 136–37,
    158n11, 167; spelman gathering,
    41n27, 52, 63, 72n70, 77, 83, 167
Biskop, Gunnel, 159n15
Bjerke, Veslemøy Nordset, 71n46
Blom, Jan-Petter, xiiin2
Boda; polska from, 50, 52, 158n11, 168;
    spelman gathering, 72n70, 83, 122
Bockfot!!!, 124n7
Bohlman, Philip, 2
Bohuslän, 41n35, 65, 66, 71n52, 151–52; as
    choreomusical style area, 24–26,
    41n35, 47, 56, 57–61, 133
Bommens Salonger, 149–56
Boot, 115
border music, Swedish/Norwegian, 55–57,
    59, 71n49
bourgeois bloc, 97, 104n63
bouzouki, 33, 63
Bowen, Jeff, 58
bow harp, 32, 100, 151
brass instruments, 20, 89
Brimi, Hans W., 57
"Byssan lull," 153
Byss-Calle, 115
Bäckström, Ola, 115, 125n20
Bälstespännar park, 147
Bäsk, 92, 115, 121, 126n41

Carlos, Wendy, 43n62
cello, 33
Celtic music, ix, xi, 60–61, 71n60, 72n61
Centrist Party, 104n63
chamber folk music, 117–19, 159n21
choir singing, 79–80
Christmas songs, xi, 30
chronotopes, 138, 141n8, 168
Cissokho, Solo, 62–63, 72n66
cittra, 125n25
clarinet, 32–33, 35, 88, 89, 125n29, 169
Classical music, Viennese 119
colonialism, 45, 104n44
Concerts Sweden, 22, 40n24, 120, 167
contrabass, x, 72n64, 88, 114, 127n53
county, 55, 68n6, 70n33
cow horn, 20, 32, 86
cultural performance, 143–44, 149
Curtis, Jamie Lee, 90, 104n43

Dahlgren, Anders, xii, 49–51, 165

Dalarna, 25, 47, 72n70, 93, 104n44; connec-
    tions to Norwegian music, 55–57; fid-
    dle style of, 20, 111, 114, 118; loca-
    tions within, 46, 63, 70–71n40, 72n67,
    167, 168; as model province, 59, 63–
    66, 72n67, 73n76, 78, 81–82; musical
    hegemony of, 20, 53, 59–61, 63–66,
    72n73, 94, 114, 118; as "traditional"
    province, 111, 114, 115
daldans, 158n10, 159n12
dance band (genre), 86; as folk music, 79–
    80, 129, 131, 137, 148, 150, 159n19
dance games, xi, 33
Dance Jon, 151–52
dance-music connection, 77, 81–83, 117,
    132, 143; in polska, x, 83, 167
Danish folk music, 54
dansband, 86; as folk music, 79–80, 129,
    131, 137, 148, 150, 159n19
Delsbo spelman gathering, 90
Den Fule, 115, 159n22
Dervish, 41n27
Dialogic Emergence of Culture, The, 16n29
didgeridoo, 33, 63
Djunovic, Ida Heinö, xii, 165
double bass, x, 72n64, 88, 114, 127n53
drone rock, 150–51, 159n21–22
drum kit, 28, 33
Dubé, Sebastian, 72n64
Du gamla du fria, 46, 68n13
durspel, 19, 86–88
Dybeck, Richard, 46, 68n13

early music, 14n7, 42n51, 121, 150–51
Edén, Mats, 115
Edström, Olle, xii, 67, 78, 87–88, 165
education theory, 8
Eikås, Sigmund, 25, 133
Ek, Helena, xii, 42n51, 149–52, 165
Ek, Magnus, xii, 31–32, 130, 137–40,
    141n7, 145, 149–56, 159–60n29, 165
Ellika & Solo, 62–63, 72n66, 92–93
emigration, 19, 67, 162
engelska, 58, 147, 158n7–8, 167
Engström, Bengt Olof, 119, 121
Enqvist, Bengt, 84
ensemble music, 29–30, 113–17, 125n30
Envallson, Carl, 9–10, 124n4
Eric Sahlström Institute, xii, 76, 159n16
Ericson, Jonas, xii–xiii, xivn11
Eriksson, Jeanette, 64, 122
Eriksson, Karin, ix, xii, 5, 23, 79, 112–13,
    165
essentially contested concepts, 5–8, 10,
    16n25, 16n28, 37–38, 130, 140,
    140n2, 145

Ethno Camp, 12
ethnomusicology, 2–3, 14n6, 43n73
European Seminar in Ethnomusicology, 118
European Union, 57, 59
Evjemoen, 27
Ewaldz, Magnus, 145, 147, 158n9–10, 158–
     59n12
exoticism, 3, 73n76, 104n44

Fahlander, Thomas, 38
Falun Folk Festival, 22–23, 28, 59–61, 63,
     167
family resemblances, 5–7, 15–16n19
feedback analysis, xii–xiii, xivn11, 140n2,
     156–57
Ferrari, André, 105n64
fiddle, ix, 23–24, 29–35, 58–59, 62–63, 83–
     86, 100–101, 114–15, 125n29, 125–
     26n32, 144, 151, 169. See also archaic
     fiddle style
Filarfolket, 34, 110, 113, 115–16, 126n41,
     144
"Final Countdown," 27
Finland, xi, 39n9, 45, 64, 72n67, 115, 162
Finnegan, Ruth, 82
Finnish folk music, 42n52, 54, 55, 100, 115,
     162
finnskogspols, 55–56, 59
Floda, 67
flute, xi, 33, 36, 117, 169
flutists, ix-x, xii, 35, 85
folk concept, 2–4, 15n13, 76–81
folk costumes, 2, 58, 62, 65, 89–92, 100,
     104n44, 111, 170. See also half cos-
     tume, knee tassels
folk dance (stage form), 47–48, 58, 76–77,
     143–49, 159n16, 168
folk dance groups, 31, 47, 53, 58, 76, 89–91,
     93, 144–49, 159n15, 167, 170. See
     also folk dance (stage form), folkdans
     vs. folklig dans
Folk Dance Ring. See Youth Ring
folkdanslag. See folk dance groups
Folkdansringen. See Youth Ring
folkdans vs. folklig dans, 76–78, 146–49,
     159n15–16, 168
folkdräkt. See folk costumes
folkhögskola, 112
folklig dans, 168; vs. folkdans, 76–78, 146–
     49, 159n15–16, 168
folklighet, double meaning of, 12, 79–81,
     102–3n17–18, 167
Folk Music Café. See Allégården
folk music contests, 20, 39n9, 102n14, 144.
     See also kappleik

folk music festivals, xii, 27, 66. See also
     specific festivals by name
folk music fusion. See Swedish folk music
     fusion
folk musician concept. See spelman vs. folk
     musician
Folk Musicians against Xenophobia, 161
folk musician vs. spelman, 110–16, 124n12,
     169
folk music Sweden, xi, xivn10, 46, 70–
     71n40, 82, 88, 98, 99, 105n64, 107,
     109, 111, 115, 119, 120, 157, 163. See
     also polska Sweden
Folkmusikboken, 15n11, 71n42
"Folkmusik—en brygd," 4, 97
Folkmusiken i Sverige, 71n42, 97, 124n7
Folkmusik i Sverige, 15n11, 54, 71n42
Folkmusik och dans (periodical), 170
folk song. See vocal folk music
folk vs. art. See axis of quality; folk vs. art
folk vs. folklig, 76–81, 102n17
folk vs. popular. See axis of commonality
Forsmark Tre, 115, 126n34
Four Man and a Dog, 58–59
foxtrot, 38n4, 76, 145
Franzén, Lars-Gunnar, xii–xiii, 36–37
Frej, 154–55
Frifot, 23
Frisell, Ellika, 62–64, 72n66, 115, 125n20,
     125–26n32
Frykmo, Ingrid, 76
Fucking Åmål, 80, 103n19
furusato, 73n77
fusion. See Swedish folk music fusion
Fälldin, Thorbjörn, 104n63
Färgfemman, 80

Galaxee, "The Crow Song," xivn7
Gallie, W.B., 5–7, 16n25
game songs, xi, 33
gammeldans, 19–20, 38n4, 47, 101, 145,
     147–48, 167, 168, 169; music of, 19–
     20, 30, 33, 38n4, 84, 86–87, 101, 113,
     147
gangar, 27
Garmarna, 113, 131, 144, 150–51
gatherings. See spelman gatherings
Gelbart, Matthew, 17n37
Gellner, Ernest, 16n19
Germany, 94–96, 97–98
Gesunda contest, 20
Goehr, Lydia, 5–6, 16n25
Gothenburg, x–xii, 57, 66–67, 70n40, 75,
     77–79, 90, 116–18, 125n27, 145–47,
     149–50, 157, 167, 168

Gothenburg School of Music, ix, xiiin1, 22,
    25, 116–17, 118, 168; world music
    program, 116–17, 126n40–41. *See also*
    Sämus
Gothenburg University, xii, 102n11, 116,
    170
Gothic Society, 8–9, 19
gramophone, 31, 38n4, 86, 118
Greece, 62
Groupa, 22, 110, 113, 115–16, 119, 126n41,
    127n50, 144
Guilbault, Jocelyne, 15n19
guitar, 24, 29, 85, 169; acoustic, 33, 88,
    125n25, 125n32; electric, 28, 33, 87,
    99
Gustafsson, Magnus, 42n51, 121
Gustafsson, Pelle, 83, 122
gånglåt, 32, 158n4
Gärdebylåten, 158n4
Gösta Rackares polska, ix–xi
Göteborgs folkdansvänner, 158n7
Göteborgs spelmansförbund, 88
Götiska förbundet, 8–9, 19

Hahn, Gunnar, 119–21, 127n50
Haitian music, 34
half costume, 91–92, 147, 158n9
Halland, ix, 47, 66
halling, 56, 99, 158n7
hambo, 19, 147, 168
Hamburgsund, 67
hammer of Thor, 98–99
hardingfela, 25–27, 41n33
harmonica, 36
harmonium, 114
Harvard University, xiii
Haugen, Bjørn Sverre Hol, 71n46
Hazelius, Artur, 46, 65, 169
Hedblom, Skölds Anders, 46, 69n14
Hedin, Johan, 115
Hedningarna, 32, 34, 42n52, 96–100, 113,
    115, 125n31, 131, 144, 150–52,
    159n22
Heimdal's spelmän, 147
"Hello You Old Red Indian," 150, 159n19
Helsingborg, 64
Helsinki, 39n9
hembygd, 66, 112, 168
Hembygden, 81, 144, 170
hembygdskänsla, 66, 73n77, 168
Hemlin, Håkan, 97–99
Hemmingsson, Merit, 99, 144
Henningson, Ulf, xii, 166
Herder, Johann Gottfried, 107, 163
herding calls, 42–43n56
heteroglossia, 7–8, 16n28–29

heteroglossic refraction, 8, 16n33, 130
hidden pathways, 81–83
Hillbratt, Martin, xii, 165
Hippjokk, 152
Hjertberg, Maja, 90
Hjort Anders, 63, 88, 167
Hoerburger, Felix, 102n4
Hogenäs, Johan, xii, 82, 165
home village feeling, 66, 73n77, 168
Horningdal, 133
Hoven Droven, 113, 150, 158n7
hummel, 125n25
hurdy-gurdy, 24, 32–33, 42n51, 100, 150–
    52, 159n19
hymns, 33
Håkansson, Lilian, xii, 103n23, 165
Hällesåker spelman gathering, 83–84, 91
Hälsingland, 20, 53, 90; fiddle style of, 20,
    111, 118, 144
Härjedalen, 56, 158n7
Höglund, Daniel, 38
Hôl i Vägga, 125n27
hörnstolpadans, 146

Iduna, 8–9
Ilmatar's Inspirations, 72n67, 162
India, 62, 143
industrialization, 19, 66–67, 73n76, 75, 80,
    86, 162
innovation as tradition, 21–25, 39n11, 123,
    129, 137
innovationism, 24, 28–30, 48–49, 51, 85–86,
    113–14, 132, 134–37, 138–39
innovation vs. tradition. *See* axis of time
instrument revivals, 23–24, 41n30, 100. *See
    also* specific instruments
International Council for Traditional Music,
    2
international culture sphere vs. nation, 55–
    63
internationalization, 67, 86, 95
interview technique, 140n2
intra-contextual conceptual shifts, 8, 130,
    141n3
Invention of Tradition, The, 40n14
Irish folk music, 58–59, 87, 135
Isaksson, Bo i Ransätt, 71n42, 97, 124n7

jazz, 86, 95–96, 99, 116, 118, 134, 158n5
Jazz på ryska, 99
Jazz på svenska, x, 99, 105n72.
Jenssen, Atle Lien, 71n46
Jinder, Åsa, 64
Johansson, Gunnel, xii, 165
Johansson, Jan, x–xi, 22, 99, 105n72, 119–
    20, 144, 158n5, 163

Johansson, Mats, xiiin4
Johansson, Olov, 105n64, 115, 125n31
Johansson, Pers Nils, xii, 89, 93, 165
Jularbo, Calle, 30, 88
Junekvartetten, 120, 127n53
June sixth, 46, 68–69n13, 89, 147–48

kappleik, 25, 26–27, 55, 168
Kaustinen, xi, 72n67
Kebnekajse, 144
Kennemark, Hans, xii, 64, 115, 117, 121, 126n34, 165
Kimberlim, Cynthia Tse, xiiin4
Kinding, Ulf, xii, 23, 87–88, 93, 165
Kjellberg, Erik, 105n72
Kjellström, Sven, 111
Klacklek, 23
Klein, Ernst, 76–78, 149, 168
knee tassels, 90, 91, 104n44
knätofs, 90, 91, 104n44
Kober, Joanna, xii, 165
kohorn, 20, 32, 86
kora, 62
Korrö festival, xi–xii, xivn11, 38, 91, 168
Kristians Kapell, 125n27
kulning, 42–43n56
Kungliga musikhögskolan, 117
Kurki-Suonio, Sanna, 42n52, 100
Kvideland, Reimund, 78
Kvifte, Tellef, xiiin2
Källman, Sten, xii, 33–34, 57, 96–97, 98, 115–17, 126n41, 165

lameness, 89–92, 104n44
landskap. See province
language games, 10–11
Larsson, Niklas, 137, 152, 159n29
lederhosen, 90, 104n43
Leidhammar, Kjell, xii, 165
Lekarlaget, ix–xii, 25, 168
Leksand, 46
Lilla Edet spelman group, 98–99
Lind, Urban, xii, 51–52, 62–63, 91, 123, 145, 147–48, 165
Lindberg, Håkan, 83
Lindroth, Bengt, 37, 43n69
Ling, Jan, xii, 62, 95–96, 118–19, 125n19, 165; and Sämus, 116, 170; writings of, 3–4, 15n11, 21–23, 39n11, 54, 71n42, 92–93, 97–99, 123, 124n7, 129, 137, 161; as a Zorn jury member, 111, 118
linguistic anthropology, 7–8, 16n29
Linköping folk music festival, 73n78
Lord, Albert, 21
lullaby, 33, 42–43n56, 153

Lundberg, Dan, 4–5, 15n11, 54, 71n42; and chamber folk music vs. drone rock, 117–19, 150, 159n21
län, 55, 68n6, 70n33
Lätt, Billy, 65
Löfgren, Orvar, 45, 73n76, 107, 124n8
Løvlid, Unni, 133

Macalester College, ix–x, xi
Madonna, 80
Malbert, Karl, xii, 82, 127–28n58, 165
Malm, Krister, 116–17, 159n21
mandola, 33
Mannervik, Svante, xii, 57, 59–60, 166
march, 32, 99, 169
Marin, Mikael, 105n64
Martinsson, Martin, 151–52, 159n29
Marton, Ference, 8
Mattsson, Hållbus Totte, 32
mazurka, 19, 168
meaning as use, 5–7, 15n16
Mellgren, Lennart, xii, 47–48, 166, 168
Mellgrens blandning, 47–48, 51–52, 168
melody vs. rhythm instruments, 28, 34
Mensah, Sowah, x–xi
midsummer, xi, 82–83, 89, 144, 148, 158n7
Miller, Kiri, xiii
Minda de Gunzburg Center for European Studies, xiii
Mitt i musiken, 36
Moderate Party, 97
"modern" dance, 20, 76, 145–46, 158n7
modernization, 19, 75, 162
Moodyson, 103n19
Morris, Sheila, xiii
multiculturalism, 61–63, 92–96, 104n54, 126n36, 161
music-dance connection, 77, 81–83, 117, 132, 143; in polska, x, 83, 167
music education, Swedish, x–xi, 75, 112, 116–18, 170
Musik vid Siljan, 64, 72n70, 121–22, See also individual gatherings by name
Myhr, Martin, 56
Månsson, Göran, xii, 42n51, 149–52, 155, 159n19, 166
Möller, Ale, 60–63, 71n60, 72n62, 92, 105n64; and the folk musician concept, 110, 113–14, 116, 169. See also World Music Orchestra

National (folk dance group), 145–49, 150, 156, 158n7, 158n10, 168
national anthem of Sweden, 46, 68n13

nationalism, 9–10, 45–46, 59, 63–64, 67;
    distrust of, 53–54, 62, 90, 92–96, 131,
    135, 161–63
national music, 9–10, 17n37, 124n4
National Organization of Swedish Spelmän,
    20, 36, 46, 53, 71n42, 126n36, 170
national romanticism, 83, 96–100, 107, 129
nation vs. international culture sphere, 55–
    63
nation vs. region, 45–54
Nazism, 94–98, 161, 163n1
Needham, Rodney, 15–16n19
neomedievalism, 23–24, 31–32, 33, 130,
    151
neotraditionalism, 21–28, 48–49, 114, 130–
    34
Newcastle, 58
New Democracy Party, 97
"new" music, 118–19
Nilsson, "Dans" Mats, xii–xiii, 15n16, 77,
    78, 102n11, 159n16, 166
Nilsson, "Sax" Mats, xii, 24, 28–30, 49,
    130, 134–38, 139, 156, 166
Nilsson, Vivi, xii, 95–96, 166, 168
Nord, Rose-Marie Landén, xii, 101, 166
Nordiska muséet, 65
Nordlek, 101, 105n74
Nordman, 97–100, 105n64, 105n73, 107,
    120, 127n50, 151, 159n22
Nordqvist, Peter, 49
Nordström, Annika, xii, 38n2, 77–79,
    102n11, 166
Norlind, Tobias, 14n8, 71n42
Norrlöf, Ida, xii, 117, 166
North Atlantic culture sphere, 57–61
Northside Records, 104n48, 114, 125n31
Norudde, Anders, 32, 125n31
Norway, 25–28, 45, 55–57, 59, 64, 65,
    69n13
Norwegian folk dance, 49, 56–57, 59, 71n46
Norwegian folk music, xiiin2, 25–28,
    41n33, 54, 55–57, 59, 71n46, 168
Norwegian-Swedish border music, 55–57,
    59, 71n49
nyckelharpa, 4, 32, 35–36, 53, 84, 88, 94,
    114–15, 125n29, 168; chromatic, 36,
    86, 97–100, 127n50, 169; older varie-
    ties of, 24, 32, 100
Nyckelharpan (book), 4
Nylin, Lars, 32
Närke, 46, 158n10
Näsåker, 63, 170
Näverluren, 146, 167, 168
Nääs, 82–83

Ohlsson, Gert, 36

Ohlsson, Gunilla, xii, 166
Olson, Lars, xiii
Olsson, Dan, xii–xiii, 22–23, 36–37, 110,
    166
Olsson, Hjort Anders, 63, 88, 167
Olsson, Pers Hans, 93, 124n7
open concepts, 4–8, 16n25, 16n28
orsapolska, 50
Orust, 58, 71n52
Oslo School of Music, 133
"O tysta ensamhet," 99
overtone flute, 87

Paulasto, Tellu, 42n52, 100
Paulsson, Kajsa, xii, 109, 166
Pekkos Per, 136–37
penis flute, 155
percussion, 24, 28–29, 33, 34, 63, 85, 99,
    125–26n32, 150–51
Pers Hans, 93, 124n7
Persson, Rolf, xii, 166
Pettersson, Harald, xii, 42n51, 105n64,
    141n7, 149–55, 159n19–20, 159n22,
    166
Pettersson, Sverker, 49
phenomenography, 8–9, 16–17n35, 129–30,
    140n2
Philochoros, 76, 145, 167, 168
polka, 19, 69n18, 99, 122, 147, 168
polkettering, 69n18
polska as metonym, 77, 82, 102n8
polska dance, 69n18, 77, 145–48; basic, 49–
    51; connection to music, x, 83, 167;
    marginalization of, 79, 91, 93–94, 96–
    97, 146–49; pedagogy of, 49–50; re-
    gional variations in, 47–49, 51–52, 56–
    57, 69n18, 77, 89, 123, 137, 158n8,
    167, 168; revival of, 47–52, 145, 148.
    See also individual types and variants
Polska Dancers, xiii, 47–52, 72n70, 77,
    102n8, 156–57. See also Mellgrens
    blandning, Skjortor och Särkar
polska dancers, social, 47, 72n70, 77, 82,
    102n8
polska music, 32–33, 116, 122, 168; connec-
    tions to dance, x, 83, 122, 167; foot
    tapping in, ix–x, xiiin2; marginaliza-
    tion of, xi, 83–84, 91, 93–94, 99–100;
    regional variations in, 12, 47–49, 55–
    57, 65, 89, 167, 168; as representative
    Swedish folk music, 30, 32–33, 65;
    rhythmic peculiarities of, ix–x, 34,
    101; three basic types, x; uneven, ix–x,
    34; vs. gammeldans music, 19, 83–87.
    See also individual variants

polska Sweden, 30, 60, 72n70, 82, 87, 89–
92, 107–8; international offshoots, 90,
104n48. *See also* folk music Sweden
Pong, Wing-Yan, 8
popular music as folk music. *See* Swedish
folk music; Swedish popular music as
popular vs. folk. *See* axis of commonality
Premberg, Göran, xii, xiii, 57–61, 65, 166
preservationism, 23–24, 35, 48, 114, 144;
reaction against, 3, 23, 36, 86, 91, 93,
112–13, 131–32, 135
professional vs. amateur, 108–13, 126n36,
148
province, 45–46, 51–55, 59–61, 64–67, 70–
71n40; vs. county, 55, 68n6, 70n33.
See also specific provinces
province vs. nation, 45–54
provincial dialects. *See* regional style variations
provincialism, 25–28, 45–61, 64–67, 131,
135–36
provincialist (puzzle-piece) nationalism, 45–
53, 59, 66

race, xii, xivn10, 63–64, 74n79, 94–96, 97–
98
Racy, Ali Jihad, xiiin4
Ramnarine, Tina, 72n67, 162
Ramsten, Märta, 31–32, 39n11, 60, 111
Ranrike spelmän, 59–60
Ransäter spelman gathering, 52, 58, 91, 168;
and debates over entrance fees, 35–38,
43n69, 156; as metonym, 52, 77, 82
Ransäterspôjker'a, 39n11
Raun, 42n51, 140, 145, 149–56; 159n20
raw vs. polished, 108–12, 117, 148, 150–51
"Ray of Light," 80
reconstructed instruments, 23–24, 41n30,
100. *See also* specific instruments
recorder, 28, 33, 36, 99, 150–52, 159n19,
169
regionalism, 25–28, 45–61, 64–67, 131,
135–36
regional style variations in music, 29, 48–
49, 55–56, 58–61, 65, 131, 134, 136.
See also polska music; regional variations in
region vs. nation, 45–54
Rehnberg, Mats, 15n13
reported speech, 7–8, 130–33
RFoD, 22, 71n42, 126n36, 170
rhythmic tolerance, x, xiiin4
Riksförbundet för folkmusik och dans, 22,
71n42, 126n36, 170
Rikskonserter, 22, 40n24, 120, 167
riksspelman badge, 20, 39n7, 111, 168–69

riksspelman gathering, 20, 169
riksspelman jury, 20, 86, 111–12, 118, 168–
69
riksspelman title, 20, 25, 35, 64–65, 72n73,
111, 125n19–20, 168–169
riksspelman trials, 20, 53, 111, 125n20, 169
Rolf, Ernst, 67
Ronström, Owe, 4–5, 38, 45, 65–66, 116–
17, 159n21
Rose, Tricia, 151
Rosenberg, Neil, 14n7
round polska dance, 47, 49–52, 69n18
Royal Music Academy, 117
rubato effect, x, xiiin4
rundpolska, 47, 49–52, 69n18
rural vs. urban, 17n44, 67, 73n76, 74n79,
80–81, 107, 123, 128n59, 148, 151–56
Russia, 45
Russian folk music, 99
Rydberg, Emma, xii, 51–52, 91, 123, 145–
46, 158n7, 166
Rydberg, Inger, xii, 92–93, 108–9, 166
Rydberg, Lisa, 122
RÅmantik, 28–29, 42n41
Rättvik, 69n14, 115; gymnasium folk music
program, 112; parish of, 72n67, 167;
spelman group, 158n4
Röjås, Maria, 105n64
Røros, 55
rørospols, 49, 56–57

Saami music, 42n52, 54, 100, 151
Saari, Wimme, 42n52, 100
sacred music, 136–37
Sandahl, Sten, 22–23
Sandberg, Björn, 84
Sandberg, Per, xii, 28–29, 85, 166
Sandberg, Sven-Olof, 67
sand dance, 58
saxophone, 24, 28, 33–34, 85, 117; players
of, 24, 28, 33–34, 57, 85, 94, 117
Scandinavium, 101, 105n74
schlager, 67, 86, 87; as folk music, 11, 67,
78, 123, 148
Schlager i Sverige, 67
scholar-practitioner feedback loop, 3–4,
14n7, 22–23, 36–38, 88, 121
schottische, 19, 33, 47–48, 147, 158n8, 168
Schultz, Louise, 42n41
second-fiddle harmonization, 20, 114, 115,
118
Selinder, Anders, 76, 78, 144, 147–48, 150,
158n9–10
Senegal, 62, 72n66
Setesdal, 27, 56
Sexdrega, 121

Shelemay, Kay, xiii, 14n7
Shetland folk music, 60–61, 72n61
Sigtuna, 9
Siljan, 65, 72n67, 72n70
Siljansnäs 115
Siljebo, Greger, xii, 24, 81–82, 108–10, 166
Silverhjelm, Henrik, 25, 168
Simonson, Jonas, xii, 115, 117, 126n40–41, 166
Singer, Milton, 143
sixth of June, 46, 68–69n13, 89, 147–48
Sjöberg, Henry, 76, 148
Sjöberg, Tommy, xiii, 69n14
Skaftölandet, 58
Skallsjö folk dance group, 82–83
Skansen, 20, 38n5, 46, 53, 65–66, 69n14, 169
Skeppis, xivn11, 77, 156–57, 169
Skeppsholmsgården, xivn11, 77, 156–57, 169
Skjortor och Särkar, xii, 49–51, 126n34
Skorpen, Joar, xii, 24–28, 30, 35, 41n35, 42n39, 48–49, 51, 55–57, 59, 130–36, 138, 139, 156, 166, 168
Skåne, 46, 47, 64, 94
slängpolska dance, 47, 158n8
Småland, 47, 151, 168
snoa, 168, 169
Social Democratic Party, 97
social polska dancers, 47, 72n70, 77, 82, 102n8
Society for Ethnomusicology, 14n6
Sol, Åsa Grogarn, xii, 1–2, 8, 51, 79–80, 93–94, 166
Soling, Jonny, 125n28
song games, xi, 33
"Sparve Lilla," 116
spelman books, 42n51, 120–22
spelman concept, 20, 38n5, 48, 66–67, 108–14, 124n12, 169. See also spelman vs. folk musician
spelman gatherings, xii, 20, 27, 31, 47, 49–50, 52, 53, 55, 56, 59, 66, 77, 82, 83–84, 89, 90, 91, 100, 102n14, 107, 109, 127n58, 146, 163, 169, 170. See also specific gatherings by name
spelman groups, xi, 20, 23, 53, 88, 89, 91, 109, 111, 113, 114, 125n27, 125n30, 144, 169
Spelmannen (periodical), 36–38, 84–85, 170
spelman organizations, 37, 46, 168, 169–170
spelmansböcker, 42n51, 120–22
spelmansförbund, 37, 46, 168, 169–170
spelmanslag. See spelman groups
spelmansstämma. See spelman gatherings

spelman vs. folk musician, 110–16, 124n12, 169
SSR, 20, 36, 46, 53, 71n42, 126n36, 170
Stake, Anders, 32, 125n31
Stensby, Marie, 64, 72n71
stile galant, 120
Stockholm, xivn11, 38n5, 46, 61, 80, 145, 147, 150, 156–57, 169
Stockholm Opera, 76, 144
Stockholm University of Dance and Circus, 148, 159n16
string bass, x, 72n64, 88, 114, 127n53
stråkharpa, 32, 100, 151
Strömblad, Ingvar, xii, 84–86, 109–10, 120, 166
Ståbi, Björn, 124n7
Suède • Norvège, 56, 71n49
Svabensverk, 64, 72n70
Sveg youth dancers, 158n7
Svenska folkdansens vänner, 76
Svenska låtar (collection), 43n58, 46, 53, 59, 69n15, 170
Svensk folkmusik (book), 3–4, 14n8, 15n11, 21, 71n42
Svensk folkmusik och folkdans (book), 14n8, 71n42
svenskfolkmusik Yahoo! discussion group, 36–38, 94–96
Svenskt musikaliskt lexikon, 9–10
Svensson, Jenny, 83
Sverigedemokraterna, 13, 70n37, 104n54, 161–64
Sveriges Spelmäns Riksförbund, 20, 36, 46, 53, 71n42, 126n36, 170
svikt, 49, 69n18
Sweden Democrats, 13, 70n37, 104n54, 161–64
Swedish bagpipe, 24, 32, 33, 35–36, 100, 151
Swedish bikini team, 90
Swedish flag day, 46, 68–69n13, 89, 147–48
Swedish folk music; in advertising, xi, xivn8; and the bourgeoisie, 2, 4, 9, 19, 38n5, 73–74n79, 80–81, 118, 144; collection of, 3, 4, 8–9, 19, 32–33, 38n2, 46, 68n13, 75, 78–79, 120–21, 151–52; collections of, 46, 59, 102n14, 118, 120–21, 170; as a concept, xi–xii, 2–5, 8–11, 14n6, 14–15n9, 15n11, 15n16, 17n44, 21, 37–38, 54, 78–79, 109, 118, 129, 145, 156, 163; definition of, 2–5, 10, 15n16, 22–24, 27, 75, 78–79, 117, 118–19, 129–40, 141n7, 154–56; and gender, 32–33, 150–51, 159n22; as genre category, 2, 4–5, 10, 19, 33, 78, 110, 112, 117, 121, 129; as ideo-

logical tool, 2, 4, 14–15n9, 21, 31–32,
73–74n79, 80–81, 97–99, 141n10,
161–63; as modal, 2, 30, 32, 85, 135;
as national music, 4, 9–10, 17n37, 48;
as peasant music, 2, 4, 19–21, 79, 80–
81, 117–18, 129; revival of, 3, 22, 31–
32, 38n2, 42n51, 47, 53–54, 97–99,
113, 144–45, 146; as romantic fantasy,
3, 22, 31–32, 37, 54, 96–100, 105n73,
107–8, 119, 124n7, 141n10; as secret
club, 81–83; Swedish popular music
as, 11, 67, 78–80, 87, 123, 129, 137,
141n7, 148, 150, 159n19
Swedish Folk Music and Dance Association,
22, 71n42, 126n36, 170
Swedish Folk Music Commission, 43n58
Swedish folk music contests, 20, 39n9,
102n14, 144
Swedish folk music fusion, xi, 32, 60–63,
71n60, 92–96, 116–19, 131, 144–45,
158n5
Swedish identity, 3, 47–48, 52–54, 80–81,
90, 93–100; as racial, 63–64, 93, 97–
100, 161–62; as rural, 65–57, 107
Swedish music education, x–xi, 75, 112,
116–18, 170
Swedish national anthem, 46, 68n13
Swedish national day, 46, 68–69n13, 89,
147–48
Swedish-Norwegian border music, 55–57,
59, 71n49
Swedish radio, 36, 67, 82, 93, 118–19
Swedish television, x, xi, 67, 79–80, 82, 94,
97–98, 104n49, 167
Swedish world music, 60–61, 159n21. *See
also* world music
SWÅP, 60–61, 71n60
Sämus, 116, 125n28, 170
Särna, 51
Särskild Ämnesutbildning i Musik, 116,
125n28, 170

tabla, 63
talking drum, 34
Tallroth, Roger, 41n27, 105n64, 125n32
tambourine, 34
tango, 38n4, 77, 145
Telemark, 25, 56
Ternhag, Gunnar, 4–5, 15n11, 38n6, 54
Texter om svensk folkmusik, 45
Thestrup, Eva, xiii
This is Spinal Tap, 105n73
timelines, African, x, xiiin2, xiiin4, 34
Titanic, 103n19
Titon, Jeff Todd, 43n73
Tollin, Björn, 32, 34, 125n32

Trading Places, 104n43
traditional instruments, 33–38, 86–88, 99,
110, 113–15; and Ransäter entrance
fees, 35–38; and the Zorn trials, 35, 86,
125n20
tradition bearers, 33, 53–54, 108–112, 138–
39, 143–44, 153–54
tradition concept, 21–24, 35–37, 78–79
tradition vs. innovation. *See* axis of time
trall, 42–43n56, 58, 151–52, 159n29
trance music, xi, xiiin7
trap set, 28, 33
Tritonus, 115
True Finns, 162
trumpet, 33
Turkish music, 135
töntighet, 89–92, 104n44

Uddevalla folk music festival, 56
Ultima Thule, 97–98
Umeå, x, 163; folk music festival, 73n78
Uneback, Sara, xii, 166
Ungdomsringen. See Youth Ring
Uppland, 47
Uppsala, 4, 9, 167, 168; spelman gathering,
73n78
urbanization, 19, 56, 66–67, 75, 80, 123,
162
urban vs. rural, 17n44, 67, 73n76, 74n79,
80–81, 107, 123, 128n59, 148, 151–56
Urkult, 63, 91, 158n7, 170

Vesterlund, Lotta, xii, 166
Vietnam War, 96
viola, 33
violin. *See* fiddle
Vivaldi, Antonio, 122
vocable singing, 42–43n56, 58, 151–52,
159n29
vocal folk music, 136–37; ballads, 33,
42n56, 149; in ensemble music, 114,
152–55, 159n22; folk chorales, 99,
137; folk songs, 42–43n56, 78,
125n25, 144; herding calls, 32, 42n56;
hymns, 33, lullabies, 33, 42n56, 153;
song games, xi, 33; vocable singing,
42n56, 151–52
Vretman, Rosa, 68n13
värendstrumma, 151
Värmland, 47, 49, 55–56, 67, 168
Väsen, 23, 41n27, 105n64, 113, 115,
125n31, 131
Västergötland, 47, 65, 66, 121
Västmanland, 68n13

Waernelius, Anders, xii, 24, 28, 166

walking tune, 32, 158n4
waltz, 19, 33, 47–48, 69n18, 93, 100, 147,
    168
Wanselius, Louise, 42n41
ways of understanding, 8–9, 16–17n35,
    129–30, 140n2
ways of understanding folk music, 8–13,
    16–17n35, 17n44, 31–32, 54–56, 66,
    78–79, 123, 124n4, 129–30, 140n2,
    161–62; as a function of the Folk, 9,
    55–56, 75–101, 109, 150; as a function
    of Nation, 9, 45–66, 124n4, 138, 149,
    161–63; as a function of Nature, 10,
    55–56, 66, 78–79, 107–23, 124n4,
    124n8, 133, 136, 138, 143, 162; as a
    function of Tradition, 9, 19–38, 48,
    55–56, 78–79, 108–9, 124n4, 133,
    138, 148–50
Wennberg, Bernt, xii, 166
Wester, Mats, 97–99
Westerlund, Annelie, xii, 65, 93, 120,
    127n50, 166
Western art music, ix, x, 25, 43n62, 118–19.
    See also axis of quality; folk vs. art
whiteness, xii, xivn10, 63–64, 72n64,
    74n79, 94, 97–98
Wieslander, Ethel, 94–95, 96
Wignall, Margareta Lundquister, xii, 166
willow flute, 87
Wiskari, Hanna, xii, 33, 35, 117, 166
Wittgenstein, Ludwig, 5–7, 15–16n19. See
    also family resemblances, language
    games, meaning as use
Wolf, Richard, xiii
work concept, 19
world music, 11, 22, 43n73, 92, 118–19,
    149; festivals of, 60–61, 63, 167, 170;
    program at Gothenburg School of Mu-

sic, 116–17, 126n40–41. See also
    Swedish world music
World Music Orchestra, 61–63, 72n62,
    72n64, 92, 104n49
World War II, 95–96
Wrethling, Tony, xiii
Wrigley Sisters, 60
written vs. aural, 117–18

xenophobia, 21, 53–54, 93–96, 104n54, 135,
    161–63

yoik, 42n52, 100
Yorkshire, 58
Youth Ring, 47, 53, 69n16, 89–90, 115,
    144–46, 148, 170; conservatism of,
    71n42, 81, 94, 113, 145–46; and the
    Zorn juries, 168–69

zither, 125n25
Zorn, Anders, 20, 169
Zorn badge, 20, 39n7, 111, 168–69
Zorn jury, 20, 86, 111–12, 118, 168–69
Zorn trials, 20, 53, 111, 125n20, 169
zouk, 15n19

Åberg, Sebastian, 63
Åkerlund, Jonas (video director), 80
Åkesson, Ingrid, 41n29
Ångermanland, 63, 170
Åström, Lotten, 158n10

Äkta spelmän, 41n27

Öckerö spelman gathering, 56, 91
Örebro, 46
Östbjörka spelman gathering, 72n70, 122
Övergaard, Einar, 56

About the Author

David Kaminsky is a lecturer at Harvard University, where he received his Ph.D. in ethnomusicology in 2005. He has also held positions at Earlham College, the McNally Smith College of Music, and the College of William and Mary. He has lived roughly one quarter of his life in Sweden, where he continues to conduct fieldwork every summer. In recent years he has written on gender and sexuality in the polska dance, the use of folk music as a propaganda tool by the Swedish extreme right, and the peculiarities of Sweden's National Folk Musicians' trials. He is also the only American ever to be titled riksspelman, or National Folk Musician of Sweden.